T0277803

Abortion

ALSO BY JESSICA VALENTI

Sex Object: A Memoir
Why Have Kids
The Purity Myth
Yes Means Yes
He's a Stud, She's a Slut
Full Frontal Feminism

Abortion

Our Bodies, *Their* Lies,
and the Truths *We* Use to Win

Jessica Valenti

CROWN
NEW YORK

Published in the United States by Crown, an imprint of the Crown Publishing Group. a division of Penguin Random House LLC, New York.
crownpublishing.com

CROWN and the Crown colophon are registered trademarks of Penguin Random House LLC.

Photographs on page 166 courtesy of MYA Network https://myanetwork.org.

Library of Congress Cataloging-in-Publication Data
Name: Valenti, Jessica, author.
Title: Abortion : our bodies, their lies, and the truths we use to win / Jessica Valenti.
Identifiers: LCCN 2024019725 (print) | LCCN 2024019726 (ebook) |
    ISBN 9780593800232 (hardcover) | ISBN 9780593800249 (ebook)
Subjects: LCSH: Abortion—Political aspects—United States. | Abortion—Law
    and legislation—United States. | Reproductive rights—United States.
Classification: LCC HQ767.5.U5 V35 2024 (print) | LCC HQ767.5.U5 (ebook) |
    DDC 362.1988/800973—dc23/eng/20240516
LC record available at https://lccn.loc.gov/2024019725
LC ebook record available at https://lccn.loc.gov/2024019726

Hardcover ISBN 978-0-593-80023-2
Ebook ISBN 978-0-593-80024-9

Printed in the United States of America on acid-free paper

Editor: Libby Burton
Editorial assistant: Cierra Hinckson
Fact checker: Grace Haley
Production editor: Terry Deal
Production editorial assistant: Taylor Teague
Text designer: Andrea Lau
Production manager: Dustin Amick
Copy editor: Janet Biehl
Proofreaders: Rives Kuhar and Tracy R. Lynch
Indexer: Stephen Callahan
Publicist: Stacey Stein
Marketer: Kimberly Lew

9 8 7 6 5 4 3 2

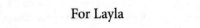

For Layla

Contents

Introduction

I'll be honest, I resent having to write this book. I'm livid that of all the things I could be doing right now, I am defending my humanity. It feels, as a friend of mine once put it, humiliating. Women should not have to convince the world that we are full people worthy of rights, protections, and the ability to control our own bodies. Yet here we are.

And here I am, twenty years after I started writing about feminism, and thirty-two years since I went to my first pro-choice march with my mother as a surly eighth grader. Today I am even more surly. Because now I have a thirteen-year-old daughter—young enough to sleep with a teddy bear, but old enough to be forced to carry a pregnancy against her will.

It was her I cried for the night the *Dobbs* decision was leaked. I remember crawling into bed with my husband and sobbing. Wailing, really. I kept saying, "My daughter, my daughter." A mother's job is to protect her children. How could I possibly do that now?

A few weeks later the Supreme Court made it official: its decision in *Dobbs v. Jackson Women's Health Organization* overturned *Roe v. Wade* and decades of protection for abortion rights.

The prevailing justices, two of whom are accused sexual predators, ruled that in order for a right to be valid, if it isn't mentioned in the Constitution, it must be "deeply rooted in this Nation's history and tradition" and "implicit in the concept of ordered liberty." Abortion, they said, was neither.[*]

Feminists, called hysterical for warning that the end of *Roe* was near, knew this was coming and spent years strategizing on what to do when it finally happened. That prescience didn't make the decision feel any less like a punch to the gut. Can you ever really be prepared for your country to tell you that you're less than human?

Because let's be clear, that's what this decision was—the decimation not just of reproductive rights but of women's citizenship. Overturning *Roe* was just a means to that end. The powerful coalition of extremist organizations[†] that spent decades working toward this moment weren't really interested in abortion, but in what ending abortion meant for their broader goals: a return to forced traditional gender roles, a forced gender binary, a culture and politics ruled by white supremacist patriarchy where women had no power, and the punishment of anyone who deviates from it all.

In short: They want to go backwards. It is not a coincidence that the abortion ban upheld in Arizona in 2024, for example, was a law adopted in 1864—a time before women had the right to vote, and when the legislature was led by a man who liked to marry twelve- and fourteen-year-old girls.

The lawmakers and activists forcing us into pregnancy and childbirth are launching a full-scale assault on our rights and freedom

---

[*]   Never mind that this country's "history and tradition" have been defined and controlled by men, or that the "social order" that the justices claimed to be protecting has fallen apart since *Roe*'s demise.

[†]   Throughout this book, I refer to different actors in the anti-abortion movement. In an attempt to be as precise as possible: *Republicans* generally means GOP legislators, and *conservatives* refers to the broader right-wing movement and players, whereas *anti-abortion* activists and groups are those who specifically hone in on abortion rights.

that they had fifty years to plan for. They know what they're doing, and they're depending on us not catching it.

That's why I started my newsletter, *Abortion, Every Day*. At first, I wasn't planning on creating a publication. I was just so angry and intent on not missing a thing.

So I tracked every ban, court case, and anti-abortion strategy I could. I read anything and everything on abortion—whether it was an article in *The New York Times*, a letter to the editor in a student newspaper, or tweets from a crisis pregnancy center. I didn't want anti-abortion legislators and groups to get away with attacking us under the cover of national overwhelm.

Most of all, I wanted to ensure that people understood what these attacks were really about, and how they were all connected. I noticed, for example, how lawmakers were undermining democracy to keep abortion banned. Because Americans overwhelmingly want abortion to be legal, these Republican leaders couldn't risk voters having a choice. So in state after state, they worked to keep abortion off the ballot.

I saw how lawmakers are eroding birth control access, running ob-gyns out of town, and enabling abusers. I uncovered anti-abortion organizations' plans to open a network of religious "maternity homes" across the country, and a secret campaign to force women to carry nonviable pregnancies to term.

I found bills that would charge women with murder if they "caused" their miscarriages, and spoke to activists defending women of color being arrested for stillbirths and miscarriages.

Again, once you understand that banning abortion is just a means to a bigger misogynist end, stories like this make a lot more sense.

Not long after I launched *Abortion, Every Day* as an official newsletter, I realized that the other common denominator for all these attacks was their sheer volume. At first I had naïvely worried that once the post-*Roe* dust settled, I wouldn't have enough news to write about daily. That never happened. It became clear, and it still is, that the overwhelm is very much the point.

The anti-abortion movement is hitting Americans with everything all at once in the hopes that those of us who want our rights back will be too exhausted and crushed to fight back. If pro-choice groups are busy trying to repeal a ban and care for desperate patients on the ground, for example, they have that much less time to keep an eye on other, seemingly less urgent issues—like the over-funding of crisis pregnancy centers* or how their local newspapers are publishing biased abortion coverage.

The same is true for everyday Americans who care about this issue. It's hard for any single person to keep track of all the anti-abortion attacks and tactics happening in different states around the country. But it's vital that we do.

Consider someone living in Arizona who decides to collect signatures for a pro-choice ballot measure. They may not know that when activists did the same in Ohio, Republican leaders worked with anti-abortion organizations to draft a biased ballot summary designed to trick voters. If they had that information, they could be on the lookout for a similar move from their own government.

Similarly, if a Utah ob-gyn knows that a bill introduced in her state contains the same sneaky language that makes it impossible for Idaho doctors to give their patients health- and life-saving abortions, she'll be that much more prepared to lobby against it. And if a New York college student knows that California campuses provide

---

* While some feminists use the term "anti-abortion center," I use "crisis pregnancy center" or "anti-abortion crisis pregnancy center" in this book because they're terms Americans are most likely to be familiar with.

cost-free abortion medication, it could inspire her to fight for the same in her school.

But the rapidly moving stories and details that change from day to day aren't all that matter; it's also the broader understanding of what these issues mean, what anti-abortion forces want, and how to *do something* about it.

There has never been a more important time to be aware and informed—whether you do abortion rights work every day or are just furious about the attacks on our rights. We can't win unless we know exactly what we're fighting against, and fighting for.

Most of all, though, those fighting to keep abortion banned are relying on Americans' fear of speaking up. Since *Roe* was overturned, I've spoken to countless people, young women especially, who care deeply about abortion rights but don't know what to say or how to say it. They worry that they sound stupid, or that they're going to be talked over or diminished. Told to calm down. Laughed at.

That's why I publish *Abortion, Every Day,* and why I've written this book.

Abortion will give you the information, language, and context you need to feel confident talking about the attacks on our bodies and freedom. It cuts through the misinformation you're likely hearing every day from the news, social media, or even your own friends and family—providing order to the chaos, and facts to back up your beliefs. I want to make sure that you don't feel overwhelmed into inaction or too unsure to speak up.

My hope is that the lessons I've learned by obsessively tracking abortion rights since *Roe* was overturned will give you everything you need to fight back—whether you're too nervous to talk about abortion or have been an activist your whole life.

Most important, in a moment when you're likely fed up with being talked over and diminished, *Abortion* is as angry as you are. Sometimes people ask me if I feel like I'm "preaching to the choir."

What I tell them, and what is true about this book, is that I'm *arming* the choir. With facts, and with fury.

No matter why you're reading this book, remember: it wasn't so long ago that political experts and pundits called feminists "hysterical" for warning that *Roe* could be overturned. They said it would never happen and that we were overreacting. Now we're watching as doctors are forced to deny dying women care, children are made to give birth, and miscarriage patients are arrested.

We're living through one of the most important moments in history for American women, and what we do now will determine what our granddaughters' lives—and the lives of their children—will look like. It's an all-hands-on-deck moment.

We can't afford to be overwhelmed or confused. We can't watch as women's experiences, their very lives, are written off as post-*Roe* statistics. The stakes are just too high.

I know this is hard. And I'm often asked how I do this work every day without crashing and burning. How can any of us, given how difficult this is, possibly keep it up? My only answer is: you just do. There's no magic solution. The moment simply requires our sustained outrage.

Because the alternative—that this nightmare becomes normalized or accepted—would mean we've conceded. And that's simply not an option. I'm not willing to live in a country where I don't have a say over my body, and I refuse to let my daughter live in a place where women are permanent second-class citizens. It's not just our health and lives on the line, but our freedom.

No matter what happens next, we absolutely can win. And the way we do it is that we *never stop resisting.*

A few things to keep in mind as you read *Abortion*. Abortion is a complicated, nuanced issue that's changing by the day. One reason I publish a daily newsletter on the topic is that that's how often news is updated, court cases are announced, and strategy shifts. I often joke that I should have called the newsletter *Abortion, Every Hour*—that's how quickly things are moving in post-*Roe* America.

What that means, though, is that some of the laws, bans, stories, and more that I write about in this book may have changed by the time you read it. And so I've tried my best to pick out examples that will stand the test of time and demonstrate a broader point or tactic.

Abortion is also very much based on the work that I've done in the last two years at *Abortion, Every Day*. It's a compilation of the research and analysis I've done at the newsletter, structured and framed in a way to be as useful as possible. That's why I've included a section containing easily accessible statistics and facts at the end of this book. If you're having a conversation with someone about abortion and want to be able to bring up an issue quickly, you can thumb to the back of the book and find what you need.

But as comprehensive as I believe *Abortion* is, abortion is a huge, complex issue that could never (ever!) be fully explained or contained in a single book.*

What I'm most interested in about abortion is not going to be what another expert or feminist is most interested in. I'm coming with my own focus, biases, and goals. In other words, this book is *my expertise and opinion* on abortion, and in no way should it be viewed as everything you need to know.

So you'll also find a list of books at the end of *Abortion* that have influenced my own thinking and activism or that have been influential in the reproductive rights movement at large. I hope this book

---

* In true obsessive form, I've already started to create a list of issues that I didn't get to cover in *Abortion* that I want to write about in my next book—like clinic violence and Christian nationalism. The hardest thing about writing a book about abortion is knowing that you could never possibly fit everything that needs talking about.

will be a jumping-off point for you to learn more about the nuances, history, and intricacies of abortion rights.

Most of all, I hope *Abortion* resonates with you, and that it reminds you that you're not alone in feeling angry, despairing, energized, hopeful, or some combination of all. If we have to be in this hellscape, at least know that we're in it together.

Abortion

Chapter 1

Abortion Is Good, Actually

Abortion is an essential freedom—necessary for the self-determination of women and anyone else with the ability to get pregnant.* It is not tragic, something to be apologized for, or a "necessary evil." It is proactively, objectively *good*.

There is no benefit in being tentative. For too long, pro-choice Americans—politicians, especially—have offered apologetic defenses of abortion. Tepid messaging certainly didn't protect *Roe,* and it ceded the most important advantage we have: the moral high ground.

After all, we're not the ones who are forcing children to give birth. We're not the ones making devastated women carry dead and dying fetuses. We're not the ones mandating that rape victims sign affidavits or that they "prove" that their attack really happened before being allowed to receive basic care.

Forcing someone to be pregnant when they don't want to be is dangerous and cruel—and voters know it. Over 80 percent of

---

* You'll notice in the book that I toggle between using "women" and "people"—that's deliberate. It's not only women and girls who can get pregnant, and it's important to be precise. Conservatives' attacks on abortion are also very much about subjugating women in particular, so when writing about the anti-abortion movement, their legislation and strategy, my language reflects as much.

Americans don't want the government making decisions about pregnancy at all. That means the extreme abortion bans going into effect across the country are being passed against voters' wishes. Why, then, are the people we elected to stop this horror show still putting out polite press releases? Why would we continue to be calm and reasoned?

America supports abortion. It's time we acted like it.

Part of the reason we're in this colossal mess is that politicians were afraid. They spoke in whispers and favored "choice" over "abortion." Instead of hammering home that we are right, and that anti-abortion legislators are horrifically, dangerously wrong, they let conservatives call themselves the party of "life." They didn't listen to years of advice of reproductive justice activists about the power of unapologetic support for abortion. Instead, they said abortion should be "safe, legal, and rare," powering Republicans' claim that there's something wrong with ending a pregnancy.

There's not.

We have the chance, right here and now, to change the conversation. We can get out of the defensive crouch and force legislators to do the same. And as awful as our post-*Roe* world is, it also gives all of us the opportunity to build something bigger and better, both legally and culturally. There has never been a better and more important moment to ensure our humanity is truly counted.

No more hesitation, no more compromise. There's no such thing as a middle ground for our freedom. Because while abortion is a necessary and normal part of reproductive healthcare—and we should fight for it as such—it's our liberation that conservatives most object to. That's why they're passing bans.

After all, if this wasn't about power, control, and punishment, why would some women be "allowed" abortions when they're raped? It's those of us who have sex willingly they want to teach a lesson to the most. The truth is that most anti-abortion sentiment and law is rooted in the idea that pregnancy is a punishment—a consequence for those who behave irresponsibly or "promiscuously."

The more ideologically pure lawmakers, those who believe in total abortion bans without exceptions for rape, incest, health, or even life, aren't any less punitive. Their push for fetal personhood, which defines fertilized eggs and zygotes as full, constitutional human beings, eradicates women's humanity entirely—rendering us mere vessels for a handful of cells deemed to be the *real* human beings. What worse punishment is there than not being seen as people at all?

That's what makes abortion good. It recognizes the humanity of women, something I truly cannot believe is somehow still up for debate.

Women have spent decades trying to convince the government that we deserve to control our own bodies. We've explained, calmly and politely, that the ability to choose if and when to have children can be the most determinative factor in a woman's life.

We've provided research showing that those who are denied abortions are more likely to stay with violent partners and live below the poverty line. We've shared our most personal experiences, recounting stories of sexual abuse and domestic violence, financial hardship, and medical trauma. We've shown that abortion is safe (much safer than pregnancy), and we've rebutted misinformation.

We've knocked on doors and raised money; debated at school, work, and on the floors of Congress. We've started organizations and research groups; we've raised awareness everywhere, from pop culture to your local hair salon. We voted: election after election, year after year.

What has it gotten us? Not only was *Roe* eliminated—forcing our daughters and granddaughters to grow up with fewer rights than we had—but somehow, we're still debating.

Why are we still trying to convince people that one in four

American women[*] aren't murderers? Do we really think that one more story of a child raped by her father will move the hearts of men who would legislate away our humanity without even bothering to learn remedial facts about pregnancy?

Asking for our rights didn't work then, and it won't work now. I refuse to explain, over and over again, that women are people. I'm done degrading myself by sharing the most intimate details of my life with strangers in the hope that perhaps one will muster a spark of empathy. Why should we beg for scraps of humanity from those who will never give it to us?

Instead of offering diplomatic explanations for why abortion is necessary to protect women's health and lives, it's past time to speak plainly: Abortion is normal and moral. Not just because abortions are common (even though they are), or because women are happy to have access to them (even though that's true).

Abortions are a proactive moral good because they allow people to control their own bodies, lives, and futures.

What's more: Abortion creates lives. Ask your friends and family how their abortions changed them. Ask what they were able to do, what path they were able to take, because they had the freedom to end a pregnancy when they needed to.

Abortion is often framed as the end of something—even pro-choicers say someone "terminated" or "ended" a pregnancy. But often it's very much the opposite. For many, abortion has been the start of something.

---

[*] Most of the abortion research we have is on women. Trans, nonbinary, and other people with the ability to get pregnant also have abortions but are far less represented in studies.

Abortion Isn't an Ending

When I had an abortion at twenty-eight years old, I was in the middle of writing my first book and just a few months away from meeting the man I would marry. The life and family I have now simply would not exist without that abortion. I would not have started a relationship with my husband, Andrew, and I would not have given birth to my incredibly loved daughter, Layla, a few years later. A world without them both would be a much dimmer life, and it's one I prefer not to imagine.

The abortion I had did more than allow me to create my family, though; it's had ripple effects. All abortions do. Because of my abortion, I wrote books and gave speeches; I did work that helped other women. And it wasn't just about feminism. When I was pregnant with Layla, I became critically ill with something called HELLP syndrome; both my daughter and I almost died, and Layla was born three months early at just two pounds. Soon afterward I wrote about the hardships of being a mom to a preemie—something I know made a difference in the lives of parents who were going through the same thing. Thirteen years later I still get emails about the pieces I wrote during that time.

Without my abortion, none of that would have happened. Without abortion, I wouldn't have the friends I have now, or the career, or even my very life. Because when I got pregnant again three years after Layla was born, the chances of my getting sick—and dying, this time—were significant. And so, I had a second abortion—one that broke my heart because I desperately wanted another child, but ensured my daughter grew up with a mother.

Those who rail against our rights like to divide women into two groups: those who have abortions and those who have children. Most often, though, we're both.

Those who would see abortion banned like to pose hypotheticals about the remarkable baby a woman could have if she just didn't get an abortion: *What if they cured cancer?* Rarely, if ever, does anyone ask if that woman herself might change the world. They don't consider that we could be the remarkable ones, if only given the chance.

But the lives and experiences abortions create don't have to be extraordinary to matter. I think less about the books I've written because of my abortions, and more about how without them, Layla's best friends never would have met her. Or how the dogs lucky enough to be walked on my block wouldn't have a lanky blond girl running up to give them pets and compliments. I think about my husband, and how he would have moved back to California had we never met, and how sad that would be for New York. I think about the dinners we've cooked, my daughter's sun-kissed cheeks on vacation, and the way we used to all fall asleep in the same bed when she was a toddler. It's the everyday moments of my life I'm grateful for most; those are moments that abortion gave me.

All abortions create something. Paths forward, lives lived, connections made. Some are hard, some are beautiful, but all are chosen. That's what we lost when *Roe* was overturned: the ability to decide our own way in the world. What's been taken from us is about more than our rights or our bodies. We've been robbed of our freedom, and our self-determination. And that, to me, is unforgivable.

Abortion, Explained

Before I go on, let's cover some basics. Abortion is a medical intervention to end a pregnancy—for whatever reason. Maybe because a miscarriage needs help to complete, because someone doesn't want to be pregnant, or because it's physically or mentally unsafe for a person to remain pregnant.

Even if that seems obvious to you, it's vital we define abortion clearly. Because for years, and increasingly since *Roe* was overturned, those who want abortion to be illegal are working hard to redefine it. That only works if Americans don't know the truth, and that's why conservatives want us confused, miseducated, and too embarrassed to ask questions. We're not going to let that happen.

There are several ways to have an abortion. Most people in the United States who end their pregnancies use abortion medication—a combination of two pills that you can take at home over the course of a few days. The first drug, mifepristone, blocks progesterone—the hormone necessary for a pregnancy to continue. The second drug, misoprostol, taken a day or two later, makes your uterus contract and empty.

Since *Roe* was overturned, the number of people using abortion medication has risen significantly. In 2023, 63 percent of abortions used medication, up from 53 percent in 2020. In part that's because as of 2024, 25 million women live in a state with an abortion ban. For them, it's often easier to have medication shipped to them than to travel elsewhere for a procedural abortion.

Women also choose abortion medication because of the privacy it affords—they can end their pregnancy at home, without traveling to a clinic. That cuts down on gas money and time taken off work, and it allows patients to avoid potential protesters.

Those who don't use medication to end their pregnancy get procedural abortions, sometimes called "surgical" abortions, even though there is no surgery or cutting involved. The type of procedural abortion someone gets depends on the specifics of their pregnancy and what's safest and standard.

For pregnancies under ten weeks, you can have a manual vacuum aspiration (MVA) abortion, also called a manual uterine aspiration (MUA) abortion. This is the procedure I had: it uses the suction of what looks like a simple syringe to empty the uterus. This kind of abortion has a history within the American feminist movement: because it's such an easily performed procedure, women in the 1970s taught each other how to do MUA abortions. (Today feminist and abortion rights groups also train people to do them, using a papaya as a stand-in for a uterus.)

Another common type of abortion is vacuum aspiration, done using an electric pump. For a pregnancy after the first trimester, the provider may use dilation and curettage (D&C) or dilation and evacuation (D&E). In such an abortion, the provider will dilate the patient's cervix manually, then remove the pregnancy tissue with a hand-operated tool or electric pump.

Those in the second trimester and beyond can have an induction abortion, in which the cervix is dilated using medication and the uterus is evacuated. Third-trimester abortions take multiple days to complete: first an injection stops the fetal heartbeat, then medication is placed in the cervix to open it, and then a procedure induces or evacuates the uterus.

Most abortions happen in the first trimester. Eighty percent are done before the tenth week of pregnancy, before the embryo becomes a fetus, and 93 percent are performed before the thirteenth week. Abortions after the thirteenth week are less common, but that doesn't make them any less important or needed. Unfortunately, there is still a tremendous amount of stigma about abortions considered "late."

Most often, the stories Americans hear about abortions after the first trimester are from women who wanted to be pregnant but received a devastating diagnosis, or whose pregnancies were endangering their lives. Since *Roe* was overturned, those stories are in the news more than ever—both because people are being denied care more often and because those are the stories that mainstream media outlets believe Americans will be the most sympathetic to. The truth, though, is that there are many different reasons someone might seek an abortion throughout their pregnancy.

Research shows that some patients don't learn that they're pregnant right away, others don't have the money to obtain an abortion as soon as they learn about their pregnancy. Some aren't sure where they can get an abortion or can't take time off of work to travel to another county or state. Ironically, a lot of these hurdles are created by the very politicians who claim to abhor "late abortions." If Republicans weren't enacting restrictions like waiting periods, bans on Medicaid funding for abortion, or parental notification requirements, there would be fewer abortions after the first trimester.

Other patients don't realize they're pregnant right away because they are very, very young. Children and teens are more likely to be sexually assaulted and more likely to be victims of incest, but they are less likely to have the resources and support to get care early in their pregnancy. They have to overcome additional financial and legal hurdles to get an abortion. They're also a demographic that's less likely to know a lot about pregnancy and their bodies.

Regardless of hurdles to care, abortion throughout pregnancy will always be necessary and important, and we must treat it that way—without shame or stigma.

Abortion Is Common and Safe

Despite anti-abortion myths to the contrary, abortions are extremely common and safe. You're more likely to have a complication from a wisdom tooth extraction than from an abortion. One in four American women will have an abortion in her lifetime, 99 percent of women who have had abortions don't regret it, and the overwhelming feeling that most describe after ending a pregnancy is relief.

When women do have negative feelings associated with their abortions, it's often not because of the procedure or decision itself but because they live in a community where abortion is stigmatized. That's why conservatives spend so much time and energy spreading misinformation about what it means to end a pregnancy—the tactic is effective!

Decades of research have shown that both procedural and medication abortions are safe, but that hasn't stopped anti-abortion groups from making false claims—focusing on abortion medication, specifically, since *Roe* was overturned.

Here's the truth: abortion pills are safe and effective, American women have been using them to end pregnancies for decades, and credible studies find them safer than Tylenol or Viagra.

In fact, when *The New York Times* examined more than one hundred studies of abortion medication, covering more than 124,000 abortions spanning twenty-six countries, it found that a vast majority of the studies reported that "more than 99 percent of patients who took the pills had no serious complications."

Still, anti-abortion groups claim the drugs are wildly dangerous, and they've taken that erroneous argument all the way up to the Supreme Court in order to restrict access to mifepristone—the first of the two drugs taken to end a pregnancy. (Two of the major studies that the groups cited to SCOTUS ended up being retracted by their publishers.)

You'll learn more about the faulty science behind the anti-abortion movement in Chapter 8, but for now let's look at one of its ominous-sounding claims—that women who take abortion medication have a 53 percent increased risk of emergency room visits compared to women who have procedural abortions.

The truth is that abortion almost never requires a hospital visit. In fact, one study showed that among women of reproductive age, only 0.01 percent of emergency room visits were abortion-related, and another showed that less than 1 percent of abortions—0.87 percent—were followed by a trip to an emergency room. I won't even get into how low these complication rates are compared to childbirth!

That means even if this statistic were true, and women were over 50 percent more likely to visit an ER after abortion medication than after a procedure, you're still talking about an infinitesimal number of women. The other fact to consider—pointed out by researchers, abortion providers, and other experts—is that women who self-manage an abortion at home are more likely to be nervous and seek care out of fear, not because something has actually gone wrong.

Think about it: you're home, without a doctor present, and maybe you're worried that you're bleeding too much. The scare tactics around self-managed abortion don't exactly help. So you go to the hospital just to be sure.

That leads us to the last important truth behind this claim: Pay close attention to the language that anti-abortion activists use. They say women are more likely to "visit" the emergency room after taking abortion medication. But a making a "visit" to the ER is very, very different from getting treatment or having a serious complication. Half the women who go to the ER after an abortion—again, an already minuscule number—are simply sent home because they're fine.

If abortion medication is so safe, why do anti-abortion groups spend so much time, money, and energy pretending otherwise? It's precisely *because* the pills are safe, easy to take, and (relatively) easy to obtain. Pregnant people can use the pills in the comfort of their own homes, self-managing their own abortions, often getting the medication through the mail using telehealth.

That kind of availability and privacy—a saving grace for those seeking abortions in states with bans—is a huge reason why the abortion rate hasn't gone down since *Roe* was overturned. That makes the pills enemy number one to the anti-abortion movement.

Even before *Roe* was overturned, though, the pills had thrown a serious wrench into the anti-abortion movement's scare tactic strategy. As safe as procedural abortion is, Republican lawmakers and anti-abortion groups had successfully spread misinformation about it for years. But the medication option made it much more difficult for them to claim that abortion is a risky, tragic "surgery." After all, it's tough to paint abortion as dangerous when someone can do it while home on the couch watching Netflix.

And that leads to the final, most insidious reason the anti-abortion movement opposes abortion medication. The pills robbed them of their favorite pastime: harassing women at clinics. Women's ability to end a pregnancy with just a few pills—safely, privately, at home, without shame—was too much for them to take. At least when we went to clinics, they could stand outside and call us "sluts."

Our progress infuriates them. Anything that eases our suffering or improves our lives makes them hate us exponentially more. How dare we have the ability to end our pregnancies with a pill. They'll show us!

Carrie N. Baker, professor and author of *Abortion Pills: US History and Politics,* points out something else—that the strategy on abortion medication and telemedicine is also related to anti-choice activists' desire to harass doctors and clinic staff:

> These telemedicine providers are entirely virtual. They don't have brick-and-mortar clinics. All they have is a website. And you know, they might go after the website, but they can't locate the doctors. They can't locate the patients, they can't scream to the patients, "You're murdering your baby." And that fundamentally undermines their strategy.

That's why these groups don't just call the safety of the pills themselves into question, but the notion that women can take them safely without the supervision of a doctor. Once again they feign concern for women's health—arguing that pro-choice activists are trying to turn every home in America into an abortion clinic, and that taking the pills without a medical provider is dangerous.

Real studies prove otherwise. A 2024 study from Advancing New Standards in Reproductive Health at the University of California, San Francisco, for example, found that telehealth medication abortion is just as safe and effective as in-person medical care. The research, published in *Nature Medicine,* looked at more than sixty thousand medication abortions across twenty states and found that 98 percent were effective and that 99.8 percent were free from "serious adverse events."

A 2023 study from the University of Tennessee Health Science Center also found that telehealth abortion was just as safe and effective as in-person care. In addition, the study's authors found that telemedicine increased access to abortion care for those living in remote rural areas, as well as those worried about privacy and stigma.

In other words, telehealth and abortion medication help those who need access the most. What happens, though, when people *aren't* able to get the care they need?

Consequences of Banning Abortion

One thing that's always struck me about the anti-abortion movement is how it talks about forced pregnancy as if it were something easy. As if being denied an abortion just means inconveniencing a person for a few months, rather than forever changing their lives, bodies, and health. But we know what the consequences are when someone is denied an abortion. And I don't mean just the physical health horrors now being reported around the country—there's much, much more.

Perhaps the most comprehensive research on the impact of

denying women abortions is the Turnaway Study,* which followed one thousand women for five years. Some of the women got the abortions they wanted, and others were denied—the study compared what happened to women in both groups. The lead researcher, Diana Greene Foster, says the sample of women was very similar to the population of those who seek abortions: 60 percent of the women were already mothers, half were in their twenties, and about 75 percent were below the federal poverty line.

The study is comprehensive and nuanced—the researchers conducted over eight thousand interviews—but the key takeaways are stark: Those denied abortions are more likely to stay with abusive partners, more likely to have serious complications in pregnancy, more likely to suffer from anxiety and poor physical health, and more likely to end up in poverty. In fact, the study found that forcing a woman into pregnancy quadruples the odds that she and her child will live below the federal poverty line.

In an interview, Foster pointed out that women's fears about unwanted pregnancies are, unfortunately, exactly right: "The things they worry about coming through are exactly the things they experience when they're denied an abortion and carry the pregnancy to term. They tell us they can't afford a baby, and we find they become poorer."

The study found that denying women abortions also has a serious impact on the children—both the ones born from that pregnancy and the already-existing children. The consequences were financial, developmental, and even related to the bond between them and their mother. Once again, women's concerns were justified. People seeking abortions are overwhelmingly concerned about

---

* The research has been published into a book that I highly recommend: Diana Greene Foster et al., *The Turnaway Study: Ten Years, a Thousand Women, and the Consequences of Having—or Being Denied—an Abortion* (New York: Scribner, 2021).

their ability to be good parents to existing and future children. "We have the data to show they're justly concerned, we see their existing kids are worse off," Foster said. "I think it's pretty important to emphasize that when parents are able to make decisions about whether to become parents, their kids do better, and that we should trust their decision-making for the good of society."

The Turnaway Study ended in 2016, so we don't know what the consequences of people being denied abortions will look like now. The landscape today is much, much different and the number of patients being denied is exponentially more. But this research, and other studies, gives us a window into what we can expect.

A 2021 study published in *Demography*, for example, estimates that the bans on abortion in the United States will lead to a 21 percent increase in pregnancy-related deaths overall—with a 33 percent increase among Black women. A 2022 report showed that states with abortion restrictions have maternal death rates that are 62 percent higher than states with abortion access—and that the maternal mortality rate was increasing *twice as fast* in states with abortion restrictions. And as you'll see in Chapter 8, a 2022 study from the University of Pennsylvania found that abortion restrictions cause a "significant increase" in the suicide rate among women of reproductive age.

The consequences are no small thing. So when you see anti-abortion activists dismiss the gravity of denying people care, remember these numbers—and remember the real stories of the people behind them.

Chapter 2

America Supports Abortion

One of the biggest myths about abortion is that it's controversial. It's not. Voters have overwhelmingly supported abortion rights for decades, support that's only grown since *Roe* was overturned. Yet somehow Americans have been successfully convinced that one of the most popular political issues of our time is something the country is irrevocably polarized over.

It's tempting to believe that ignorance over abortion's popularity isn't all that dangerous in the grand scheme of things—it's certainly not the most extreme anti-abortion lie out there. But the myth that Americans are evenly split on the issue undergirds all others about abortion—and it allows anti-choice lawmakers to hide the fact that they're passing abortion bans against voters' wishes.

After all, if people understood just how popular abortion rights are, they'd also realize that a small group of extremist legislators are passing laws that people don't want. It's a lot easier to dismantle democracy under the cover of darkness.

Abortion by the Numbers

Abortion rights are more popular than they've ever been in American history. Eighty-five percent of voters say abortion should be legal in some or all circumstances, more than 70 percent want abortion medication to be legal, and over 80 percent believe abortion should be unregulated by law, that it should be a decision solely between patient and doctor. In November 2023 a *Wall Street Journal* poll found that 55 percent of voters, including one-third of Republicans, want abortion legal "for any reason." Those are incredible numbers.

That massive support doesn't end at the polls. Ever since *Roe* was overturned, angry voters have been showing up for election after election to support abortion rights—from the 2022 midterms, where post-*Roe* fury drove voters out to stop a Republican "red wave," to pivotal state Supreme Court races in swing states like Wisconsin and Pennsylvania. And, of course, the ballot measures: in the two years following the fall of *Roe,* any time abortion was directly on the ballot, abortion rights won every single time—even in states like Kansas and Kentucky.

That's because regardless of how people feel personally about abortion, they overwhelmingly don't want the government involved in the decision—even in red states, and even among conservatives. A 2023 poll out of Tennessee, for example, found that 65 percent of Republicans want their state ban loosened, as did 56 percent of those who identified as conservatives and 54 percent who identified as evangelicals.

Voters don't just oppose bans; they support abortion protections. In Florida, most Republican voters said they'd support a ballot measure to restore abortion rights in the state. And when voters passed Ohio's abortion rights amendment, Issue 1, nearly one in four white evangelicals voted in support of the measure.

Because the polling and the election results are inarguable, Republicans no longer bother denying that Americans want abortion to be legal. Instead, they claim that voters want some kind of restriction on abortion, pointing to the fact that support for abortion decreases after the first trimester—from 69 percent to 37 percent.

Conservatives claim that this drop in support is proof that Americans want a "middle ground" when it comes to abortion rights. (Please keep in mind that what they call a compromise is anything but. As of the spring of 2024, Republicans' proposed federal abortion ban would force women to carry doomed pregnancies to term.)

But here's the thing they don't mention: in just the last five years, support for the right to abortion throughout pregnancy has actually risen by nearly 10 percentage points. In 2018 only 28 percent of Americans supported abortion in the second trimester—but now 37 percent do. And while 13 percent of voters in 2018 supported abortion in the third trimester, now 22 percent do. A jump that size in such a short amount of time is a sign that Americans aren't just becoming more pro-choice, but more knowledgeable about abortion rights.

Consider what happened when the polling group PerryUndem asked voters to choose between two hypothetical ballot measures: one that would protect abortion up until "viability,"* and another without restrictions. Despite conservative claims that Americans want some kind of legal limit on abortion, respondents were 15 percentage points more likely to choose the measure without the viability standard. (This surprised pollsters so much that they ran the numbers twice, with the same results.)

Tresa Undem, co-founder of PerryUndem, said that while just a few years ago people supported a viability mandate, today "people are saying, 'I don't want the government involved in this at all.'" Again, these numbers indicate that Americans are seeing abortion in a more nuanced way. They increasingly understand that pregnancy is too complicated to legislate at any point.

---

* It's important to know that "fetal viability" is not a medical term. The truth is that there's no straightforward medical standard for viability because every pregnancy is different. The popular notion of viability as we know it was actually created by a law clerk!

Some of this shift is the natural arc of progress, but it's safe to assume that the overturning of *Roe* has played a big role as well. After all, the nightmare stories coming out of anti-choice states have overwhelmingly been from patients who are later in their pregnancies.

Every time a voter reads about women who get a devastating diagnosis just to be denied care, whenever someone sees a patient explain how they were refused treatment for a miscarriage—those stories are consistent reminders that abortions are needed for all sorts of reasons, at all different times.

What's especially heartening about the increase in support for abortion throughout pregnancy is that it's young voters driving the trend. According to 2023 Pew numbers, 74 percent of adults under thirty believe abortion should be legal in most or all circumstances, and nearly 40 percent believe abortion should be legal in all circumstances.

We also see just how pro-choice Americans are when pollsters stop using an anti-abortion framework. Too often, polls will ask voters at what point in pregnancy they believe abortion should be legislated—a question that starts from the default assumption that the government should be involved in pregnancy. But when asked *if* pregnancy should be legislated rather than *when,* Americans give a clear, overwhelming response.

When a 2023 ABC News/*Washington Post* poll asked voters whether abortion should be regulated by law, for example, nearly 80 percent responded that abortion should be a decision between a woman and her doctor. Just as incredible, 58 percent of Republicans agreed, as did 60 percent of self-identified conservatives and 75 percent of Catholics.

A 2024 *Axios*/Ipsos poll that asked the same question came back with similar results: 81 percent of Americans agreed that the government shouldn't be involved in abortion, including 65 percent of Republicans.

We've known for years that Americans support abortion rights. Asking the right questions makes it clear just how overwhelming that support really is.

Abortion at the Ballot Box

The truth is that you don't need to read polls to understand that Americans support abortion—just look at what's happened in elections since *Roe* was overturned.

The 2022 midterms, held just a few months after the Supreme Court's decision, became a referendum on abortion rights. Abortion was on the ballot in five different states—and abortion won in every single one of them.

Even in GOP-controlled Kentucky, voters quashed a ballot measure that would have amended the state constitution to explicitly state that it doesn't protect the right to abortion. If pushed through, it would have been near-impossible to restore abortion rights in the state. By rejecting it, Kentuckians made clear that they wanted the ability to make abortion legal again.

What's more, nationwide, Republicans' expected "red wave" never materialized: they barely took back the House and performed badly across gubernatorial and other state races. Instead, post-*Roe* fury sparked a massive turnout and drove voters to Democrats across the country. Exit polls showed an incredible turnout from voters under thirty—who supported Democrats by over 70 percent in key states—and that abortion was a top issue for voters. It was number two behind inflation, with 27 percent of respondents saying it was the most important issue for their midterm vote.

Now in 2024—after years of ignoring feminists who pointed out that abortion is a winning issue—you'd be hard-pressed to find a Democrat who isn't running on reproductive rights. Candidates finally understand that abortion isn't a "controversial" radical feminist issue: it's about family, health, and the economy. Most of all, abortion reminds voters about basic human compassion—or cruelty.

When red state Kentucky governor Andy Beshear won reelection in 2023, it was in large part because he focused on the anti-abortion extremism of his Republican opponent, Daniel Cameron. Beshear's campaign ran a television ad featuring a young woman, Hadley Duvall, who had been raped as a child. In the video, Hadley looks straight into the camera: "This is to you, Daniel Cameron," she says. "To tell a twelve-year-old girl she must have the baby of her stepfather who raped her is unthinkable."

In Governor Beshear's victory speech, Hadley Duvall was the first person, after his family, whom he thanked, noting that "because of her courage, this commonwealth is going to be a better place."

The power of abortion in red state elections didn't stop there. In 2024 Marilyn Lands, a licensed mental health counselor, flipped an Alabama House seat by running on repealing the state's ban. Lands didn't just campaign on abortion—she campaigned on *her own* abortion and won by twenty-five points.

Like Beshear, Lands put out a pro-choice ad featuring a young woman sharing a personal story: She had to drive ten hours out of state for an abortion after finding out her fetus had a fatal condition. In the ad, Lands then shared that she had a "nearly identical situation" years ago but "was able to get the care I needed close to home." The campaign spot reminded voters that their daughters and granddaughters don't have the same access to healthcare that they did.

For decades, anti-abortion activists and legislators counted on Democrats to treat abortion like a controversial, third-rail issue. And just a few years ago, a candidate in Kentucky or Alabama campaigning on abortion rights would have been unthinkable. But when politicians stopped being apologetic and started talking about abortion the way most Americans feel about it—positively—it changed the game.

I just wish it hadn't taken the end of *Roe* for politicians to figure out what feminists have been saying for decades: that abortion wins elections because Americans support abortion.

The Myth of a Divided America

If most people support abortion rights—if young people and Republicans and people in red states support them—why is the myth that Americans are split on the issue still so strong? If abortion is so popular and only getting more so, why does the lie persist that the country is divided?

In part, it's because anti-abortion organizations and conservative activists have spent a tremendous amount of money and energy embedding that lie in American culture. It's important to them that voters believe that abortion is something we're evenly split on, because it's a lot less controversial to strip away a long-standing right if you can convince the public that half of the country agrees with you.

After all, if Americans truly realized just how popular reproductive rights are, they'd also understand how attacks on abortion rights are attacks on democracy. (More on this later in this chapter.)

The other reason the anti-abortion movement wants people to believe that the country is split on abortion is that *support begets support.* Conservative lawmakers know that how your friends and neighbors feel about an issue impacts your own beliefs. Essentially, if voters knew that the people around them were actually pro-choice, they'd be a lot more comfortable thinking the same. (And vice versa: when people believe that their communities are "pro-life," they also feel social pressure to think similarly.)

That's one reason Republicans have been so obsessed with using words like "consensus." It's not just to cover up the fact that they're passing laws against voters' wishes—it's to give Republican voters the impression that they're in the majority.

The good news is that voters are starting to realize how pro-choice the country really is. In early June 2022, a few weeks before *Roe* was overturned, a study found 69 percent of anti-choice voters believed that most Americans opposed abortion. By December of the same year, only 43 percent thought the same. Voters have learned the truth, and quickly.

The other reason the myth of a divided America persists is a media problem—specifically the obsession with "both sides" journalism. If you were to learn about abortion only by reading a mainstream news-paper or magazine, you might get the impression that Americans are evenly split over the issue. Studies show that for years, media outlets have ignored majority support for abortion rights, with most of them covering the issue as "divisive, debatable, charged, controversial, or other similar terms." It's only been recently, as outrage has grown since *Roe*'s demise, that some publications are making clear that bans are being passed against voters' wishes.

That's because mainstream journalists have been trained to give equal space to "both sides" of an issue. On the surface, that seems like a good idea: of course reporters should be truthful, and readers should know all credible information on an issue. And at a time when accusations of "fake news" abound, it's understandable that publications and other news outlets want to be as careful as possible.

But there's a difference between being truthful and being "balanced." The latter suggests that journalists need to provide equal consideration to different sides of an issue and story—even when one side is clearly, unequivocally inaccurate. (Trump's presidency is perhaps the best recent example of how dangerous this kind of framing can be.)

Journalists favoring "balance" over truth have painted abortion as divisive instead of popular, and have given equal weight to those who oppose abortion—even as their position has become more and more out of step with public opinion. A 2020 study by Global Strategy Group and NARAL Pro-Choice America (now called Reproductive Freedom for All) found that only 9 percent of articles about abortion mentioned that most Americans supported *Roe*.

Essentially, the media's attachment to faux notions of objectivity means that they present abortion as far more polarizing than it actually is and opposition to abortion as far more common than it is.

In November 2022, for example, *The Washington Post* published a piece that looked at how college students were feeling about the end of *Roe*. The piece was framed as if students were split down the middle: "For some, the changes are joyful, a protection of human life. For others, they are terrifying, pushing them to consider scenarios that would have been unthinkable just months ago."

The truth, however, is that young people are the most pro-choice demographic in the country—overwhelmingly so. Three-quarters of eighteen-to-thirty-year-olds believe abortion should be legal in all or most circumstances. A 2023 poll from Harvard University's Institute of Politics found that adults under thirty are twice as likely to describe themselves as "pro-choice" than "pro-life."

The *Post* article made no mention of young people's staggering support for abortion rights.

When it comes to abortion rights, mainstream outlets and editors are so desperate to appear objective that they routinely ignore or downplay the truth. There's also a self-fulfilling problem with this kind of coverage; once the idea that America is evenly split on abortion becomes culturally accepted, reporters are more likely to buy into the idea themselves and to tailor their coverage accordingly.

Publications often use anti-abortion rhetoric and messaging without any context. They cover "heartbeat" bills without mentioning that cardiac activity isn't possible so early in pregnancy. They refer to medical facts as pro-choice "beliefs" rather than as scientific reality. One study found that language "personifying the fetus" appeared more often than women's abortion stories, which were present in only 4 percent of articles. (In other words, the media are more likely to humanize fetuses than women.)

Journalists sometimes reinforce myths that are downright dangerous. A 2017 report found that half the news articles it examined contained stigmatizing language about abortion; 15 percent used language claiming abortion is a dangerous procedure despite facts showing just the opposite; and 15 percent included statements suggesting abortion providers were murderers or just trying to make money.

Add all this up, and what we're left with is a national conversation on abortion that's dangerous, incoherent, and wildly divorced from reality. All because mainstream publications believe that in order to be unbiased, they have to give equal space and credibility to absolute nonsense.

Against Our Wills

Once you understand that abortion is massively popular—and that the vast majority of Americans want the right protected—it becomes easier to understand that abortion bans aren't just bad laws. They're attacks on democracy.

That's why I don't waste time "debating" people about abortion. Yes, it's partly because I think it's beneath me: I shouldn't have to convince someone of my humanity. But I also won't get into a back-and-forth on abortion rights with an anti-choicer or a Republican because I don't have to in order to win. Hearts, minds, and votes are already on our side.

This is not an issue of needing to persuade people to support abortion; it's a problem of a small group of powerful legislators and lobbyists banning abortion against our wills. Despite all the media myths and conservative messaging to the contrary, America is a pro-choice nation. So why talk about abortion rights as something people need to be convinced of?

Spending activist energy trying to sway those who will never be swayed—especially when we already have the votes we need—is exactly what anti-abortion groups want us to do. What better way to waste our time and resources?

The truth is that Republicans should be trying to convince us that their position is the better one; it's their policies, after all, that are causing so much suffering. It's their laws that Americans keep voting against. The real question is, if Republicans believe that America is a "pro-life" country, then why are they working so hard to keep voters from having a choice?

Instead of defending their abortion bans or trying to change hearts and minds, conservative lawmakers and the anti-abortion movement have focused their efforts on preventing voters from having a say at all. Given how popular abortion rights are, they figure it's better not to risk it.

After *Roe* was overturned, abortion rights activists in multiple states started to propose pro-choice ballot measures—amendments that would protect abortion rights in their state constitutions. Just as quickly, conservatives started spending millions of dollars to stop voters from having a say.

A refresher for those who need it: Ballot measures are a way for citizens to vote directly on an issue—whether it's abortion, marriage equality, legalizing marijuana, or something else. Forty-nine out of fifty states allow legislative-led ballot measures, proposed amendments that are suggested by state representatives and then put to voters.

Half the states also allow citizen-led initiatives, where everyday voters who collect enough signatures can put an issue on the ballot. The abortion rights ballot measures we've seen since *Roe* was overturned have primarily been citizen-led measures.

If Republicans truly believed that they were passing abortion laws that voters wanted, they would have no problem with this kind of direct democracy. Instead, they've pulled out all the stops to keep voters as far away from abortion as possible. They know that when voters have a say, they protect abortion—and they're just not willing to let that happen.

In early 2023, for example, Mississippi Republicans decided to restore the citizen-led ballot measure process in the state—but only if voters couldn't use it to bring back abortion rights. That's right, they said it was fine for voters to have a say, just not about abortion.

There was a reason that Mississippi Republicans were worried about voters making abortion legal. In addition to the clear message voters sent in the 2022 midterms, Mississippi voters had overwhelmingly rejected an anti-abortion ballot measure over a decade earlier, in 2011. They soundly defeated an attempt to add fetal personhood into the state constitution even before widespread post-*Roe* anger and a massive increase in support for abortion rights. Mississippi Republicans knew that if it were up to voters in the state, abortion would be legal.

The clearest—and perhaps most egregious—example of anti-abortion leaders working to stop voters from having a say came out of Ohio. After *Roe* was done away with, Republicans there passed a six-week abortion ban—that is, a near total ban. In response, pro-choice groups started collecting signatures to get abortion on the ballot for November 2023.

Ohio's Republican legislators—working alongside powerful conservative anti-abortion organizations—immediately got to work. First, they tried to raise the standard for ballot measures: they wanted to require amendments to get 60 percent of the vote in order to pass, instead of a simple majority. They also wanted to mandate that pro-choice activists collect signatures from every county in the state, as opposed to half of them. A rule like that would have allowed a single rural county with just a few residents to shut down a law that every other Ohioan wanted.

Republicans were so intent on making this happen that they held a special election that cost taxpayers $18 million, while arguing that it had nothing to do with abortion. (A leaked letter would later show that to be false and that the effort was entirely about abortion.)

At the same time, anti-choice organizations also sued over the ballot measure, arguing that the amendment should be split in two—a way to require that petitioners start over and gather twice as many signatures.

Thankfully, both efforts failed. The lawsuit was quashed, and Ohio voters overwhelmingly defeated Republican attempts to raise the ballot measure standards. But that didn't stop the state GOP. They then turned their attention to the ballot measure summary—the language that voters read before deciding whether to support or oppose an amendment. (In this case, Issue 1.)

Secretary of State Frank LaRose—the state's top election official—drafted an incendiary and false summary that changed the term *fetus* to "unborn child," left out the fact that the amendment would protect rights other than abortion (like miscarriage care and fertility treatment), and inverted language about restrictions later in pregnancy to say that the amendment would "always allow an unborn child to be aborted at any stage of pregnancy, regardless of viability," if a doctor deemed it necessary.

LaRose later admitted that he drafted the summary with anti-abortion groups. During a GOP event, he inadvertently admitted that his office worked on the summary with Susan B. Anthony Pro-Life America, the Center for Christian Virtue, and Ohio Right to Life—all groups that led the campaign opposing the pro-choice amendment.

That means when Ohioans went to cast a vote on the pro-choice measure, they didn't see the measure itself. Instead, they saw an anti-abortion distortion of the amendment that the state's top election official had crafted specifically to trick them, conspiring with the anti-abortion groups that spent millions of dollars and months of activism to oppose the measure.

At the same time that Ohio Republicans were undermining democracy, anti-abortion groups launched a multi-million dollar disinformation campaign in the state. They claimed in advertisements, interviews, and public appearances that Issue 1 would eradicate parental rights—allowing children to have abortions—and even gender-affirming surgery—without parental consent.

With abortion rights more popular than ever, the hope was that anti-trans bigotry would be better received than anti-choice talking points. But that doesn't mean they stopped those either.

These groups and lawmakers also falsely claimed that Issue 1 would allow for abortion "up until birth," despite clear language restricting abortion throughout pregnancy. And just in case that messaging didn't make its way into the public consciousness, conservatives told voters that they didn't need to support Issue 1 because abortion was already legal in Ohio. (It was a half-truth: the state's six-week ban was blocked, meaning that at the time abortion was legal up until twenty-two weeks. But without the protection of Issue 1, the near total ban would go into effect.)

What's more, the misinformation was being disseminated using taxpayer funds. An investigation conducted by the Associated Press found that lies about Issue 1 were being spread by a state-run website. And because that site is run by the government, it was prioritized in online search results.

To recap: Republicans spent millions of taxpayer dollars to try to require 60 percent of the vote instead of 50 percent, sued to force petitioners to collect twice as many signatures, colluded with anti-abortion organizations to draft ballot summary language to trick voters, and launched a multimillion-dollar disinformation campaign. All in order to keep voters from having a say on abortion rights.

Oh, and a few days before the vote on Issue 1, Republican leaders purged 26,000 voters from the rolls.

If you want to know how popular abortion rights really are, consider that despite all this incredible time, money, and energy spent to keep abortion illegal—in spite of all those attacks on democracy—Ohio voters passed Issue 1 resoundingly. That's how much people want abortion to be legal.

And that's how incredible pro-choice activists in Ohio are; they were able to win with huge margins despite all those insane state-driven hurdles.

Republicans launched similar attacks on democracy in every state considering or working on a pro-choice ballot measure. In Florida, where Republicans passed a six-week abortion ban, Attorney General Ashley Moody petitioned the state supreme court to reject a pro-choice ballot measure based on the language of the proposed amendment. She didn't want Floridians to be able to vote on it at all, even though Republicans there are in a strong position: Florida requires 60 percent of the vote to pass a ballot measure. But the state's abortion restrictions are just that unpopular, and Moody knew it. (Even the majority of Republicans oppose a six-week ban.) Thankfully, that effort failed and as this book goes to press, the issue is heading to voters.

In Missouri, Republicans tried to stop any abortion rights amendments from getting to voters by holding up the process for pro-choice signature collecting. The state attorney general refused to sign off on a legally necessary cost estimate for a measure, which voters see when they vote on a proposed amendment. Attorney General Andrew Bailey claimed that restoring abortion rights would cost the state billions of dollars rather than the $51,000 listed by the state auditor. Bailey had to be forced by the state supreme court to give his approval for the real estimate. Even then, he said if voters passed the pro-choice amendment, he would refuse to enforce it. Instead, Bailey threatened, the state would need to hire outside counsel to the tune of $21 million—an estimate he wanted included in, you guessed it, the ballot summary that would go in front of voters. The hope was to convince voters that abortion rights are too costly to support.

When legal hold-ups didn't work, Missouri anti-abortion groups tried a different tack. They sent voters text messages warning that pro-choice petitioners were trying to steal their personal data. The texts told Missourians to "protect yourself from fraud and theft" by refusing to sign any petitions. How much clearer can they be that they don't care what voters want?

Today Republicans have another democracy problem to contend with: now that abortion rights ballot measures are getting so much national attention, people in states that don't have citizen-led initiatives are asking why they can't vote directly on abortion.

It's a moment that abortion rights advocates predicted. In 2022, Planned Parenthood president Alexis McGill Johnson sparked a conservative media firestorm when she said that abortion would "save democracy." McGill Johnson—quoting Mini Timmaraju, president of Reproductive Freedom for All—was talking about the fight over pro-choice ballot measures, and how voters were seeing "how it's possible that you can have a state where there is majority support, but you actually can't have the laws that you want."

The idea was that with Americans getting a front-row seat to the Republican attacks on democracy, it would only be a matter of time before voters would get very, very pissed off. Now, here we are. In the wake of the winning vote in Ohio and the upcoming vote in Florida, Americans across the country are asking why they can't vote directly on abortion, too.

Remember, only about half the states allow citizens to bring a ballot measure forward; the other half depend on their legislators to put issues on the ballot.

But because abortion has been front page news since *Roe* was overturned, voters who haven't necessarily thought about ballot measures before are suddenly interested.

A columnist at Louisiana's *Times-Picayune,* for example, wrote in September 2022 that after Ohio activists put abortion on the ballot in their state, readers had been contacting her en masse wanting to know how to do the same. She had to tell them that Louisiana state law didn't allow it. Still, Louisiana voters were so interested in having an abortion rights ballot measure that the question came up in a 2022 gubernatorial debate—candidates were asked whether they'd change the rules to allow citizen-led initiatives. The sole Democratic candidate, Shawn Wilson, was the only one who said yes.

Similarly, in Mississippi, the Democratic candidate for secretary of state in 2023, Ty Pinkins, called out incumbent Michael Watson and other Republicans over ballot measures—saying they "stripped away our ballot initiative process, completely eliminating our right to take issues directly to voters."

Wilson and Pinkins, both long-shot candidates, didn't win their elections. But the fact that the issue was forced to the table in deep red states is important. In Mississippi, Republicans were even nervous enough that Watson changed his ballot measure stance—saying the state should revive the initiative process.

Voters in other states have been asking about ballot initiatives, too. The Iowa publication *Bleeding Heartland* reported in 2023 that readers were increasingly questioning why Democrats weren't trying to put abortion on the ballot, given that the majority of voters want to see it legal. And in North Carolina, the editorial board of *The Charlotte Observer* called out Republicans, issuing a specific challenge: "Come on, North Carolina Republicans. Put abortion on the ballot. What are you afraid of?" After all, they pointed out, Republicans were assuring voters that the recently passed twelve-week abortion ban was reasonable, mainstream legislation that the majority of North Carolinians supported. "If that's true," the board wrote, "they shouldn't have a problem with putting it to a test."

This kind of pressure on GOP lawmakers is growing. It's going to get ever more difficult for them to claim they support "common-sense" abortion policies in line with the majority of Americans while simultaneously refusing to allow those Americans to have a direct say. The hypocrisy isn't lost on voters, who are watching in real time as their elected officials work to pass laws that most of them oppose.

Still, Republicans don't seem to have gotten the memo. After Ohio's pro-choice ballot measure won, for example, former senator and conservative pundit Rick Santorum said the quiet part out loud: "Thank goodness that most of the states in this country don't allow you to put everything on the ballot, because pure democracies are not the way to run a country."

As Maya Angelou said, when someone shows you who they are, believe them.

This is not what democracy looks like. Americans deserve the right to make their voices heard on abortion rights without interference or obstruction. And if Republicans are so sure this is a "pro-life" nation, what are they so afraid of?

I think we know the answer. They're afraid of us. The good news is, they should be.

Chapter 3

"Pro-Life" Language Is a Sham

In 2023, Senator Mitch McConnell (R-KY) held a closed-door meeting of Senate Republicans about retiring the term *pro-life,* so afraid of voters' anger that they considered doing away with a label they've proudly donned for decades. The discussion came after a poll McConnell had commissioned showed that Americans associated the term *pro-life* with extremism.

Senator Kevin Cramer (R-ND) told NBC News that Americans understood "pro-life" to mean "being against all abortions . . . at all levels." (Which is accurate.) "Pro-choice," however, was seen as meaning a variety of things; voters understood it as a far more nuanced label.

What made this such an important moment is that for years, the prevailing political wisdom was that conservatives had won the language war, particularly around abortion. Let's be honest, *pro-choice* just doesn't have the same power as *pro-life;* one resonates far more than the other. But thanks to decades of Republican extremism, the GOP's long-winning label had become poisonous.

America was not prepared for the confusion and tragedy that would follow the fall of *Roe.* And anti-abortion lawmakers—confronted with the grim reality they've created and poll after poll showing how horrified voters are—are desperate to avoid responsibility. They know having their name attached to preventable medical tragedies is terrible politics. But while Republicans don't want the suffering of rape victims and miscarrying women laid on their doorstep, they also have no interest in changing their policies. So, they lie, mess with language, and make up nonsense terms.

What anti-abortion lawmakers and lobbyists don't seem to understand is that their problem isn't messaging, but policy. There's no label in the world that would make voters okay with watching cancer patients and child rape victims be denied abortions. But that hasn't stopped them from trying to throw themselves back into the language war, hoping that changing the way Americans talk about abortion might help change the way they feel about abortion (which, as you know, is very pro-choice).

Redefining Abortion

One of the boldest language moves from the right has been its attempt to redefine the term *abortion*—ignoring science, medicine, and reality in an effort to make the word more politically beneficial. They've been at this in one way or another for years, but since *Dobbs,* they've ramped up their efforts tenfold. Their primary strategy? Claim that some abortions aren't really abortions.

Specifically, conservatives claim that *abortion* refers only to ending unwanted pregnancies. They don't want it to mean treatment for ectopic pregnancies, miscarriages, or life-threatening pregnancies. Sometimes they don't even want to use the word when talking about ending rape-related pregnancies.

In late 2022, for example, Catherine Glenn Foster, president of Americans United for Life, told the House Judiciary Committee that a ten-year-old who terminated a pregnancy after being raped wasn't actually getting an abortion. "I believe it would probably impact her life," she said. "And so therefore it would fall under any exception and would not be an abortion."

When a puzzled Democrat asked her to clarify, Foster repeated herself: "If a ten-year-old became pregnant as a result of rape and it was threatening her life, then that's not an abortion."

Erin Hawley, senior counsel for Alliance Defending Freedom—the group responsible for the end of *Roe*—made the same claim about ectopic pregnancies (when a fertilized egg implants outside the uterus, usually in a fallopian tube). "That's not an abortion, because it does not have the intent to end the life of the child," she said.

That word *intent* is key—it is used often by Republicans and anti-abortion activists. In 2022 the conservative media outlet *The Federalist,* for example, published a piece arguing that treatment for ectopic pregnancies and miscarriages "has nothing to do" with abortion: "Abortion is an elective choice to kill an unborn child. Treatment for ectopic pregnancy and miscarriages do not constitute abortion because the intent is to save lives, not take them."

Similarly, in 2022, when Alexandra DeSanctis Marr of *National Review* responded to stories of women being denied abortion despite life-threatening conditions, she wrote that there's a "difference between necessary women's health care and intentionally killing a baby."

Abortion is a medical intervention; "intention" has nothing to do with it. After all, doctors will perform it in the same way regardless of how you feel about your pregnancy. But the focus on intent is telling; it reveals how those who oppose abortion split women into two groups: Those who deserve care, and those who don't.*

---

* If abortion is an intention rather than a medical intervention, if it's based on a feeling, then Republicans' definition also opens the door to broader criminalization. Consider what an abortion as an "intention" would mean for a woman who Googled "abortion" soon after she found out she was pregnant, then later had a

In Republicans' view, women who want to be pregnant, adhering to traditional gender roles that say women should be mothers, deserve abortions. Those who don't want to be pregnant, shunning their proper "place," are murderers. That's why in 2024, after the Alabama Supreme Court defined frozen embryos as "children," so many Republicans rushed to defend fertility treatments and IVF: Women who want to be mothers are "good" and deserve care.

It's also not a coincidence that conservatives exclude the most popular kind of care from their definition of abortion. Support for IVF and abortion in cases of rape, incest, and health conditions is extraordinarily high—defining abortion as an intention allows them to both demonize women who "want" abortions while appeasing as many voters as possible.

Most important, redefining abortion this way feeds voters—Republican women, specifically—a lie that they're desperate to believe: that if *they* needed an abortion, they could get one. That's why Republicans have been enshrining this false definition of abortion in legislation, under the guise of "tweaking" abortion bans in order to help the women they deem deserving.

When women started coming forward after *Dobbs,* with stories about being denied miscarriage care or left to bleed for days on end because doctors were too afraid of the law to help them, Republican legislators used that moment to their advantage.

Lawmakers in states like South Dakota and Idaho said they would "clarify" the abortion ban for doctors, to ensure that they could give women the healthcare they needed. But instead of adding so-called exceptions (more on these soon) or laying out when abortions were legal, legislators instead changed what abortion meant.

This allowed Republican lawmakers to get good press for

---

stillbirth. That Internet search could be used to argue that her stillbirth wasn't a stillbirth at all, because maybe her "intent" had been to end the pregnancy.

"softening" on the issue and supposedly making it easier for doctors to help women. In reality, their language changes did little to change care on the ground.

In 2023, for example, Idaho Republicans got glowing headlines for "clarifying" the state's abortion ban with language on life- and health-saving abortions. But doctors saw it for the farce it was. Boise-based maternal-fetal medicine specialist Dr. Lauren Miller said that politicians were "trying to make it look like something happened, when in fact, this makes no meaningful change."

Unfortunately, it's even worse than that. Nearly every state that passed an abortion ban since *Roe* was overturned has added this kind of "clarifying" language to their legislation. They're codifying— over and over again, in state after state—a false definition of abortion. One that tangibly and seriously hurts women.

Made-Up Medicine

If treatment for life-threatening pregnancies and miscarriages isn't abortion, what is it? According to anti-abortion groups, they're "maternal-fetal separation procedures."

As you can probably guess, this isn't a medical term, but a phrase invented by anti-choice extremists. The first time I noticed it was in a 2023 Iowa bill; the legislation defined "medically-indicated separation procedure" as such: "[A] medical intervention, the purpose of which is not to terminate a clinically diagnosed pregnancy of a woman, that is necessitated by a medical emergency . . . a 'medically indicated separation procedure' is not an elective abortion."

Soon the language of "separation" was coming up in bill after bill, law after law. Anti-abortion activists began to use it in earnest as well. Students for Life president Kristan Hawkins said, "When you're looking at a case where a woman's life is at risk, where the physician believes that she can no longer safely carry her child in her womb, or she may lose her life—we wouldn't consider that an abortion . . . it's a 'maternal-fetal separation.'"

Perhaps you're thinking, who cares what Republicans call abortion so long as women are getting the care they need? Does it really matter if they want to call it "separation"?

It absolutely does, for two main reasons. The first is that anti-abortion legislators are desperate to divorce abortion from healthcare; they argue that abortion is never necessary to save someone's health or life. "Separation" is a semantic way to enshrine that lie. The second reason we must call abortions *abortions* is that when we don't, people get hurt.

When Republicans started passing laws that called abortions "separation procedures," legislators also began outlining the *type* of procedures they'd consider acceptable means of "separation"— namely, induction of vaginal birth and C-sections.[*]

To be crystal clear: Republicans want women with life-threatening pregnancies—even when they're very early on—to be given major abdominal surgery, or be forced into unnecessary and traumatic vaginal delivery, rather than get a ten-minute abortion.

Abortion is quicker, safer, less painful, and less traumatic, but to those who believe fetal rights are more important than women's lives, that truth doesn't matter.

When I tell people about these mandates, the first question is often, why? Why in the world would anyone want to do this? When you're talking about someone who is fifteen weeks or even twenty weeks pregnant, it's not as if the fetus is going to survive. Why put patients through hell when their pregnancies aren't viable to begin with?

---

[*] Idaho's law specifically names C-sections and vaginal deliveries as "separation" procedures. Other states stick with "maternal-fetal separation" and let doctors intuit the rest.

The truth is that none of it makes sense until you understand that conservatives' goal has never been to help women or babies. It's always been about control and punishment—and what better way to inflict both than to force surgery on someone?

Again, the primary political tactic is to divorce abortion from healthcare. Anti-abortion lawmakers and activists want to prove that abortion is never necessary to protect a pregnant person's health or life. By mandating that doctors give women C-sections or induce vaginal labor, they think they can make that talking point true.

The Charlotte Lozier Institute, one of the nation's largest and best-funded anti-abortion groups, explicitly recommends that treatment for emergency abortions "be done by labor induction or c-section," which they call "medically standard." (It is absolutely not standard.)

The group claims a C-section is "a more appropriate method of separation" because it "shows greater respect for the human dignity of the fetus, even if she is too young or sick to survive." Unsurprisingly, dignity for women isn't mentioned.

This is not some future danger; it's already happening. Soon after *Roe* was overturned, a Louisiana woman's water broke just sixteen weeks into her pregnancy. She was made to spend hours delivering a nonviable fetus rather than be given an abortion. Her doctor reported in an affidavit that the woman not only hemorrhaged and lost close to a liter of blood but "was screaming—not from pain but from the emotional trauma she was experiencing."

In March 2024 the abortion rights group Lift Louisiana released a report showing that doctors were increasingly giving patients who had life-threatening and nonviable pregnancies C-sections in order to steer clear of breaking the law.

One doctor spoke about the fear ob-gyns were experiencing: "Our attorney general, Jeff Landry, sent us all a letter saying, 'I will put you in jail if you break these rules.' Literally, *I am out to get you, so don't break these rules.* So you do feel a little bit like there's a target on your back because you want to do what's right for the patient. And these aren't situations that happen infrequently, these aren't clinical scenarios that happen once a year. They happen all the time. Every time I'm on call, I have a patient that's considered to potentially be in a life-or-death situation."

Louisiana's abortion ban is one of the strictest in the nation. Doctors who perform abortions can face fifteen years in prison. So in order to, as one doctor put it, "preserve the appearance of not doing an abortion," they give women C-sections.

One patient was just twenty weeks pregnant when her water broke—far too early for a fetus to survive. She wasn't given a choice, just surgery. A Louisiana emergency medicine physician explains, "This person has had a C-section, . . . and that means that she's at higher risk for any future pregnancies. She can no longer deliver vaginally. . . . The appropriate thing to do . . . would be a D&E . . . without subjecting the patient to this unnecessary abdominal surgery. But my colleague didn't feel like she could do that while remaining in compliance with the law or appearing to remain in compliance with the law."

When we don't stop attacks on language early, they become part of our cultural lexicon. Consider what happened with "partial-birth abortion"—which isn't a scientific term, nor is it a real medical procedure. Anti-abortion groups coined the phrase in the 1990s, and had Republicans use it over and over again—on cable news, on statehouse floors. Soon it became a commonly used term.

If we don't fight back now against conservatives' latest made-up terms, we run the risk of the same thing happening with abortion as an "intention" and all of the related language that goes with it.

That said, part of the reason the term "partial birth" spread is because it had to do with abortion later in pregnancy, something Democrats are historically terrified to talk about or take on. That fear and defensiveness helped Republicans: Without anyone willing to talk about what abortion later in pregnancy really is, conservatives and anti-choice groups were able to paint their own picture.

Something similar is happening now with Republican lies about "abortion up until birth." Because Democrats are still loath to talk about abortion later in pregnancy—other than to say it's rare—conservative groups are once again taking advantage of that silence to create their own language.

Republican candidates and anti-abortion groups repeat the phrase "abortion up until birth" as often as possible because they're desperate to paint Democrats as the real extremists, especially as their own laws wreak havoc among American women. But the conservative obsession with so-called late abortion goes beyond finding a successful talking point; they're strategically redefining what "late" abortion means.

It's important to understand that there is no such thing as a "late abortion"; it's not a medical term. Regardless, when Republicans use the phrase, there is still a cultural understanding of what they're talking about; what most Americans imagine is a pregnancy in the third trimester.

But in May 2023, the president of March for Life Action, Jeanne Mancini, wrote an op-ed characterizing "dangerous and extreme late-term abortions" as anything after twelve weeks of pregnancy.

More recently, anti-abortion lawmakers and groups have started to slickly define "late abortions" as anything past fifteen weeks. Why that particular marker? Because Republicans are pushing national- and state-level fifteen-week bans, of course.

In late 2023 the Charlotte Lozier Institute put out a paper in support of a national fifteen-week ban, calling it a "Federal Limit on

Late Abortion." The paper was written by Ingrid Skop, an extremist ob-gyn whom anti-abortion groups trot out when they need false medical justifications for their bans. In her paper, Skop uses a constantly shifting definition of "late abortion."

The framework of the report is that any abortion after fifteen weeks of pregnancy is a "late abortion." But Skop also uses several examples that characterize anything after the first trimester as a "late abortion." There's even a section on "extremely late" abortion where Skop writes about abortions at twenty weeks, twenty-four weeks, and twenty-eight weeks.

Here's the thing: because "late abortion" is not a real medical term, Skop—and the anti-abortion movement more broadly—can define it however they want. Indeed, in a footnote, Skop admits that there is "no standard medical definition" for "late abortion." Still, she writes, "this discussion will consider 'late abortions' to be those performed after the first trimester and 'extremely late abortions' to be those performed after viability (late second trimester and third trimester)."

The Charlotte Lozier Institute is an extremely powerful group that directs Republicans on what kind of legislation to propose and what language to use. What the group says about "late abortion" will make it into Republican bills.

Just as concerning is the cultural impact of their lies. When anti-abortion legislators give interviews saying that they only want to ban "late abortions," most Americans will think they mean banning abortions in the third trimester. They likely don't imagine that the legislators mean banning abortions after twelve weeks. It's a clever way to trick voters.

It's not just the definition of *abortion* that conservatives are mucking with—all terms that have to do with pregnancy are now up for grabs. Since *Roe* was overturned, anti-abortion activists and groups have taken notice of phrases and words related to fatal fetal abnormalities, because those diagnoses are so often followed by abortion.

Nonviable, for example, has become "previable." *Lethal* has become "potentially life-limiting." The point is to make it seem—to both patients and voters—that doomed pregnancies aren't really fatal after all. And thanks to lobbying efforts by powerful anti-abortion groups like American Association of Pro-Life Obstetricians and Gynecologists (AAPLOG), this language, too, has made it into state legislation. Conservatives have even started to refer to nonviable fetuses as "disabled children"—a way to shame women thinking about ending their pregnancies.

Conservatives' hope is to eradicate exceptions for fatal fetal abnormalities altogether, forcing people to carry doomed pregnancies to term. And thanks to their use of certain innocuous-sounding terms in bills—like "prenatal counseling" and "perinatal hospice" which actually mean anti-abortion crisis pregnancy centers—voters largely don't know the difference.

But here's the good news. Every new term that Republicans come up with, every new message they try to embed into the public consciousness, is a hint. They're giving the people who care about abortion rights a road map—a dictionary, really—of what they're planning on doing next. Once you understand anti-abortion terms and talking points, their strategy becomes very, very clear.

Post-*Roe* Translations

Here's former South Carolina governor Nikki Haley talking about her abortion position on the campaign trail for the 2024 presidential primary: "The only way we're going to do it is if we find consensus on the federal level. I think we will find consensus on banning late-term abortions."

During her campaign, Haley had made a point of always talking about abortion using this kind of language; mentioning "compassion," "consensus," and other key words that gave the impression that she'd be more reasonable on the issue than other Republicans. And unless you'd been following abortion rights closely, you might have thought her remarks were fairly ordinary.

The truth, though, is that conservative legislators and anti-abortion leaders have spent the last few years creating a new language to talk about abortion—terms and phrases meant to come across as reasonable and moderate, while actually signaling extremism to hardcore anti-abortion voters.

"Consensus" is actually just another word for abortion ban. And as you know, "late abortion" means anything after twelve weeks of pregnancy. So what Haley was really saying in this seemingly innocuous statement is that she'd support a federal abortion ban after the first trimester, which is very far from what most Americans want.

Republicans and anti-abortion activists know that Americans overwhelmingly support abortion rights, but they're unwilling to change their policies, so they're changing their language instead. Presenting themselves as far more moderate than they actually are is a way for them to feign reasonableness while maintaining the same extremist beliefs. (Consider that conservatives now call "crisis pregnancy centers," which try to trick women out of abortions, "maternal wellness centers.")

Perhaps the most striking example is that since *Roe* was overturned, anti-abortion legislators, lobbyists, groups, and candidates will not use the term *abortion ban* at all. Let that sink in: they are so afraid that Americans oppose their agenda that they won't even call their own bans "bans" anymore.

Instead, Republicans now say they're just supporting "standards" on abortion, or that they're seeking a "consensus" and "reasonable limits." All those words are a stand-in for *ban*.

But this isn't just fearful messaging and avoidance; eradicating the word *ban* is a proactive strategy to trick voters.

When you're passing laws that Americans overwhelmingly don't want, what better word to use than "consensus" to give the impression that those laws are actually popular? And if you're pushing for extremist bills, best to call them "reasonable limits." Anything to avoid telling the truth about what your policies would actually do.

Eradicating *ban* started with Marjorie Dannenfelser, president of Susan B. Anthony Pro-Life America, who after the 2022 midterms began replacing the term *national ban* with "national standard" or "national consensus." In a statement about Donald Trump's stance on abortion, she told *The New York Times,* "We will oppose any presidential candidate who refuses to embrace at a minimum a 15-week national standard."

Responding to a speech from Nikki Haley on abortion, Dannenfelser used the word again: "When Ambassador Haley talks about national consensus on late-term abortion, we are in agreement. The consensus already exists. Polling shows 72 percent of Americans support limiting abortions by at least 15 weeks. . . . The pro-life movement must have a nominee who will boldly advocate for this consensus."

Soon we saw terms like "consensus" and "standard" everywhere. In 2023 Senator Lindsey Graham (R-SC) announced that he'd "introduce legislation soon, creating a national minimum standard of 15 weeks." And when Representative Elise Stefanik (R-NY) held a press conference to announce that House Republicans would be pushing a fifteen-week ban, she also didn't use the word—instead, she said that lawmakers have a role at the federal level regarding "building consensus" on abortion.

The terms come up most often, however, when Republicans who don't want to admit they support bans are asked about their abortion position. At a CNN town hall during the Republican presidential primaries, former New Jersey governor Chris Christie said, "I want to see that consensus, and then as president, I want to build off that consensus. Let's leave it to the states and if a consensus emerges, we'll know it." In an appearance on *Meet the Press,* Republican National Committee chair Ronna McDaniel said that Republicans can win on a message of "consensus" and "reasonable limitations." And Virginia governor Glenn Youngkin pushed for a fifteen-week ban that he called "consensus" legislation.

By the summer of 2023, Marjorie Dannenfelser had redefined *ban* so that it wouldn't apply to any abortion legislation in the United States. She said, "*Banning* is not the word that we use because it's not accurate. . . . *Ban* means everything."

Her claim was that if an abortion law had an exception—for women's health and lives, for example—it wasn't a "ban," but a "limit" or a "restriction." A ban would mean no abortion, no matter what. Under this definition, Texas and Tennessee don't have abortion bans. (In truth they have the strictest bans in the country, only allowing abortion when women are in imminent danger of death.)

In fact, by Dannenfelser's logic, there are no abortion bans in America at all. In an op-ed in *The Hill,* she made that claim specifically, writing that "the dictionary definition of 'ban' is 'to forbid someone to do something.' . . . In no state are all abortions forbidden."

To be clear: this is the president of the most powerful anti-abortion group in the country arguing that the United States has no abortion bans.

By then, Republicans across the country had gotten the message. In a 2024 debate between Ohio Senate Republican candidates, participants objected to a question about abortion that used the word *ban*. Businessman Bernie Moreno said, "To be clear, you're using that word, I'm not," and then went on to talk about "commonsense restrictions." Ohio secretary of state Frank LaRose said, "I don't use the word *ban*."

In North Carolina, when lawmakers were trying to frame their twelve-week ban as a "reasonable compromise," sponsor State Senator Joyce Krawiec said, "This is a pro-life plan, not an abortion ban." When Virginia Republicans were running for office in 2023, most put out ads about Governor Glenn Youngkin's fifteen-week abortion ban proposal, insisting that it wasn't a ban at all. An ad from State Senator Siobhan Dunnavant said, "I don't support an abortion ban, period." And Virginia governor Younkin released an ad with a voice saying, "Here's the truth: there is no ban."

When a pro-choice activist went undercover at a 2024 anti-abortion event, she secretly taped an exchange with Representative Andy Harris (R-MD), who said: "We think the use of the word *ban* is a bad idea. You mean a bill that limits abortion? I think we can. We should never use the word *ban*. That's the word they use."

He also explained why Republicans call *bans* "limits": "The majority of Americans believe there should be 'limits.' That's the word we have to use because the majority of Americans agree."

In an interview with *The Nation,* James Bopp, general counsel for the National Right to Life Committee, called the term "the big ban word," saying that polls showed that using the word *ban* made abortion policies much less popular. In the same piece, political director Karen Cross told reporter Amy Littlefield, "We want to talk about 'protections' and not 'bans.' "

Now, it would be one thing if anti-abortion activists and legislators simply didn't want to use the word *ban,* but what makes the post-*Roe* war on language different is that these groups and lawmakers want journalists to stop using *ban,* too. Conservatives launched a pressure campaign on mainstream media outlets to stop using *ban,* claiming that doing so was a sign of pro-choice bias.

The argument—made by groups like Dannenfelser's—is that because there are no abortion bans in America, calling any piece of their legislation a ban is a sign that journalists are taking a side in the abortion debate.

E. V. Osment, vice-president of communications at Susan B. Anthony Pro-Life America, chastised her *Hill* interviewers for using the word *ban*: "I wouldn't use the word *ban* because I think it's really misleading for the American people . . . when you say *ban* . . . then they think there's not exceptions."

Later in that *Hill* article, reporters described a fifteen-week national ban as "restrictions on the procedure at 15 weeks, with exceptions at the federal level." That sounds a whole lot different—and less extreme—than *ban*. Which, of course, is the point.

By October 2023, the pressure had reached *The Washington Post,* which covered a proposed fifteen-week ban in Virginia as a "limit." When the *Post* article did mention the word *ban,* it put it in scare quotes. Similarly, in 2024, ABC News called Republicans' proposal for a national ban a "limit" that "cap[ped] abortion at 15 or 16 weeks."

Let's be clear: When reporters adopt anti-abortion language, they are doing conservatives' work for them—namely, misinforming voters.

To the pundits and reporters who don't know about the anti-abortion movement's strategic language shift, Republicans calling a ban a "consensus" may seem like a mere equivocation. They may not realize that Republicans are still calling for a ban, just using different terminology. Ignorance isn't any less dangerous, though.

In 2023 the National Republican Senatorial Committee was "encouraging Republicans to clearly state their opposition to a national abortion ban and support for reasonable limits on late-term abortions when babies can feel pain with exceptions for rape, incest, and life of the mother."

Mainstream publications like *The Washington Post* and *The New York Times* took this statement at face value, reporting it as evidence that Republicans were moving away from supporting a national ban. But if you understand the language game conservatives are playing, you know that's just not true.

Like "consensus" and "national standard," "reasonable limits" is just another euphemism for *ban*. (They use the terms interchangeably, but all refer to abortion bans while sounding a whole lot better and less unpopular.) And you know what "late abortion" means to them. So while major publications were telling their readers that Republicans were moving away from a national ban, the NRSC was telling candidates to support a national ban on abortion after twelve weeks—and signaling to Republicans that they should lie about it.

Because they define *ban* as a total ban without exceptions, they had plausible deniability.

In short, Republicans' claim that they don't support a national ban means nothing. Pundits and reporters need to ask candidates if they support federal legislation of any kind on abortion, and how they define *ban*. Most of all, publications need to stop taking Republicans' word for it and learn what these terms really mean.

The good news is the anti-abortion movement's effort to redefine ban means they're on the defensive, literally running from their own policies. Some Republicans have even begun to adopt pro-choice rhetoric, calling their twelve-week abortion bans "plans to legalize abortion up until 12 weeks."

But the fact that Republicans are coming from a place of weakness doesn't make their attacks on language any less dangerous. They're using these words to trick Americans, making them believe that these laws are far less extreme than they actually are—and are counting on mainstream media outlets to help them solidify their lies.

This isn't just about talking points and messaging; the language powerful people use has a real-life impact on pregnant people every day. What's more, when false and misleading language—like the

GOP's fake definition of *abortion*—makes its way into legislation, there's a long-term danger: The longer those definition and words remain in legislation, the more fake terms they put in bills, the easier it is for anti-abortion organizations to argue to judges and courts down the line that these lies are part of the country's history and tradition. It's a way for them to forever enshrine their bullshit at women's expense. And nowhere is that clearer than in the next chapter.

Chapter 4

They're Banning Birth Control

In early 2023, Lindsey wanted to get an IUD, a common form of birth control. So the twenty-nine-year-old Georgia resident—who had just given birth two months earlier—set up an appointment with her ob-gyn. But a few days before she was scheduled to get the contraceptive placed, her doctor called with bad news: Lindsey's insurance company wouldn't cover the IUD unless it was "medically necessary."

"I feel that it's necessary to not have any baby," Lindsey told me. "It was mentally, physically, and emotionally very challenging, and I cannot do it again. Why is that not necessary?"

Her insurer's answer? They considered it a "sanctity of life" issue. If Lindsey wanted the IUD, she would have to pay $2,000 out of pocket.

When I tell people that Republicans are banning birth control—not in the future, but right now—they don't always believe me. That's because they're imagining a singular law explicitly outlawing contraception, not a scenario like Lindsey's. But that's how this happens, not with an obvious attack but with a slow, methodical chipping away at our rights. Through small indignities and limitations of access that we won't immediately see as a "ban" or deliberate attacks.

Republicans know that openly outlawing birth control would be a political disaster. Ninety-nine percent of American women have used contraception, voters are already angry over abortion bans, and Republicans are losing by huge margins at the polls because of their attacks on reproductive rights. If voters understood that lawmakers were targeting contraception, too, the blowback would be unprecedented.

Republicans know they need to hide their extremism from voters. Their beliefs about birth control aren't just unpopular—they're bizarre. Consider one of the arguments that the anti-abortion movement makes about IUDs and birth control pills: that the contraceptives are abortifacients because they make a uterus "inhospitable" for a fertilized egg.

Human Life International, for one, says that the pill "transforms the endometrium from a welcoming, lush forest into a barren, sterile desert," causing a "silent abortion." The group also claims that IUDs "irritate" the uterine lining "and make it inhospitable to the blastocyst . . . which is an abortifacient effect."

If "abortion" is simply your body being "inhospitable" to a fertilized egg or embryo, imagine how broadly that redefinition could be applied. If you don't take prenatal vitamins, are you making your body inhospitable and therefore having a "silent abortion"? What about if you drink alcohol? Or exercise strenuously?

This isn't fearmongering. In 2006 the Centers for Disease Control and Prevention released guidelines instructing all women of childbearing age—whether or not they were pregnant, and regardless of whether they had plans to be—to take folic acid supplements, not smoke, not "misuse" alcohol, maintain a healthy weight, refrain from drug use, and avoid "high risk sexual behavior." The idea was that anyone who had the ability to get pregnant should be making their body as hospitable as possible to a potential pregnancy.

All of which is to say: The things that may sound absurd or insane—beliefs that we think no one could possibly take seriously—

have, in many cases, already been floated in the corridors of power. And for as much as conservatives claim that they have no interest in banning birth control, you'd be hard pressed to find a single one willing to protect or expand access.

And so instead of taking on that risk with a clear-cut birth control ban, Republicans have launched a quiet war against contraception. They know that the slow erosion of a long-standing right is much harder for people to spot than a single sweeping law. Either way, the result is the same: death by a thousand cuts still kills you in the end.

This attack on birth control is happening in two major ways (and Lindsey's story exemplifies both): First, Republicans are eradicating access to contraception. Day by day, state by state, they are passing laws that allow insurers to deny coverage for certain kinds of birth control, allowing pharmacists to refuse to dispense emergency contraceptives, and replacing real reproductive health clinics with "crisis pregnancy centers" that refuse to discuss contraception. It doesn't matter if birth control is legal or not if it's impossible to get.

The second way the GOP is banning contraception is by lying about what birth control actually is, claiming that IUDs, the morning after pill, and sometimes even the Pill are not birth control at all—but abortifacients. It's a strategy that's been years in the making.

I hate to say it, but these tactics are smart. The first one allows Republicans to pretend they support birth control while doing everything in their power to ensure no one can get it; the second allows them to say they're banning not birth control but abortion.

Both strategies give lawmakers and activists plausible deniability to claim they would never, ever ban contraception. That means that when feminists or pro-choice lawmakers warn about Republicans' war on contraception, they're made to seem ridiculous.

When an Ohio Democrat raised the alarm about the danger to birth control in 2023, for example, the president of Ohio Right to

Life, Mike Gonidakis, hit back by calling it fearmongering, saying, "She can't cite a piece of legislation that bans contraception." They're counting on Americans continuing to think of banning birth control as that single piece of legislation. That's why it's so critical that we know what the attack on contraception really looks like.

Chipping Away at Access

If your pharmacist has the right to refuse you emergency contraception, it's irrelevant whether the medication is legal or not. Given that you have only a short period of time when the medication works, if you live in an area with just one or two pharmacies—and no pharmacist will give you the medication—it might as well be banned.

If your insurance company can deny you coverage for an IUD, who cares what the law says? You can't afford it anyway. Legality is theoretical; it's access that determines whether someone can actually get the care they need. The people most likely to be impacted by attacks on access will be the most vulnerable, like young women and those who are low income. What's also important to know is that some women who might want an IUD or birth control pills will be pressured into getting long-acting, reversible contraception (LARC) or sterilization instead. Women of color, immigrant women, and poor women—those who Republicans deem undesirable communities—have long been pressured and forced in this way.

Because so many of these attacks on access are happening at the state level—and because they overwhelmingly impact the most marginalized communities—they're not getting the same kind of media attention that the broader war on abortion rights receives.

When a small program offering free birth control gets cut, the story might get some local coverage, but the media will rarely contextualize it within the bigger, more deliberate targeting of contraception.

In short, not enough people are connecting the dots. So let's do it for them, using the GOP's biggest and most expensive attack on access as an example: anti-abortion crisis pregnancy centers.

Since *Roe* was overturned, ob-gyns have been fleeing anti-choice states en masse, and abortion bans have shut down the places that are often a community's only reproductive health clinic. At the same time, conservative legislators have launched a massive expansion of crisis pregnancy centers, claiming that they will fill that healthcare gap (that is, the gap that their own policies caused).

When I say that the expansion is massive, I mean massive. After *Dobbs,* Tennessee boosted state support for crisis pregnancy centers from $3 million to $20 million; Florida raised it from $4.5 million to $25 million, and Texas went from giving the groups $5 million every two years to giving a whopping $100 million for 2022 and 2023.

The Republicans funneling all that money to these religious groups frame it as proof that they care about women's health. Iowa governor Kim Reynolds described her state's uptick in funding as evidence that Republicans are "supporting healthy families." Mississippi governor Tate Reeves said it's about the state doing "everything in its power to deliver the support moms and babies deserve."

And while most people understand that crisis pregnancy centers are anti-abortion, many don't know that they're also anti-contraception. I don't just mean they can't prescribe birth control, though that's certainly true. (After all, they aren't real medical clinics.) The staff at these centers can't even talk about birth control or refer women to anyplace that does. Republicans are essentially funding a multimillion-dollar gag rule on contraception.

In Louisiana, "eligible maternal wellness centers" must be affiliated with one of three large anti-abortion networks, all of which prohibit their affiliates from dispensing or "promoting" birth control.

The law in Texas is similar. Anti-abortion crisis pregnancy centers and "maternity homes" funded by the state are explicitly prohibited from providing or "promoting" contraception. Regardless of how many different Republicans claim they're not attacking contraception, their laws make it clear that they're investing heavily in crisis pregnancy centers largely *because* they're anti–birth control.

When crisis pregnancy centers do talk about birth control, they lie. Study after study shows that crisis pregnancy centers spread misinformation about contraception. A 2023 report on centers in Ohio found that not only do they refuse to discuss contraception, but that staff at one center told women that birth control "causes an abortion." And in Maryland, a staffer said she couldn't give a referral for birth control because contraception is "next to aborting your baby."

These aren't one-off examples. Opposing birth control is a major pillar of these centers' beliefs. In 2022, a *Mother Jones* reporter went to a conference of anti-abortion centers where staffers were trained how to handle a "young, unmarried female client" who had a pregnancy scare.

They were told to warn her "about the side effects and risks of hormonal birth control," to claim that barrier methods like condoms are ineffective, and ultimately get to the point that "the goal of birth control is preventing sexual intercourse from resulting in its natural, intended biological result: children."

Crisis pregnancy centers are growing at an exponential rate: they already outnumber real health clinics by a factor of three to one. Those numbers are only going to increase with the influx of state funding.

Consider what the attack on birth control access looks like in an anti-choice state that overfunds crisis pregnancy centers. Imagine being a teenage girl or young woman in a small town in Iowa. You know birth control is legal, and you remember that a few years ago your older sister went to Planned Parenthood to get on the Pill.

The problem is your local Planned Parenthood clinic shuttered after *Roe* was overturned. You don't have health insurance, you don't have the money to pay for birth control out of pocket, and you have no idea that Iowa has a program to help low-income people get contraception.

That's because a few years ago, the state decided to discontinue its participation in the federal Medicaid family planning network as a way to strip Planned Parenthood of state funding. The state created its own program instead, but because it decided not to spend any money to advertise or promote that program, people simply don't know about it. (There's been a nearly 83 percent drop in Iowans using this program's services since they made the switch.)

With no other place to go, you remember the crisis pregnancy center that gave you a free physical back when you were in middle school. Or maybe you did a quick Google search for "clinics" in your area. Either way, you end up in a building with people who look like doctors—they're wearing lab coats. You ask them how you can get on the Pill or get an IUD.

These seem-to-be doctors tell you that hormonal birth control could be life-threatening. It could give you a stroke, they say. They also tell you that IUDs cause abortions. Because you know abortions are illegal, that freaks you out. Maybe they lie some more, saying a minor can't get birth control without parental permission, or that there's no other place that will give you contraception. And while you don't quite believe their assertions that your body should be allowed to do its own "natural" thing, you're not sure what else you can do.

So you leave, defeated and resigned. You just hope your boyfriend will agree to use condoms.

Redefining Birth Control as Abortion

For years, conservative organizations, activists, and lawmakers have been laying the groundwork for this moment, arguing in legislation, lawsuits, and culture that certain types of contraceptives are actually abortifacients. They claim, falsely, that emergency contraception and IUDs disrupt the implantation of a fertilized egg and are therefore abortifacients. (They say pregnancy begins at fertilization.) Science doesn't back that up, but even if the morning-after pill and IUDs did stop the implantation of a fertilized egg, the American College of Obstetricians and Gynecologists defines *fertilization* as the first step in a series of events "that leads to pregnancy"—not as the beginning of pregnancy itself.

Unfortunately, the truth hasn't mattered much here. Conservatives and the anti-abortion movement have been successful with their birth control lie at the highest levels. In 2014 the retail chain Hobby Lobby argued that it shouldn't have to cover employees' contraception costs because IUDs and the morning-after pill end pregnancies. That's just not true, but the company still won their SCOTUS case: it wouldn't have to cover employees' contraception.

This isn't just a redefinition tactic, and it isn't just happening rhetorically or theoretically. This lie is being used to actively prohibit real women from obtaining birth control. Consider the employees at Hobby Lobby, Lindsey's inability to get her insurance company to cover her IUD because of the "sanctity of life," and the pharmacists who refuse to dispense emergency contraception.[*]

This happens to women every day.

And it's not just happening in red states. In 2023 Oregon Right to

---

[*] There have been an increasing number of lawsuits seeking to protect pharmacy workers who believe birth control is abortion and refuse to prescribe it. The legal tactic isn't just meant to reduce access to contraception, but further enshrine the lie that certain kinds of birth control are abortifacients.

Life sued the state over a law that requires insurance plans to provide contraception coverage. Citing the Hobby Lobby Supreme Court case, the anti-abortion organization argued that it needed an exemption from the law because emergency contraception and certain kinds of IUDs are abortifacients. In fact, the group refused to even call them birth control, referring to them in the filing as "abortifacient 'contraceptives.'"

Republican state lawmakers are relying on that myth to stop any efforts to increase the availability of contraception. In Colorado, they tried to stop a program that provided free IUDs, and in Missouri they fought to prevent Medicaid from covering IUDs—both arguing that IUDs weren't really birth control but abortifacients.

And when Mississippi Democrats tried to pass a law protecting birth control, a Republican lawmaker (who just so happened to have crafted the state's abortion ban) said he opposed the effort because it would allow for "morning-after abortions." He meant emergency contraception.

That said, most of these efforts are happening quietly and behind closed doors—Republicans want voters to believe they support birth control, not oppose it. That's why whenever reporters ask Republicans if they support contraception, they should also ask, *What kind of contraception do you support?*

Republicans are even pushing this abortifacient myth under the guise of providing *more* birth control. In 2024 Indiana lawmakers were advancing legislation that would increase the availability of long-acting reversible contraception for Medicaid recipients, but before the bill made it to a state senate committee, all language referring to IUDs was removed.

Behind the scenes, anti-abortion activists had successfully persuaded legislators that IUDs are abortifacients. When Republican state representative Cindy Ledbetter was asked why they took out the IUD references, she responded that it was because "we are a strong pro-life state." In other words, anti-abortion legislators pushed the contraception-as-abortion lie even in a law meant to provide birth control.

It's important to know that extremist state legislators and activists aren't the only ones spreading this lie. National Republican leaders—even those considered "mainstream" GOP—are lining up behind the "abortifacient" myth.

During Amy Coney Barrett's Supreme Court confirmation hearings, Senator Ted Cruz (R-TX) said that the Affordable Care Act— which mandates coverage for contraception—was trying to force religious groups to "pay for abortion-inducing drugs." And Representative Mike Johnson (R-LA), who became House Speaker in 2023, believes that birth control is actually abortion. In fact, during a 2013 panel, Johnson said outright, "The morning-after pill, as we know, is an abortifacient."

It's not just a few extremist activists or groups that say birth control is really abortion. Every major anti-abortion group and activist believes it. Some groups, like Students for Life, are open about that belief. There is a whole page on its website dedicated to explaining "abortifacient" and "non-abortifacient" contraceptives. In short, they claim that any hormonal contraceptive or IUD is abortion. The only birth control they consider non-abortive are barrier methods.

But most anti-abortion organizations hide their true beliefs for the same reason that Republican legislators do—they understand that Americans would be horrified. Susan B. Anthony Pro-Life America takes great pains to avoid talking about birth control. But it opposes any legislation that would increase access to contraception, and it supports lawsuits—like *Hobby Lobby*—that redefine contraception as abortion. The same is true for groups like the Heritage Foundation and Americans United for Life; they avoid talking about their position but use their tremendous power and capital to ensure that this lie is embedded in American legislation and politics.

How They're Doing It

Given the popularity of birth control—and the ridiculousness of anti-abortion claims—you may be wondering how in the world Republicans' attacks on birth control could possibly be successful. After all, Americans are outraged over abortion bans—why would we turn a blind eye to the attack on contraception? The truth is that conservative groups and legislators have put a lot of time and effort into hiding that attack from us. They've carefully planned this moment, choosing to target contraception in a way that attracts the least attention.

Republicans are betting that Americans will be too distracted by the more obvious attacks on abortion rights to notice their quiet war on birth control. The anti-abortion movement knows that ever since *Dobbs*, the pro-choice movement has been doing triage to reduce the harm the abortion bans are causing, to stop the constant attacks on democracy, and to prevent any further damage as we close in on the 2024 presidential election. As a result, the movement is completely overwhelmed.

That means there is no better time for the anti-abortion movement to push through restrictions on contraception, hoping that their efforts will go unnoticed in the chaos. Remember the metaphor about the frog being slowly boiled alive?

Unfortunately, that strategy is working. The GOP's attempts to redefine and reduce access to contraception have been largely overlooked. The mainstream media aren't covering the effort in earnest; nor are Democrats pointing out that the attack on birth control is not some future danger—it's happening now. And it's happening strategically.

When Republicans talk about contraception-as-abortion, they tend to focus on emergency contraception. There's a reason for that—they know the morning-after pill is a medication that people are already confused about. In fact, the vast majority of Americans don't understand the difference between emergency contraception and abortion medication. (Emergency contraception prevents pregnancy, while abortion medication ends pregnancy.)

A 2023 poll found that 73 percent of Americans believe that emergency contraception can end a pregnancy. And so the anti-abortion movement is stoking confusion whenever possible, believing that if it can make Americans think emergency contraception is the same thing as abortion medication, it will be that much easier to ban both.

After *Dobbs,* colleges both in pro- and anti-choice states started installing vending machines stocked with emergency contraception. But because the anti-abortion movement can't tell the truth—which is that it opposes birth control—its activists planted quotes in the media about these vending machines, conflating emergency contraception with abortion medication.

In the summer of 2023, a representative from Susan B. Anthony Pro-Life America told the *Washington Examiner* that "providing dangerous abortion pills on college campuses is reckless, puts women in grave danger, and is not the answer to an unplanned pregnancy." The machines stocked the morning-after pill, not abortion medication. (I wish!) Anti-abortion activists knew the truth, but they deliberately tried to misinform already-confused Americans. They repeated that lie about vending machines again and again, and within just a few weeks, Fox News published an article with the headline "Abortion-by-Vending-Machine Is Much Worse Than It Sounds."

Really, it's no wonder that so many Americans don't understand the difference between abortion medication and emergency contraception—there's an incredibly powerful, well-funded movement working to keep them ignorant.

And to be clear, tactics like this have a direct impact: I get frequent messages from college students asking if they're breaking the law when they buy emergency contraception. The disinformation works. And that's what the anti-abortion movement is relying on for its most ambitious attack yet: hormonal birth control.

Killing the Pill

The birth control pill is the most popular form of contraception in the United States, behind sterilization. So if anti-abortion groups want to eradicate contraception, it makes sense that this is where they'd start.

For women who grew up before the Pill, the advent of hormonal contraception was a miracle. But if you've spent any time on social media recently, you've likely seen some of the widespread misinformation about and disdain for hormonal birth control. Supposed "health" influencers make videos saying that the medication interferes with your body's "natural" rhythms. Conservative pundits claim that the Pill is changing women's sexual preferences. There's even a new generation of young conservative women romanticizing housewifery—"tradwives"—who claim that the contraceptive is one of modern women's major woes.

All of this, brought to Americans via an insidious cultural campaign meant to sow distrust in a safe and popular form of birth control.

At the 2023 Turning Point USA's Young Women's Leadership Summit—a gathering for ultraconservative youth—young women and girls in the audience were urged not to use hormonal birth control. The group even set up a mirror at the conference, made for selfies, that was made to look like a magazine cover; one of the headlines read, "Birth Control Is So Last Year."

Following in the footsteps of conservative women like Phyllis

Schlafly, who told women to stay home while she herself went out and became a successful writer and speaker, the pundit and podcaster Alex Clark told conference-goers that hormonal birth control was one of the feminist movement's "lies." She blamed it for "fracturing" American families by "coercing" women "outside of their natural roles as mothers into the workforce." (That word *natural* comes up a lot.)

Similarly, in a 2023 appearance on Fox News, podcaster Mikhaila Peterson—daughter of misogynist extraordinaire Jordan Peterson—said that the Pill was to blame for men's decreasing workforce participation. Hormonal birth control pills, she said, were "majorly impacting relationships between men and women." Women, she said, "choose more feminine men when they're on the Pill." Such choices, "could impact people generationally."

The message would be laughable if it weren't taking off. That same claim has been repeated again and again in conservative media.

The most explicit aspect of this cultural campaign is the rise of tradwives—young, mostly white women who create online content that yearns for the days of 1950s housewifery. They claim that modern feminism made women's lives worse. The movement has grown exponentially, largely because of how much young sexist men love it.

For anyone who lived through that time—or knows anything true about it, at all—the content being put out by these young women is easy to pick apart. Their idealized version of housewives never really existed outside of advertisements and television shows. In reality, housewives were trapped.

They had no financial security, no ability to apply for a line of credit or even have a bank account. They were victims of domestic violence, which was illegal in name only. They could be institutionalized by their husbands or fathers if they deviated from the norm. They were often medicated unnecessarily and/or were depressed and anxious. (No-fault divorce brought women's suicide rate down 20 percent!)

And that's just the women who had husbands with enough money that they could stay at home. Women like my grandmother, who worked in bars and factories, didn't have a white picket fence and starched aprons. Women of color didn't have access to this "dream" of American womanhood either; they were more likely to be domestic help for white women. As you can imagine, the panoply of Pinterest board images never seem to feature housewives with domestic help. I suppose saturated images of poodle skirts and roasts are better marketing than the reality of what white supremacist patriarchy really looks like.

Instead, these videos and creators say that feminism decreased women's happiness, and that those who return to the domestic sphere have easier, more fulfilling lives. That would never be a harmless message, but it's especially dangerous given the timing: This resurgence of housewife iconography comes at the same time abortion rights have been stripped from American women. What better way to quiet the next generation of girls, growing up in a country without reproductive rights, than to tell them it's actually progress? That not having access to birth control would be *good,* actually? They're making sexism aspirational.

I'd be less worried about this cultural trend if it were just "tradwives" spreading misinformation about birth control. But increasingly, seemingly politically unaffiliated influencers are also talking about the dangers of hormonal birth control—and touting "natural" family planning instead.

When researchers at the University of Delaware looked at YouTube influencers who spoke about birth control, they found that 74 percent of the content creators talked positively about stopping hormonal birth control and that a common theme was touting "natural" family planning or claiming birth control pills negatively impacted their mental health.

What's also distressing is that this cultural pacification campaign relies on feminist rhetoric to lure in young women—whether it's a website for natural family planning urging women to "listen to their bodies," or influencers using the very real issue of medical sexism to argue against contraception, or preying on the understandable financial and existential distress women feel under capitalism to push for traditional gender roles. Some videos even suggest that becoming a stay-at-home wife is "making patriarchy work for you"—a subversive way for women to get one over on men!

All of this is a deliberate effort to lay the groundwork for Republicans to ban birth control while insisting it's for our own good. Think I'm reaching? Consider that one of the most viral "tradwife" videos of 2022 was published by an influencer who launched a billionaire-backed wellness company that provides women with health tips based on the dates of their menstrual cycles. The conservative women's magazine, *Evie*—which published an article in 2023 claiming that the Pill triggered a cortisol response in women's bodies that was "similar to PTSD"—is also connected to the same company.

That's right, the people who are pushing out content about how bad birth control is are founding apps to gather and track women's period data.

Their messages may be working. A 2023 study showed that while emergency contraception sales were increasing, other kinds of birth control use were decreasing. A poll from *The Skimm* that same year found that a third of women who weren't on birth control said they'd stopped taking it within the last year. Ob-gyn and researcher Dr. Kate White told the *Financial Times*, "There is a lot of distrust about highly effective methods of contraception, especially those with hormones in them."

Birth Control Is a Winning Issue

Here's the good news. The numbers are on our side: not only do the vast majority of voters support abortion—they support birth control even more. A 2024 survey from Americans for Contraception reported that 80 percent of voters say protecting access to contraception is "deeply important" to them—and that even 72 percent of Republicans support birth control.

Just as important, 64 percent of voters were less likely to support Republican candidates when they were told that the legislators voted against the Right to Contraception Act. That means birth control is a really dangerous topic for Republicans, and that Democrats should be talking about it all the time. Not just because it polls well but because Republicans are, in fact, attacking contraception.

Americans for Contraception even pointed out the GOP's targeted attacks on certain types of birth control, recommending that people who care about reproductive rights talk specifically about those different kinds of contraception. The survey urges, "Don't shy away from talking about all forms of contraception, including I.U.D.s and emergency contraception like Plan B. Contraception is popular, and voters want to be the ones making the decisions on what methods they use. They do not draw distinctions between types of birth control, and neither should we."

In other words, we shouldn't just be talking about birth control—but publicly asking Republicans what they think of certain kinds of contraception.

That includes mainstream media outlets, who too often neglect to ask difficult or specific questions about contraception. When *The Atlantic* did a glossy profile on Students for Life president Kristan Hawkins in 2023, for example, the reporter didn't ask a single question about birth control access—nor did the publication report on the group's birth control stance.

This is a powerful organization actively and openly fighting to make contraception illegal, yet their extremism is never mentioned whenever the group is quoted or covered. We need to demand that mainstream media outlets, whether they're magazines, radio stations or cable news shows, do their jobs and tell the truth about what these organizations really want for Americans. The same is true for all of us; whenever possible we have to lay Republican extremism bare, and make clear what the consequences are for turning a blind eye.

Chapter 5

"Exceptions" Don't Exist

Mississippi has an abortion ban exception for rape victims. At least, it's supposed to. But in 2022, when investigative reporters from *Mississippi Today* went looking for a doctor who would provide a rape or incest victim with an abortion, they couldn't find one. Not a single doctor in the state was willing to end the pregnancy of a sexual violence victim. And that's the truth of "exceptions" in a nutshell; they exist only on paper. To put it simply: they're not real.

In Louisiana, a woman was denied an abortion despite the fact that her fetus was diagnosed with anencephaly, a fatal condition specifically named in the state's list of "exceptions." And even though Texas's ban allows abortions if someone's life is endangered or if there would be a "substantial impairment of major bodily function," Amanda Zurawski wasn't given an abortion until she was in the ICU with sepsis. Another Texas woman, a twenty-five-year-old whose doomed pregnancy was making her increasingly ill, was told by doctors she'd need to have a stroke before she could come back for an abortion. And these are just the stories we know about.

None of these nightmares was an accident. Abortion ban "exceptions" are deliberately crafted to be impossible to use. In fact, the only reason they exist at all is to make Republicans seem a little less punishing. As the Guttmacher Institute's Elizabeth Nash says, "Exceptions function mainly as PR tools to make abortion bans seem less cruel than they are and [to] distract from the inhumanity of the ban itself."

The truth is that when Republicans sit down to write "exceptions," they do so with the sole intent of excluding as many people as possible.*

Rape and Incest "Exceptions"

What's one of the best-known facts about sexual assault survivors? That they overwhelmingly don't report their attacks to law enforcement. The shame, fear of victim-blaming, and trepidation over the criminal justice system keeps more than two out of three victims from going to police.

So when Republican legislators write a law that's supposed to help these victims get care, what do they do? They include a requirement that the attacks must be reported to law enforcement. That's what I mean when I say lawmakers are carefully crafting these laws to never be used.

We also know that it often takes rape and incest victims time to come to terms with their attack; trauma isn't processed overnight. It's common for those who've been attacked to be in denial about a rape-related pregnancy; this is especially true when victims are younger or have been assaulted by a family member. So, Republicans add in a time limitation for rape victims to get care.

In some states, GOP legislators have written "exceptions" that

---

* If your state has an exception, you should still try to use it, if needed. There are organizations listed at the back of the book that can help.

purposefully terrify sexual violence victims. Before a South Carolina doctor can perform an abortion on a rape victim—assuming you can find a doctor willing to perform an abortion at all—they have to inform the patient that their name, information, and the details of their allegation will be reported to the local sheriff.

Leaving aside for a moment that outrageous breach in confidentiality, this is a clear way to scare rape victims away from having abortions. The law forces victims to go to the police regardless of whether they want to, and it contains an implied threat. Telling victims they'll be reported to police gives the impression that if they're not believed about their attack, they'll be punished. It's bullying.

Some Republicans are eager to make that threat of punishment even more explicit. Tennessee doesn't have an abortion ban "exception" for rape victims, but when Republicans were briefly considering one, it included this telling mandate: any woman who the state believed made a false report would be guilty of a felony and would have to serve a minimum of three years in prison.

And in case you weren't already convinced that this was about punishment, consider that Republicans included an additional requirement that the woman be made to serve the full sentence.

That means a rape victim, knowing that people in her situation are routinely disbelieved, would have to risk years in prison in order to get care. Not to mention, what constitutes a "false report" is vague. Women have been accused of false reports simply because a police officer didn't believe their allegations. We've also seen women accused of false reporting because they decided not to pursue charges, or because they recanted their accusation. (Victims recant for a variety of reasons, such as being pressured by their attacker or by law enforcement.) As is the case with any kind of criminalization, it's women in marginalized communities—women of color and poor women—who are most likely to be disbelieved.

To put it plainly, anti-abortion legislators are relying on American victim-blaming to ensure that victims can't get care. Iowa's state medical board guidelines require doctors who are considering giving a victim an abortion to determine whether the attack is "prosecutable."

And these are just the laws that apply to adults. The week that I sat down to write this chapter, Tennessee Republicans voted to force children twelve and under to carry pregnancies to term after being raped. Every single House Republican voted down an "exception" that would have allowed raped children to get care. (I'll tell you more about the laws targeting children in Chapter 7.)

Anti-abortion lawmakers and activists also claim that pregnancy after rape is rare—a claim designed to hide their utter cruelty, and to pivot when asked about abortion ban exceptions. Some even say that women can't get pregnant from a rape at all. Students for Life president Kristan Hawkins—who has been celebrated as the future of the anti-abortion movement—says that "sexual assault actually helps prevent a lot of pregnancies itself because of your body's natural response."

There's a reason that conservatives consistently downplay how many women and girls are raped: they know that Americans very much oppose sexual violence victims being forced into childbirth. Anti-abortion lawmakers and activists believe that if they pretend that rape-related pregnancy—or rape in general—is rare, they can hide their extremism.

But a 2024 study estimated that there were 65,000 rape-related pregnancies in the fourteen states that banned abortion after *Dobbs*. *Sixty-five thousand.* The researchers used data from the CDC, the Bureau of Justice Statistics, and FBI Uniform Crime Reports to come up with their estimate.

One of the study's authors, Dr. Samuel Dickman, told NPR he

was "horrified" seeing the numbers. "Sexual assault is incredibly common—I knew that in a general sense. But to be confronted with these estimates that are so high in states where there's no meaningful abortion access? It's hard to comprehend."

"Exceptions" for Nonviable Pregnancies

One of the more brutal Republican policies are so-called exceptions for fatal fetal anomalies—conditions that will result in a fetus dying in utero or after birth.

Since *Dobbs*, anti-abortion groups and lawmakers have launched a quiet campaign to do away with any exceptions for fatal fetal conditions and to pressure women in states with exceptions to carry their nonviable pregnancies to term, regardless of the law.

Republicans have to be sly about this particular initiative. They know that Americans are furious over stories like Kate Cox's, the Texas woman denied an abortion despite a life-threatening pregnancy.

Cox's story went internationally viral in 2023 after she was unable to get an abortion in her home state, even though she was diagnosed with a dangerous and nonviable pregnancy. With the help of the Center for Reproductive Rights, Cox filed for an emergency order asking for an abortion, a plea to prevent her baby's suffering and to end her own.

In a just world, it would be unthinkable for a woman to have to beg the courts for such a thing. But Cox doesn't live in a just world—she lives in Texas. And so she and her lawyers hoped that her obviously dire circumstances would clear the way for her to get care.

Instead, the state fought Cox's request: lawyers for Texas claimed her life wasn't sufficiently at risk, arguing that "countless women . . . give birth every day with similar medical histories." As if this nightmare pregnancy was just business per usual. The state didn't even bother to address the fact that the pregnancy was nonviable, because Texas doesn't have an exception for fatal fetal conditions.

Still, a sympathetic judge—who got emotional during her ruling—granted Cox's request. She called what the law was doing to Cox a "genuine miscarriage of justice." That ruling didn't stand for long, though. Texas attorney general Ken Paxton soon sprang into action, asking the state supreme court to reverse the judge's decision. All to prevent one single woman from getting care.

Paxton was so intent on forcing Cox to carry this pregnancy, in fact, that he sent letters to three hospitals in Houston, threatening them with criminal charges if they provided or assisted in giving her an abortion.

Cox's story sparked fury across the country. Americans saw, firsthand, exactly what anti-abortion politicians wanted for them and their families.

Republican legislators tried to run from questions about Cox—in one case, literally. When a reporter attempted to ask Senator Ted Cruz what he thought about Cox's experience, the senator took off in a sprint. Nikki Haley said she believed the Texas law should be changed, but neglected to mention that she supported a national ban that would do to all American women what Texas did to Cox. One after another, Republicans showed their true colors.

In the end, so did Texas. The state supreme court ultimately sided with Paxton, reversing the judge's order and blocking Cox from getting an abortion in her home state. And so the thirty-one-year-old mother of two did what most people in her situation would do if they had the ability—she left Texas to get the care she needed.

Cox said she didn't want to watch her baby have a heart attack or die of suffocation, and she didn't want to put her health or future fertility at risk. That she had to explain herself at all is a nightmare. Imagine, though, if there had been no other state for Cox to go to. What if instead of being forced to travel to a neighboring state—an impossible hurdle for many Americans—Cox had had to travel to a nearby country? That's what the anti-abortion movement wants for all of us.

In addition to trying to do away with exceptions for nonviable pregnancies altogether, Republican legislators make those "exceptions" impossible to use. One of the GOP's tactics is to claim that exceptions exist for nonviable pregnancies, while narrowly defining what constitutes a *nonviable pregnancy* so that virtually no one can qualify.

North Carolina's abortion ban, for one, requires severe fetal abnormalities to be "uniformly diagnosable"—an impossible black-and-white standard that applies only to a small handful of nonviable conditions. Other states define a nonviable pregnancy as one in which a newborn would die immediately upon birth or "imminently" thereafter. That language is vague enough that legislators can argue that a newborn who would live only for a few days doesn't have a "fatal" condition.

Then there are the states that deliberately include no language at all about what constitutes a fatal diagnosis. The point here is to put doctors in the position of having to decide if they're willing to risk their license and freedom on the chance that a fetus isn't viable—and that a court of law would agree with that diagnosis.

What this means in reality is truly shocking: Parents forced to "prove" that a baby born without a skull is, in fact, going to die. Mothers wondering if their daughter's condition constitutes being "lethal" because she'll survive a few days rather than a few hours. People who might otherwise be able to grieve and recover at home in peace being forced to make their cases with lawyers in courtrooms. How is any of this "pro-life"?

And imagine what this kind of cruelty and confusion looks like on a national level: Every year about 120,000 pregnancies are diagnosed with fetal abnormalities, and congenital malformations are responsible for thousands of infant deaths per year. Are Republicans prepared for a country where thousands or tens of thousands of women are suing for the right not to be treated as "walking coffins"? Do they understand what it will mean when neonatal intensive care units are overloaded with dying babies, or when families go bankrupt from medical costs and baby funerals?

What's most shocking about these "exceptions" is that they allow conservatives to pretend as if they're generously allowing vulnerable women abortions, even as they force them to beg for care. Cultivating that illusion of empathy is central to everything the GOP does when it comes to abortion.

That's why Republicans frame their "exceptions" as policies that help and protect women. Anti-abortion states increasingly require that women with nonviable pregnancies be given resources about what the law calls "prenatal counseling" and "perinatal hospice care." This sounds innocuous enough, and legislators frame the mandates as a way to help patients deal with horrific news. But those terms are code for something much more insidious: anti-abortion groups posing as counselors and experts.

Take Indiana's abortion ban, which requires that doctors tell patients with nonviable pregnancies about "perinatal hospice services." That would be reasonable if the services were nonideological and offered as part of a full spectrum of care, including abortion. But the brochure that healthcare providers are required to give women actually directs them to organizations like the Charlotte Lozier Institute and includes this language: "If an abortion is performed this late in the pregnancy, it significantly increases the risk of death or complication. Mothers may also risk complications with future pregnancies, including premature birth and low birthweight after an abortion."

The brochure also tells women that parents have found that giving birth to a dead baby is "a beautiful, profoundly meaningful, and healing journey." The brochure features an image of a baby's footprints and the quote, "There is no footprint too small to leave an imprint on this world."

Indiana Republicans added even more guilt and shame to the mix, requiring that women with nonviable pregnancies certify in writing that they are choosing not to offer their fetus hospice care.

If you had any remaining doubts that the intention is to guilt women into carrying doomed pregnancies to term, consider what one anti-abortion neonatologist says she tells patients after they've just found out that their fetus will not survive: "Congratulations."

Dr. Robin Pierucci, who works with the "prenatal counseling" group Be Not Afraid, says, "I love reminding them that the first diagnosis is 'It's a baby,' and no other diagnosis ever negates diagnosis number one. The baby is inherently valuable and worthy of our love."

Imagine getting perhaps the worst news of your life—finding out that your pregnancy isn't viable—and having a cheerful doctor come into the room and say "congratulations." Now imagine that women weren't just directed to people and groups like this—they were required to be "counseled" by them. That's what anti-abortion organizations and lawmakers are working on right now.

Kristen Day, the executive director of Democrats for Life of America, says that her group is in the process of drafting legislation that would require "training and increasing the number of perinatal hospice nurses to support and inform the women who receive a prenatal diagnosis."

Let me clue you in to what that "training" looks like: it's not mental health experts learning how to best care for patients. It's crisis pregnancy centers teaching volunteers how to lie to and shame women until they're too afraid or guilty to get an abortion.

Anti-abortion crisis pregnancy centers are ground zero for this initiative: they are the groups that coordinate and provide the so-called prenatal counseling and perinatal hospice "training," and their activists have volunteers on the ground in communities around the country. (Crisis pregnancy centers are a central part of Republicans' broader anti-abortion plans—that's why legislators are increasing state funding for them so steadily.)

When patients go to these "counselors," they'll be lied to—much as crisis pregnancy centers lie every day to women seeking abortions. Some women will be told that it's perfectly safe to carry a nonviable pregnancy to term, even though serious mental and physical health risks are involved. Others will be warned that having an abortion is dangerous and might kill them. And no matter what these patients' tests and ultrasounds say, these anti-abortion counselors will tell women that they might be aborting a healthy pregnancy. In fact, these activists won't even use the term *nonviable*; they'll tell women that their pregnancies are "potentially life-limiting."

And while women who agree to carry their doomed pregnancies to term will get some sort of memento, like a photograph or a footprint, women who decide to end their pregnancies will get no such keepsake. Surely if the point were to help and comfort women, this service would be offered to anyone who wanted it, right?

All this cruelty and misinformation, of course, assumes that a state has an exception for fatal fetal abnormalities at all. Most states with abortion bans don't.

And despite Republicans' insistence that their proposed national fifteen-week ban is a reasonable middle ground that most Americans can get behind, that ban contains no exception for fatal fetal anomalies. That means a woman like Kate Cox who had a nonviable pregnancy wouldn't just have to leave her state for care—she'd have to leave the country.

One question I'm often asked about this particular "exception" is why. Why would anyone—even someone anti-abortion—want to force a person to carry a nonviable pregnancy to term? It's not as if there's going to be a healthy live baby at the end of the pregnancy. I wish I had an answer. The truth is that this has never been about the health of women, babies, or families. It's about imposing extremist Christian nationalism and controlling and punishing women.

Republicans know what they're doing. They know their laws will hurt and kill women. And for all their rhetoric about saving babies, they also know that more infants will die as a result of this work. But they don't care. In fact, some anti-abortion groups see that as a sign that their laws are working.

After Texas banned abortion, the state's infant mortality rate went up by over 11 percent. According to Michael New from the Charlotte Lozier Institute, that rise in infant deaths meant that Texas's law was "preventing unborn children from being aborted due to their medical condition."

Health and Life "Exceptions"

Even if rape victims or patients with nonviable pregnancies can't get abortions, surely Republicans would want those whose health or lives are endangered to be able to get care. Surely? Not even close.

Every woman who has come forward with a painful story of being denied care has lived in a state that claims to make allowances for women's health; but when push comes to shove, they're unable to get care. They're not sick enough, or not close enough to death. Doctors around the country find themselves in the position of weighing their medical license and their freedom—against whether or not they should provide an abortion at that moment, or wait until their patient is just a little bit sicker.

If you were risking years in prison—decades, even—what would you choose?

There's perhaps no better example of the failure of health and life exceptions than Tennessee. When *Roe* was first overturned, the state didn't even have an allowance for women's lives—that's right, there was no exception if a pregnant person would die. Instead, the state had an affirmative defense mandate: a law that required doctors giving life-saving abortions to break the law and then later prove it was necessary.

In 2022 a Tennessee woman with an ectopic pregnancy had to wait hours while lawyers at the hospital put together a legal justification for her treatment. Ectopic pregnancies are nonviable and deadly for the pregnant person. But because of Tennessee's law, doctors had to stop and prepare a legal defense before giving her care.

As the woman described to the *Nashville Scene,* she, her husband, and other family members spent those hours trying to find hospitals in another state in case she was refused. In the end, the doctors treated her, but they had to break the law in order to do so: "It's a felony, what they did, and that is crazy to me. . . . So while I'm recovering from surgery, and trying to emotionally process all of it, another layer of it was, what if my case wasn't severe enough, right? And what if a prosecutor decides, 'Well, we want to make an example.' Like, what if I wasn't bleeding internally enough?"

When Tennessee Republicans finally decided to pass some kind of exception to protect women's health and lives, the "pro-life" organization in the state, Tennessee Right to Life, fought them every step of the way. Will Brewer, a lobbyist for the group, accused Republicans of trying to "weaken" the law and claimed that dangerous conditions during pregnancy can "work themselves out" without medical intervention and that doctors should "pause and wait this out and see how it goes."

The group opposed language that would allow doctors subjective decision making power on when an abortion was necessary, even claiming that a woman hemorrhaging was not an "objective" medical standard. If a patient bleeding out doesn't require abortion care, what does?

Because of the outsize influence that Tennessee Right to Life has in the state, legislators made the changes that the group wanted—effectively watering down the bill into something that didn't help doctors at all.

Maternal-fetal medicine specialist Dr. Sarah Osmundson wrote, in an op-ed in *The New York Times,* that the law was "intended to be ambiguous and confusing, to make physicians scared to provide abortion care." Osmundson continued:

> We have denied abortion care to women with cancer and other complex medical problems who find out they are pregnant. Women with pregnancies affected by life-limiting fetal anomalies—anencephaly (no skull or brain), renal agenesis (no kidneys, no proper lung development)—have had to seek abortion care out of state. One patient I managed who was unable to receive abortion care ultimately required an emergency hysterectomy and delivered an extremely premature infant, 14 weeks early.

Unsurprisingly, even after the "exception" was passed, Tennessee doctors continued to struggle. Dr. Osmundson sits on the abortion committee at Vanderbilt University Medical Center—the group of ob-gyns and maternal-fetal medicine specialists who decide whether a patient is close enough to death to warrant care. She told *ProPublica* reporter Kavitha Surana how the committee members send each other urgent text messages, at all hours, to sign off on emergency life-saving care.

She recounted cases where the committee had to deny women care despite serious illness, like a patient whose pregnancy complications meant she could end up with an ostomy bag or sepsis. The issue was that the woman wasn't in *immediate* danger. If she was given an abortion, a conservative prosecutor could later decide that the patient hadn't really needed it and that doctors were guilty of a felony.

Some doctors refused to even discuss abortion because of how great the risk was. Surana reported on an oncologist reluctant to give a pregnant patient cancer treatment, and a hospital cardiologist who refused to sign off on an abortion even though their patient had heart failure.

This is just one state, and the politics of just under two years. The same thing is happening everywhere. When Idaho Republicans wrote language to "clarify" the state's abortion ban, they declined to include an exception for "life-threatening conditions." Why? Republican state representative Julianne Young said, "The list was endless when we began considering the decisions that would fall under that language."

That's right, when faced with the fact that there are an "endless" number of things that can go wrong during pregnancy and put someone's life at risk—conservative lawmakers simply opted to leave out any allowance for them at all.

Why Bother?

If the point is to ensure that patients can't use abortion ban exceptions, why include them at all? The truth is that when it comes to abortion rights, Republicans are desperate. The GOP has been struggling with how to talk about abortion at all, and conservative strategists think "exceptions" are the answer. Because the only thing more popular than broad access to abortion rights is abortion for sexual violence victims and those whose health and lives are in danger.

The polling is astronomical, even in red states, and even among Republican voters. By focusing on exceptions, Republican legislators would finally have an abortion stance that's popular. (That's why Donald Trump has been talking so much about exceptions in the lead-up to the 2024 election.)

Best of all for lawmakers, exceptions allow them to feign empathy and "reasonableness" without actually giving anything up policy-wise because they know that their exceptions don't work. For them, it's a win-win.

The other reason Republicans love "exceptions," though, is that they allow them to tap into American misogyny. After all, the very idea of exceptions is built on the notion that some women deserve care while others don't. Those who have sex willingly are bad girls who should be punished; those who were forced, or who are sick, get a reprieve.

This is where Democrats and the pro-choice movement have a real opportunity to push back. We should be raising the alarm again and again about how exceptions aren't real; but we also have the ability to point out the misogynist absurdity and hypocrisy of exceptions. If a fertilized egg is a life, and abortion is murder, why do the circumstances for abortion matter? (At least the anti-abortion extremists who don't want exceptions at all are ideologically consistent.)

What that means, however, is that Democrats need to get comfortable advocating for zero government interference in pregnancy. We have to let go of "exceptions," too. There's never been a better time to do so. In fact, it's downright shameful we haven't already.

Given how unpopular abortion bans are, how is it possible that the GOP is still framing the debate on abortion? It's absurd that the national conversation has become a question of when it's fair to legislate someone's body. With voters more furious and pro-choice than ever, the most effective message is also the only appropriate answer: never.

Every abortion denied is a tragedy. You don't have to go into sepsis to be forever harmed by an abortion ban. You don't need to be raped to have control of your body stolen from you.

And while the most extreme consequences of abortion bans do happen with shocking regularity, they are still outliers: Most people seek out abortions because they don't want to be pregnant. And that's okay—in fact, it's critical.

Reproductive rights and justice isn't about who "deserves" care, or who has endured enough suffering to have "earned" an abortion. Forcing anyone to be pregnant against their will, for any reason, is immoral and cruel. Yet somehow in the hubbub of polls and bills, talking points and politics, the power of this fundamental truth has been pushed aside.

Chapter 6

The Punishment Is the Point

As Brittany Watts cried, recounting the details of her miscarriage to a police officer, a nurse at the hospital rubbed her shoulders. Brittany later told a reporter, "I'm wondering, 'Why is a police officer coming in here? I don't recall doing anything wrong.'"

What Brittany didn't know was that the reason she was being interrogated amid this traumatic moment was because the very nurse comforting her—the woman rubbing her shoulders—had called the police. That nurse's 911 call set off a chain of events that led to Brittany being arrested and charged with "abuse of a corpse." All because Brittany flushed her miscarriage.

Before I tell you more about Brittany's 2023 case, what's most important to know is this: In a country where a fetus is more important than a woman, this could happen to anyone. And while the people targeted and punished most often will be Black women, poor women, and those from other marginalized communities, it would be a mistake to believe that privilege can fully protect someone.

For years, anti-abortion legislators and groups have claimed that they have no interest in seeing women arrested for abortion. And for just as long, women have been targeted anyway. Even before *Roe* was overturned, women were being arrested and prosecuted for abortion, stillbirth, miscarriage, and more.

In 2015 in Indiana, for example, Purvi Patel was sentenced to twenty years in prison for feticide—despite the fact that Purvi said she miscarried, and there was no trace of any abortifacient in her system. In Utah, Melissa Ann Rowland was arrested and charged with murder after one of her twins was stillborn. The reason? She had refused a C-section.

Rennie Gibbs was just sixteen years old when she was indicted in Mississippi on charges of "depraved-heart murder" after delivering a stillborn baby; prosecutors claimed she used drugs. A Louisiana woman was charged with second-degree murder after going to the hospital with unexplained vaginal bleeding. She spent over a year locked up before medical records proved she had a miscarriage. Like Brittany, these were patients in the middle of medical traumas who needed help—not jail.

Prosecutors have even targeted women who lost their pregnancies after being injured.

In Iowa, Christine Taylor was charged with attempted feticide after she fell down the stairs at home. In Indiana, Bei Bei Shuai lost her pregnancy after trying to end her own life. Within just a half hour of her suicide attempt, a homicide detective was arresting her for murder.

And in 2019, Alabama charged Marshae Jones with manslaughter after she was shot in the stomach and miscarried. Lawyers for the state claimed that she had put herself into a dangerous situation.

Over and again women—women of color, especially—have been punished for their pregnancy outcomes. What's more, all of this happened under the protection of *Roe v. Wade*. Imagine what criminalization will look like now.

We're already getting a glimpse. As soon as the *Dobbs* decision came down, Republicans around the country started to introduce bills that would allow them to charge women with murder for having abortions. In some, even miscarriage patients could be charged with homicide if they were found to have somehow "caused" the end of their pregnancy. Others laid the groundwork to make using certain types of birth control punishable as murder.

These bills weren't one-offs or anomalies. At one point in 2023, I was reporting on legislation in Kentucky, Alabama, South Carolina, and Georgia that would all classify abortion as homicide and make it punishable as such. If South Carolina's bill had passed, abortion patients could be given the death penalty. At the time, governor Henry McMaster dismissed the legislation as far outside mainstream Republicanism—claiming that "no one that I know wants to criminalize women." Yet he made that comment just a few weeks after a woman in his state had been arrested for taking abortion medication.

The bill in Alabama wouldn't just allow prosecutors to charge abortion patients with murder; if they believed a woman miscarried because of "reckless" or "negligent" behavior, the state could charge her with murder, too. Think about how broad that language is, and what a zealous prosecutor could do with it. If you lost your pregnancy after lifting something heavy, they could say you were being "reckless." Didn't take your prenatal vitamins? That's "negligence."

The bill also deliberately defined personhood as beginning at the moment of fertilization, which opened the door for prosecuting women who use IUDs and emergency contraception. Remember, conservatives believe these types of birth control prevent the implantation of a fertilized egg. And if contraception is actually "abortion," you could go to jail for using it.

And while the Alabama bill noted that a woman shouldn't be charged with murder if she loses a pregnancy after being violently raped or beaten during a domestic violence incident, there was a caveat. Such a defense wouldn't be available if "the actor intentionally or recklessly placed [themselves] in a situation." It is not hard to imagine a scenario where a woman would be blamed for staying with an abusive partner who caused her miscarriage. (Think of Marshae Jones, who was charged with murder after being shot and mis-carrying.)

Anti-abortion groups are eager to distance themselves from efforts like these; they know that putting patients in jail doesn't go over well with voters. That's why after the *Dobbs* decision was leaked, a coalition of anti-abortion organizations—ranging from Americans United for Life to Susan B. Anthony Pro-Life America—released a letter claiming that "we do not support any measure seeking to criminalize or punish women and we stand firmly opposed to including such penalties in legislation." The truth, however, is far more sinister.

While so-called mainstream anti-abortion groups would like us to believe that these kinds of bills are rare, or the result of single extremist legislators, that's simply not true. The South Carolina bill that would have made abortion punishable by the death penalty had two dozen co-sponsors. And anti-abortion lawmakers and activists are increasingly coming out in support of the notion of "equal protection," which calls for fetuses to be treated the same as people in cases of homicide, wrongful death, child endangerment, and more. That means charging abortion patients as murderers.

The "equal protection" movement has rapidly gained traction across the country. In fact, over twenty-five anti-abortion groups signed a letter in the *National Review* calling for "equal protection in the womb," including some of the groups that signed on to the first letter, the one that claimed to oppose the punishment of women.

The other vital thing to note is that anti-abortion lawmakers are deliberately introducing radical legislation more and more often, even though they know the bills won't pass. Some will even reintroduce the same bill session after session. Why work so hard to push legislation that has no chance of advancing? Because by continually reintroducing radical legislation, they can numb Americans to their anti-abortion extremism. It doesn't matter if the bills pass or not; the more the legislation is out in the world, the more it becomes normalized.*

It's not only patients or women who are targeted. Conservatives' broader goal is to prosecute anyone who supports an abortion patient. They're going after the helpers, from bills designed to ban pro-choice websites to so-called anti-trafficking laws that criminalize aiding someone receiving out-of-state care.

Before getting into that, though, let's start with what the anti-abortion movement is most afraid for Americans to know about: the arrest and prosecution of individual women.

Anatomy of an Arrest

Back to Brittany Watts's case: Every single step of her experience perfectly captures the cruelty of criminalization and the devious way it operates. And while Brittany didn't have an abortion, what happened to her was very much the result of her state's abortion law and the way zealous legislators, prosecutors, and law enforcement use fetal personhood to target women for any pregnancy outcome at all.

When Brittany's water broke twenty-one weeks into her pregnancy—far too early for a fetus's survival—her ob-gyn warned that there was a "significant risk" to her health and life. And so, like anyone would do, Brittany went to the hospital for help.

What Brittany needed to protect her health and life was clear. As

---

* In 2023, an anti-abortion "abolitionist"—someone who believes women should be charged with murder for ending their pregnancies—won a state senate seat in Oklahoma. And remember that even Donald Trump said he believes women should be punished for having abortions, saying in 2016 that women should suffer "some form of punishment."

one doctor wrote at the time, "My recommendation instead of waiting until mom is on death's door before proceeding with treatment, [is] to deliver this baby."

The hospital in Warren, Ohio, however, was religiously affiliated. So doctors and administrators at Mercy Health-St. Joseph's Hospital spent hours debating the "ethics" of giving her care. Officials were also concerned that treating Brittany—even given the risk to her life—would constitute an abortion and put them at legal risk.

After waiting for over eight hours with no treatment, Brittany finally decided to go home. And that's where she miscarried in the early hours of morning—home and alone because the hospital she went to for help wouldn't give her timely care. Brittany bled so heavily from what she'd later find out was life-threatening hemorrhaging that she went back to the hospital. There, she told a nurse what happened.

Brittany explained how she had miscarried into her toilet and tried to separate out what she thought might be fetal remains. But because Brittany was only halfway through her pregnancy—and because of all the blood, tissue, and feces involved—she wasn't sure if she had.

Imagine the trauma of all this: you are alone, twenty-one weeks into your pregnancy after being denied help, and as you're heavily bleeding and in shock, you try to find a fetus in a mess of bodily fluids. It's unthinkable.

But the nurse, after hearing Brittany recount this nightmare, called 911, claiming that there was a "baby . . . in a bucket" in Brittany's backyard. (Incredibly, when *The Washington Post* called Mercy Health for comment, a spokesperson declined to comment "out of respect for patient privacy." Now they cared about privacy?)

———

Unfortunately, it's not unusual for a nurse to turn someone in for a negative pregnancy outcome. In fact, studies show that it's most often healthcare providers who report women in cases like these. The reproductive rights lawyers I've spoken to also tell me that the patient-to-prison pipeline is becoming worse and worse: hospitals—emergency rooms, especially—have a close relationship with law enforcement. Some even have police stations inside the same building. But it's that initial betrayal of trust between a provider and patient that most often kicks things off.

In a 2023 report, the reproductive rights legal group If/When/How found that in cases where people were turned in for self-managing their abortions, 45 percent of the time it was a healthcare provider who had reported them. The next most likely group to report was acquaintances, at 26 percent.

Another vital piece of information about Brittany's case is that she is Black. Again, women of color—Black women in particular—are disproportionately targeted in cases like this. In part, that's because of how criminalization in America works in general; people of color are more likely to be arrested and prosecuted. But it's also because women of color and women from other marginalized communities are more likely to be seen as cold and uncaring when they lose a pregnancy.

Indeed, that's what happened here: When Brittany's nurse called 911, she told the emergency operator that Brittany didn't want the baby, which is something Brittany had never said. Later, after a medical examiner testified that Brittany's fetus had had no chance of survival and that it had been dead before it hit the vaginal canal, a Warren County prosecutor argued that that was irrelevant. The issue, this prosecutor said, wasn't whether Brittany had caused the end of her pregnancy, but that the fetus was "left in that toilet and she went on [with] her day." In other words, he was offended that Brittany didn't seem sufficiently traumatized when she lost her pregnancy.

This focus on patients' demeanor is a common tactic when women are brought up on pregnancy-related charges. If/When/How's report found that those who were arrested were targeted for "subjective personal factors" such as "their demeanor during inter-rogations and hearings, feelings they expressed about the pregnancy, actions they took or did not take during their pregnancy, and past histories of abortion and pregnancy loss." For example, someone who did a Google search for abortion clinics early in their pregnancy might be more likely to be charged if they later had a stillbirth.

The prosecution's characterization of Brittany as somehow cal-lous or cruel was also repeated by local publications and television stations, which offered sensationalized and often false coverage of her case. Ohio television station WKBN claimed that Brittany had been arrested because investigators "found a baby stuck in a toilet." Other publications reported that police were called to Brittany's house because the toilet was clogged with a large fetus, and that she had tried to "flush" and "plunge" it before it got stuck in the pipes. The idea was to demonize Brittany.

The truth, however, is that after her nurse called 911, police went to Brittany's home and tore her bathroom apart, disassembling her toilet to look for fetal remains (all while she was being treated for life-threatening hemorrhaging). Imagine the humiliation and hor-ror of that: strange men taking apart your toilet and sifting through your bodily fluids to prove you committed a crime.

Grace Howard, assistant justice studies professor at San Jose State University, told the Associated Press at the time: "I just want to know what [the prosecutor] thinks she should have done. [Are we] going to require people to collect and bring used menstrual prod-ucts to hospitals so that they can make sure it is indeed a miscar-riage?"

It was these gory details that reminded me of what it means to have men running newsrooms and prosecutors' offices. How many leaders in criminal justice and journalistic institutions know what a miscarriage actually looks like? How many have seen a birth or a stillbirth? How often do police or reporters target and blame women because they simply don't understand pregnancy, what it looks like, and all that can go wrong?

Here's the thing: there is no legal standard for how to handle a miscarriage in Ohio or anywhere else. Nor should there be. This is not something we want law enforcement, or the state to be involved in. Yet because of misogyny, racism, and fetal personhood laws and culture, Brittany was mistreated and tortured by the people meant to care for her. Traci Timko, Brittany's lawyer, told me, "No one should be criminalized or punished for their miscarriage. Brittany should be able to focus on taking care of herself after losing her pregnancy, but instead she is being forced to defend her actions in a moment that should have never been made public."

The last strategy that prosecutors used to go after Brittany was one that groups like Pregnancy Justice and If/When/How have flagged for years: they pursued charges that are seemingly unrelated to miscarriage or abortion, such as "abuse of a corpse," unlawful practice of abortion or medicine (after someone takes abortion medication, for example), child abuse or endangerment, or even homicide. Targeting women in this way allows prosecutors to get around state prohibitions on arresting women for abortion, while still being able to dole out punishment.

If/When/How's 2023 report details one case where an adult was charged with child abuse and reckless endangerment after helping a teenager obtain abortion medication. In another similar case, the prosecutor admitted to the media that they were using different charges as a way to punish the person who had helped a teen: "This is a very disturbing case. It makes you humble as a lawyer because there are certain situations when the law doesn't have a good way of dealing with [a defendant's actions]."

For anti-abortion groups that claim they don't want abortion patients punished, this tactic gives them a rhetorical out. After a Nebraska teen who self-managed her abortion was jailed, for example, anti-abortion groups in the state insisted that she wasn't prosecuted for her abortion, but for "concealing or abandoning a dead body." (More on her story shortly.) It's a way to shirk responsibility for arresting women. And there's no place that relies on this strategy more than Alabama.

Alabama Leads the Way

Alabama's abortion ban, the Human Life Protection Act, explicitly states, "this bill would provide that a woman who receives an abortion will not be held criminally culpable or civilly liable for receiving the abortion." Indeed, when *Roe* was overturned, Alabama's attorney general Steve Marshall went on television to assure voters that the law "is not a criminal offense against the mother." He might as well have been crossing his fingers behind his back.

While reporting for *Abortion, Every Day* a few months after *Roe* was overturned, I found a local conservative blog whose readers were upset that the law didn't allow for the punishment of women. But the reporter assured his audience that they didn't have to worry: a representative from the Alabama attorney general's office told him that the state planned to use a law other than the abortion ban to put women behind bars.

A spokesperson for Marshall said that even though the Human Life Protection Act exempts women from being prosecuted, it "does not provide an across-the-board exemption from all criminal laws, including the chemical endangerment law."

Now, Alabama's chemical endangerment law was written to punish adults who expose children to "an environment in which controlled substances are produced or distributed." In other words, parents who bring their children to drug dealer's houses. But the attorney general saw this law as an opportunity get around the prohibition on arresting women for abortion: he planned to prosecute women who took abortion medication with the "chemical endangerment" of their fetus. The tactic would have a broad impact: Abortion medication accounts for 63 percent of abortions and is the primary way women in anti-abortion states circumvent bans.

This use of "chemical endangerment" isn't new in Alabama; prosecutors had already been using the law to arrest and imprison pregnant women they accused of using drugs. Like twenty-three-year-old Ashley Banks, who slept on a jail floor for three months in 2022 as she endured severe vaginal bleeding without treatment, all because the police found a small bag of marijuana in her car.

Another woman, Stacey Freeman, was incarcerated for "chemical endangerment of a child" after she allegedly used drugs while pregnant. But here's the thing: she wasn't even pregnant. The county jail was forced to release her, but a sheriff investigator warned her that if she did get pregnant, she'd be brought up on additional charges.

After I wrote about the Alabama attorney general's office, my story was picked by local and national media, forcing Marshall to publicly reverse course. He said he wouldn't use the "chemical endangerment" law to arrest women who take abortion medication. Pregnant women who haven't used the medication, however, are still being arrested.

And that's the last thing you need to know about the way criminalization operates: prosecutors target those they think most Americans won't care about. Pregnant women accused of using drugs top that list. This is, unfortunately, a smart tactic. Law enforcement deliberately brings cases against people they believe are potentially unsympathetic so they can test out criminalization methods without drawing too much attention or outrage. If Americans think that those being arrested somehow "deserve" it, they'll be much less likely to cause a fuss—and much less likely to think it could happen to them or people they know.

Conservatives have spent a lot of time, energy, and money on the lie that abortion bans won't send women to prison. The last thing Republicans need is for voters, who are already mad about the end of *Roe,* to start thinking about the women they love behind bars. That's why another one of their strategies directs punishment not at individual women, but those who help them.

Targeting the Helpers

There's a famous quote from Fred Rogers (Mr. Rogers, as you're more likely to know him) that I think about often when I write about abortion. Mr. Rogers told the children who watch his show that when he was younger and would see scary things on the news, his mother would tell him: "Look for the helpers. You will always find people who are helping."

Since *Roe* was overturned, we've seen so many helpers: Abortion funds raising money and coordinating travel for those who need to leave their states for care; doctors taking legal risks to ship abortion medication to anti-choice states; volunteer pilots flying women to the states where they can get abortions; clinic escorts, activists, and so many others.

Since *Dobbs,* anti-abortion legislators and groups—desperate to punish whoever they can—have sought ways to target these helpers. Sometimes they're attacking helpers explicitly—like proposing legislation that would characterize someone who ships abortion medication as a drug trafficker. For the most part, though, legislators and activists would never admit what they're doing. They know it would make them look awful; so they frame their attacks as benevolent moves to help women. Most recently, that's come in the form of "anti-trafficking" laws.

The first so-called abortion trafficking law was passed in Idaho in 2023. Soon after, near-identical bills advanced in states like Tennessee and Oklahoma. (As I write this, Tennessee's bill is headed to the governor's desk to be signed into law.) Republicans claim these laws protect minors from predatory adults who bring their teen victims across state lines for abortions in order to hide evidence of rape. In reality, the laws label and prosecute anyone who *helps* a young person get an abortion as a trafficker. Tennessee's legislation would make it a felony to take a minor out of state for abortion care. That means a friend, aunt, or grandmother who helps someone get an abortion could be sent to prison for fifteen years.

But it's not just taking a teenager out of state that would be illegal—it's helping them in any possible way. You could be arrested for lending a teenager gas money or even just for texting them the URL of an out-of-state clinic. These laws deliberately define "abortion trafficking" as broadly as possible, stating that anyone who "recruits, harbors, or transports" a minor for the purpose of getting an abortion is guilty of "trafficking."

In fact, that's why the Idaho law was blocked in 2023: a judge ruled it violated the First Amendment. An amicus brief filed by twenty attorneys general in opposition to Idaho's travel ban offered this example: "A teenage girl in Moscow, Idaho, calls her aunt in Pullman, Washington, less than ten miles away, to say she is pregnant and feels she cannot safely tell her parents. If the aunt tells her niece about a clinic in Pullman that offers abortion care and counseling, is that 'recruitment'? What if the aunt texts her niece a web link to the clinic's informational material? Or if the niece books an appointment and the clinic's office manager emails her a preappointment information sheet? If the aunt pays for her niece's bus ticket to

Pullman, is that 'transportation'—or, as the Idaho law would have it, 'trafficking'?"

Some of the legislators behind these efforts don't bother hiding the fact that they're defining "trafficking" as broadly as possible. When Oklahoma Republican Sen. Nathan Dahm was interviewed about his travel ban in 2023—asked specifically about these broad interpretations like lending a teen gas money—this is how he responded: "If they did it knowingly that they would be circumventing the parents and committing a crime. It's no different than if you gave somebody gas money for them to be the getaway driver for committing some other crime or something else like that. You're becoming an accessory in the violation of a crime [sic]."

If you think this effort is just about stopping teens from traveling, you're wrong. Multiple Texas counties have passed similar anti-abortion "trafficking" bans that allow civil suits to be brought against anyone who helps a patient—regardless of age—leave the state for an abortion. Anyone who lends a woman money, recommends a clinic, or provides logistical help could be in the law's crosshairs.

All these laws go beyond targeting individual helpers—they're looking to attack abortion funds and pro-choice groups as well. After all, who helps people leave their state? Who gives them money for gas? Who provides information about out-of-state clinics? Abortion funds do, of course. That's why Alabama attorney general Marshall argued in a court filing that groups helping pregnant women leave the state for abortion are participating in a "criminal conspiracy."

Under his interpretation of the law, simply telling a pregnant woman about a clinic where she can get care would be a crime: "One cannot seriously doubt that the State can prevent a mobster from asking a hitman to kill a rival because the agreement occurred through spoken word. So too here for conspiracies to obtain an elective abortion." Leaving aside the fact that Marshall likens an abortion to a mob hit, the point was to characterize abortion funds—vital community services—as criminal organizations.

In addition to passing travel bans, Republicans are proposing all sorts of legislation that makes it easier for them to prosecute abortion funds. In 2023 Texas Republicans introduced legislation to make pro-choice websites illegal, specifically naming organizations that ship abortion medication. The legislation would also have allowed the state to charge abortion funds using the RICO Act, a federal law meant to target organized crime rings.

Even those who refuse to go after the helpers could be punished. Since *Roe* was overturned, Republicans have been passing laws that would allow them to remove any district attorney who declines to prosecute abortion cases. District attorneys are elected officials who have been put in office because voters want them to use their discretion on what cases to pursue. This means legislators are overriding the will of the people in order to ensure that only district attorneys willing to prosecute abortion "crimes" hold office.

In Florida, Governor Ron DeSantis suspended Andrew Warren, a district attorney who made clear he wouldn't prosecute so-called abortion crimes. After Warren was effectively fired, he sued Florida. Not only did DeSantis fight back, he had the support of other conservative leaders: fifteen Republican state attorneys general signed onto an amicus brief to back DeSantis, arguing that the First Amendment doesn't apply when the state wants to remove prosecutors. That means attorneys general in fifteen states believe it's their right to fire any district attorney who won't prosecute abortion "crimes."

In Texas, Republicans have pushed multiple bills that would make it easier to remove district attorneys who refuse to prosecute abortion cases. (They would also make it easier to remove judges that the state deems too progressive.) They're not just arresting the helpers, they're systematically removing anyone who isn't willing to punish them.

Protecting Ourselves and Our Communities

Here's the good news about anti-abortion activists and lawmakers targeting helpers: it means they know that we're actually helping. It also means that despite their rhetoric about being pro-family or pro-community, conservatives are actively trying to prevent communities from supporting each other. That's why they're passing laws that allow people to sue each other over abortion, and why they're trying to make it illegal to help someone get an abortion or even share information about abortion. Republicans want us to be afraid. They want us to be too scared to help each other, too anxious to share our abortion plan with a friend, too scared, even, to get medical help when we need it. It's heartbreaking: they've criminalized community.

What's more, they're depending on us to turn on each other. People often ask me how Republicans plan to enforce travel bans. Are they going to check people's cars at the state border to see if there's a pregnant teen inside? The truth is that they don't need to do that. Their entire enforcement plan is *us*.

There's a reason that Texas passed "bounty hunter" laws, which give citizens a $10,000 reward for successfully suing anyone who violates abortion bans, and why so many other states are following suit. The sad truth is that Republicans probably didn't even need to attach a financial incentive to their legislation, because some people simply enjoy tattling. That's especially true when it comes to abortion, an issue hypercharged with misogyny, racism, and classism.

Even worse, conservatives are encouraging people to betray those closest to them. Anti-abortion legislators and activists know that for every friend or family member who is willing to support a woman through an abortion, there's someone else in her life—an abusive ex-boyfriend, an estranged mother-in-law—who is eager to use the power of the state to punish her or anyone who helps her. Conservatives are relying on Americans' appetite for punishment to enforce a cruel and divisive agenda, hoping that we'll prioritize adherence to the state over the safety and health of our own communities.

That's what makes this all so distressing: the people who claim to stand for "family values" are depending entirely on our willingness to turn on each other. They're incentivizing the breakdown of family and community trust and codifying betrayal. It's a way to make us feel disconnected from each other, and to make women feel as if they aren't safe anywhere or with anyone. In this way, abortion bans don't just do damage to individual patients; they're hurting the faith we have in each other.

So how do we stop them? First, by being good community members. (As my dad used to say, snitches get stitches.) It's vital that we help each other, even when we're afraid, because fear is central to the GOP's plan. That means as scared as we are, and as honest as we are about the legal risks in anti-choice states, we have to steer clear of spreading misinformation and scare tactics. In a moment when Republicans are introducing terrifying bills by the day, folks are eager to spread the word on what's happening over social media. That's great, but more times than I can count, I've seen videos go viral that tell women such-and-such is now illegal, even if the legislation hasn't been adopted, or they quote from a politician about what they'd *like* to do. Now more than ever, we need accurate and up-to-date information.

Speaking of misinformation, something that we can all do, on a local or national level, is hold media outlets accountable. As we saw with Brittany Watts, media coverage that stigmatizes and villainizes women plays a deliberate role in criminalization. Conservatives know that the only way to arrest women without stirring too much public outrage is to paint them as the bad guy.

Consider the Nebraska teenager I mentioned earlier, who was arrested after self-managing an abortion. Multiple publications honed in on the girl's Facebook messages, which law enforcement had obtained as evidence. They reported that the teen wrote about how she "can't wait to get the 'thing' out of her body," and that she said "I will finally be able to wear jeans." But that wasn't true.

While the young woman did say something about wearing jeans (which seems pretty on brand for any teenager), she didn't say she couldn't wait "to get the 'thing' out of her body." That sentence appears nowhere in her Facebook messages; in fact, it was actually a police officer's interpretation of the teenager's conversation. But when journalists wrote about the case, they literally put the officer's words in the teen's mouth—presenting his biased belief about the young woman as a fact.

Later, as the story went national, that lie was repeated again and again by credible media outlets like the Associated Press. Instead of reading the actual Facebook messages, reporters across the country used language that was meant to make the teenager seem callous and cold.

That's why we need to demand that abortion cases be reported carefully and accurately. It's especially important that when local or national news outlets cover these stories, they're not taking the word of law enforcement or prosecutors as the truth. Just because a district attorney says that a case is not about abortion, for example, doesn't make that true. A publication uncritically reporting it as such is not doing its job. A reporter who writes about an abortion-related arrest or prosecution by only relaying the version presented in a police report, too, is failing their readers. Pay attention to the way your local newspaper covers a story of someone being criminalized; look for telltale signs of racism, misogyny, and abortion stigma, and *call it out*.

You can also protect yourself and your community by supporting abortion funds, which are doing vital work on the ground, and by being mindful of your digital privacy. You'll find digital safety tips and best practices in the Resources section (page 165), along with other places for support and advice, including a free legal helpline if you have questions.

Chapter 7

Teens Are the Canaries in the Coal Mine

In 2024, every House Republican in Tennessee voted to force child rape victims to carry pregnancies to term. And when I say child, I mean *child*: the lawmakers voted to mandate rape victims twelve years old and under to give birth. I wish this was hyperbole: Tennessee's abortion ban, one of the strictest in the nation, doesn't allow for abortions in cases of rape or incest, even when the victims are children.

That's why in 2024, Democrat state representative Gloria Johnson introduced a bill that would have allowed rape victims under thirteen to obtain care. She implored her colleagues, "Please think of the children." Republicans resoundingly killed the legislation. We're talking about girls who are little more than babies being forced into childbirth, something that's dangerous even for adult women. For a small ten- or eleven-year-old body, it's downright life-threatening.

Incredibly, in the same session, Republicans advanced legislation that would make it a felony to help teens obtain an abortion in any way—the so-called anti-trafficking law I outlined in the previous chapter. Remember, under these laws, an aunt who got abortion pills for her niece—or even texted her the URL of an out-of-state clinic—could be sent to prison for fifteen years. Tennessee's version would even allow one parent to sue another if they helped their child obtain an abortion, or imprison someone who lent a teen gas money to leave the state.

Lawmakers claimed this cruelty was done in protection of minors—legislation to stop sexual abusers from bringing children out of state. In truth, it was a travel ban, a way to trap teens in Tennessee and force them into pregnancy against their wills.

Why focus on minors? Because anti-choice groups and politicians know that their bans are incredibly unpopular, and that voters increasingly see Republican lawmakers for the misogynist extremists that they are. To counter that opposition, legislators hope that feigning concern over children will distract Americans from the terror their laws are causing.

That's why they use words like "trafficking" that produce an emotional reaction in people, especially parents. In addition to the travel bans, Republican leaders are targeting Planned Parenthood. In 2024 Missouri attorney general Andrew Bailey brought a lawsuit against the organization, claiming that it was allowing and helping children get out-of-state abortions. What better way to drum up outrage than to accuse the group of aiding in the "trafficking" of children?

But anti-abortion policies focused on young people aren't just a PR strategy; they're a political move, too. By passing particular restrictions on children, Republicans can test out their radical policies without too much public backlash. It's a key part of a chipping away strategy for people of all ages: on abortion, travel, birth control, and more.

Law professor Mary Ziegler, author of *Roe: The History of a National Obsession,* put it this way: "Starting with a law centered on minors may make justifying other such travel-related laws easier down the line, even if states try to apply them to adults. But the distinction between minors and adults does not matter in the big picture. The point of this law, and others like it, is to restrict access to abortion as much as possible. Today, it may be minors whose rights are on the line, but if the anti-abortion movement has its way, it will soon be the rest of us."

In other words, minors are the canaries in the coal mine. When it comes to abortion rights, what happens to them today comes for us tomorrow.

Ziegler pointed out that this isn't a new strategy. When parental notification and parental consent laws were spreading in the 1980s and 1990s, Americans largely saw them as an issue not of abortion but of parents' rights. That's why anti-abortion lobbyists and lawmakers have been framing so many of their post-*Roe* restrictions as "parental rights"; they're trying to divorce their legislation from abortion, which they know is incredibly popular.

A case in point: California governor Gavin Newsom put out an ad attacking Tennessee's "abortion trafficking" bill. It featured a teen rape victim who was shackled to a hospital bed and unable to get the abortion care she wanted. In response, Tennessee Republican state representative Jason Zachary, who had sponsored the "trafficking" legislation, accused Newsom of "gaslighting." He said, "We are running an important parental rights bill. . . . [It] doesn't prohibit providing healthcare to any pregnant woman, period," as if the proposed law had nothing to do with abortion at all.

One of the clearest examples of this strategy is the conservative response to pro-choice ballot measures. After *Roe* was overturned, Republican candidates took an ass-kicking in the 2022 midterms. Every time abortion rights was put directly to voters, abortion rights won.[*] So, when more states started proposing pro-choice amendments, conservative groups and lawmakers knew that their usual

---

[*] This is true as of spring 2024—it might change come November 2024 when states like Florida and Arizona have abortion on the ballot.

anti-abortion talking points weren't going to work. Instead, they put most of their messaging effort into "parental rights."

It started in November 2022 in Michigan, where voters were set to vote on Proposal 3, a constitutional amendment to ensure the right to abortion. By October, groups who opposed Proposal 3 were putting out ads claiming that the amendment would allow children "as young as 10 or 11" to get what they called "gender change therapy" without parental consent. Even though the ballot measure had nothing to do with gender-affirming care, conservatives made a bet that anti-trans talking points would be more popular than anti-abortion ones. (At the time, Republicans were stoking an anti-trans panic across the country, claiming that LGBTQ people were trying to indoctrinate children through school and library books.)

Abortion rights ended up winning in Michigan. But the following year, when a pro-choice measure was advancing in Ohio, conservatives tried the same strategy. Right after the state attorney general approved Issue 1's proposed language, three separate anti-abortion groups sent out simultaneous press releases, all claiming that the measure would eradicate parental rights.

Soon afterward these groups and anti-abortion activists claimed that the measure wouldn't just let children get abortions and hormone therapy but gender-affirming surgery without parental consent. One anti-abortion group, Protect Women Ohio, spent millions in ads repeating this messaging. One TV spot showed an image of a drag queen, telling viewers that supporting Issue 1 would "keep this madness out of Ohio classrooms."

The Heritage Foundation even weighed in, calling the measure a "Trojan horse" that would allow children to have abortions and make "gender decisions" without their parents. By the way, this is a group that put out a policy paper decrying the "non-marital teen birth rate," as if teen pregnancy wasn't a problem so long as they were married. (That lines up with Republicans' refusal to vote for child marriage restrictions; they want to make it easier for rapists to make "honest women" out of little girls.)

It wasn't just anti-abortion organizations and activists pushing this rhetoric. Ohio state senator Theresa Gavarone said the amendment entailed an "assault on parental rights." And Secretary of State Frank LaRose—the state's chief election officer—wrote an op-ed explaining why he was voting "hell no" on Issue 1: "Until recently, one thing we didn't worry so much about was whether underaged girls could be secretly convinced to get abortions or even sex-change operations without their parents even knowing. But if the radical Issue 1 amendment passes, this will be a new and horrifying fear for every parent of younger girls in Ohio."

Abortion rights eventually won in Ohio, but anti-abortion rhetoric around parental rights has been successful elsewhere, even in pro-choice states. In Oregon in 2023, Democrats "compromised" on minors' reproductive rights in order to end Republicans' six-week walkout. It's often the rights of the most vulnerable that are first on the chopping block.

When we talk about minors, we're talking about a community of people who have few or no legal protections, who have no say over what happens to their bodies, and who suffer disproportionately when forced into pregnancy and childbirth. Young people don't have close to the same level of access to abortion that adults do. They don't have money, and if they have healthcare, they're probably on their parents' plan, which makes privacy difficult if not impossible. Teens are also much less likely to have transportation to get to an abortion clinic, and if they need to travel a long distance, they don't have the ability to take time off; they have to skip school. If they want to order abortion medication online, they'll need a credit card.

And that's all assuming their state allows minors to have

abortions to begin with. It's hard to imagine a starker hypocrisy than parental notification or consent, the idea that a minor must have a parent's permission before obtaining an abortion because they're too immature to make that decision on their own. In what universe is someone too young to consent to taking a pill or undergo a ten-minute procedure but old enough to have a child?

Parental consent and notification laws also don't account for the teens who are being abused by someone in their own home, or who have parents who might hurt them if they were to find out about the pregnancy. But for anti-abortion legislators, young victims are an afterthought. In 2022, when South Carolina legislators were debating an abortion ban, Republican state representative Doug Gilliam said that teenagers have "choices," even sexual violence victims. "There's a morning-after pill," he said, "that's available in Walmart." When asked how a young girl who has been raped by her father would get to a Walmart for emergency contraception, Gilliam responded, "The ambulance."

In some states, judicial bypasses allow teens to obtain care without their parents knowing, but that process is onerous and often humiliating. Imagine being that young and having to go in front of a judge—sometimes an anti-abortion judge—and explain why you deserve care.

In Florida in 2022, the *Orlando Sentinel* reported that judges were approving fewer abortions for teens. One young woman was told that her poor grades were proof that she wasn't mature enough to decide to end her pregnancy. Another was denied because she didn't have a learner's permit or a car. Once again: how these seeming marks of immaturity would impact a teen's capacity for parenthood wasn't even discussed.

For teens who don't have a legal parent—if they're in foster care, for example—the state becomes their parent, opening up a whole new can of worms in terms of parental permission and notification. But the overall issue remains the same: young people are deprived of any bodily autonomy or choice.

These laws never stop with minors. The entire point is to use children as an excuse to strip rights from all of us. Remember, the "anti-trafficking" travel bans being passed or advanced in states like Idaho, Tennessee, and Oklahoma are now being adopted in Texas county ordinances that apply to people of *any age*. Under these ordinances, driving an adult woman out of state for an abortion, lending her money for an abortion, or giving her information about an out-of-state clinic could open you up to civil charges.

This slow roll toward restricting all women—not just minors—from leaving anti-choice states is the entire point. The same thing is happening with attacks on birth control. They're coming for teenagers first, with an eye toward all of us.

In early 2024, the Fifth Circuit Court of Appeals upheld a Texas law that requires teens to have parental consent before they can access birth control. The question before the court had been whether the parental consent law ran afoul of Title X, a law allowing teens to get birth control at federally funded clinics. The (notoriously conservative) court ruled that it didn't.

We were meant to believe this ruling was decided in "protection" of minors, but one of the judges let something slip that made clear what it was really about. During oral arguments, Judge Stuart Kyle Duncan said that he'd be upset if his daughter were able to get birth control because it would allow her to escape pregnancy as a punishment for sex: "If she did receive contraceptives without my knowledge, that interferes in a dramatic way with my ability to parent, because the child now has a means of engaging in sexual activity and avoiding certain consequences of it."

The impact of that one ruling reached far beyond Texas: it

opened the door for other states to restrict teens' ability to get contraception.

Once again teens are the canaries in the coal mine. As we saw in Chapter 4, Republicans are already years into their attack on birth control. Just as legislators are defining certain types of contraception as abortion and are reducing access to birth control, they are attacking teens' ability to obtain contraception as part of that broader chipping-away approach.

And while conservatives claim right now that preventing teens from getting birth control is about parental consent, the truth is that this is a trial balloon for how to ban contraception for all of us. They're just testing out their strategies on teenagers first, because they assume we won't protect them.

This is what you can expect to see: soon Republicans will "question" the safety of hormonal birth control specifically for young people. In the same way the anti-abortion movement (falsely) claims that abortion medication is dangerous and needs to be regulated accordingly, Republicans will push anti-contraception policies under the guise of "protecting" young women's health.

Conservatives have already laid the groundwork through their campaign claiming that the Pill is dangerous and that women should abandon it. The other work they've been doing to prepare for this moment connects to their anti-trans bigotry: conservative groups and lawmakers have managed to ban gender-affirming care for minors in certain states. (In Nebraska, the ban on gender-affirming care for teens is *the same law* as the state's abortion ban.) If *those* hormones aren't safe for teens, what makes anyone think the hormones in birth control aren't next?

The Increase in Indoctrination

Pretending to care about children while passing laws that hurt them is one hypocrisy, but there's another when it comes to abortion and young people: the idea of indoctrination. Conservatives have long accused groups like Planned Parenthood of indoctrinating or "grooming" children, because reproductive rights groups and activists want young people to have access to comprehensive sex education and the contraception they need to protect themselves.

But as is often the case when it comes to anti-abortion groups and lawmakers, this is all projection. Even as they hurl accusations of indoctrination at abortion rights activists and Democrats, they are working overtime to brainwash young people and children. Some of that propagandizing is well-known: like what children are taught in church groups, religious schools, or abstinence-only education classes. Since *Roe* was overturned, though, anti-abortion groups have been emboldened. They're expanding their reach into public schools and communities—and doing so under the guise of teaching "science" and "health."

In 2023, for example, a woman named Brooke Stanton wrote an op-ed for *Newsweek,* arguing that the reason Republicans kept losing on abortion was because of "faulty science standards." Stanton is the CEO of Contend Projects, a group that describes itself as "a secular, nonpartisan, science education nonprofit with the mission to spread accurate information and awareness about the biological science of human embryology," and that works "to make the essential scientific facts easily accessible and to educate people in a simple and positive way."

It sounds fairly innocuous until you understand that this group is an anti-abortion organization disguising itself as an educational institution.

If Republicans are losing elections on abortion because of "widespread scientific ignorance," she wrote, the answer is to change the national educational guidelines around what schoolchildren are taught about human development. "Science education in schools is the most effective way to shape future generations," she wrote. "If pro-life leaders want to win the battle against abortion, they need to recognize and release the untapped potential of K-12 science education standards, by ensuring human embryology is in America's science classrooms. If they fail to do so, the abortion industry will continue its winning streak at the ballot box for many generations to come."

When I first read this passage, the reference to "untapped potential" made my blood run cold. As you've likely gleaned, Stanton isn't interested in showing students what pregnancy and abortion actually look like. She wants to lie to young people about human development in an attempt to convince them to oppose abortion or, at the very least, to ensure that they feel a deep sense of shame if they ever do get abortion care.

This focus on children is strategic. The anti-abortion movement knows that one of its biggest problems is generational, that young people are the most pro-choice demographic in the country. As I've mentioned previously, 74 percent of adults under thirty believe abortion should be legal in most or all circumstances, and nearly 40 percent believe abortion should be legal in all circumstances. And a 2023 poll from Harvard University's Institute of Politics found that adults under thirty were twice as likely to describe themselves as "pro-choice" than "pro-life."

In other words, the anti-abortion movement knows that its support is dying, literally. So, activists and lawmakers are ramping up their efforts to indoctrinate children as early as possible. And to reach a broad swath of the population, they need to insert themselves into public school classrooms. Enter groups like Stanton's.

What makes her organization and others like it so dangerous is that they're presenting themselves as credible education and scientific organizations. Anti-abortion groups and lawmakers are also targeting science classes, in particular. Embedding their beliefs in science education not only frames them as more credible but also allows anti-abortion activists to avoid roadblocks that are specific to sex education, like parental opt-outs. Whereas many school districts allow parents to remove their kids from a sex ed lesson, there is no such option for science classes.

Indoctrinating children in public school isn't just some strategy or future plan—it's already happening. Several states, including North Dakota and Tennessee, have passed a law that would require public middle schools to teach "human growth and development" by showing students a video produced by Live Action, one of the most extremist anti-abortion organizations in the country, best known for creating misleading and false videos. (One of its leaders even had a multimillion-dollar judgment levied against him after he published deceptively edited videos targeting Planned Parenthood.)

The video that Republicans want to mandate in public school classrooms is made to look as if it's an ultrasound, or images of an actual fetus, but it's not; it's computer generated. And while Live Action claims that the video has been "reviewed and certified" by healthcare providers, the "experts" they're referring to are all anti-abortion activists affiliated with the Charlotte Lozier Institute. Other so-called medical experts who signed off on the video are from American College of Pediatricians (ACPeds), an anti-abortion, anti-LGBTQ organization that's been designated as a hate group.

All of which is to say, these are not just conservative groups who disagree about abortion. They are scary, dangerous organizations that are vastly out of step with the views of nearly all Americans. They would rather women die than have abortions. And that's who Live Action and groups like Stanton's got to back up this video that they're putting in public school classrooms.

What's more, in some states the legislation mandating this video has another rule: schools that decline to teach it can be punished. A bill advancing in Kentucky allows the state attorney general to bring civil action against any public school district that refuses to use the video in their health classes, and allows parents to do the same.

Anti-abortion lawmakers and lobbyists know what they're doing. They know if they want to change the trend of young people being overwhelmingly pro-choice, they need to reach children earlier. They also know that accurate information about pregnancy directly correlates to support for abortion.

Research presented at the Southern Political Science Association Conference in early 2024 found that the more someone knows about pregnancy, the more likely they are to be pro-choice. That means that anti-abortion activists have a vested interest in keeping students ignorant about the reality of pregnancy and fetal development.

Meanwhile Students for Life—which began as an organization for college students—has started expanding its work into middle schools, bragging about "reach[ing] young people during the crucial developmental years." Students for Life is an extreme anti-abortion organization that wants to see birth control banned. Its curricula tells fifth to eighth graders that fetuses "have lost their value because of physical characteristics, just like slaves and Jewish people did before."

They teach students that "one million children are being killed every year," and that if they oppose that killing, they must be "pro-life": "If you are against abortion, you are pro-life. Pro-life people assign value to all human persons despite age, gender, size, level of development or location. And believe it is wrong to kill children who are different than you and me."

While groups like Students for Life and Live Action are embedding their disinformation and scare tactics in schools, anti-abortion crisis pregnancy centers are doing "outreach" to children in local communities. One of the more recent tactics of the nonmedical religious groups is to offer free sports physicals for female students—who are often required by their schools to have an exam. The groups consider it "a way to engage early with a population that might become pregnant and consider abortion." More accurately: they're using false pretenses to target children with propaganda. Instead of allowing young people's rights to be the first to go, we need to start putting minors' ability to access care and freedom first. Not just because what happens to them will eventually come for us—but because it's the right thing to do.

Chapter 8

They Don't Care About Women

Jaci Statton was told to wait in the parking lot of an Oklahoma hospital until she was just about to die. Only then, doctors said, could she come in to get an abortion. In Texas, the mother of a twenty-five-year-old woman was told that her daughter, who had a nonviable pregnancy that was making her ever sicker, couldn't come back for an abortion unless she had a stroke. Another woman in Texas was forced to carry a dead fetus for two weeks. "I felt like a walking coffin," she said.

Nancy Davis, a mother of three in Louisiana, couldn't get an abortion even though her fetus had anencephaly and was missing part of its head. The same thing happened to Heather Mayberry in Kentucky, whose fetus also had anencephaly. In Texas, Samantha Casiano's fetus was diagnosed with the same issue, but unlike Heather and Nancy, she couldn't afford to leave the state for an abortion. She had to carry a dying baby to term and watch her daughter take pained last breaths. When she recounted that moment in a lawsuit against the state, she vomited on the stand.

Then there's Kelsie Norris-De La Cruz, a Texas woman who was denied treatment for an ectopic pregnancy and ended up needing emergency surgery to remove most of her right fallopian tube. An ob-gyn said that if they'd waited much longer, she would have been "in extreme danger of losing her life." She was luckier, though, than Mayron Michelle Hollis in Tennessee, who needed an emergency hysterectomy. She nearly died after being denied an abortion.

In Alabama, Ashley Caswell was forced to sleep on the floor of a county jail and was refused help when she went into labor. She delivered her baby in the jail shower, passing out in a pool of blood from a life-threatening placental abruption.

In Kentucky, a mother of five with cervical cancer went before a hospital committee to beg for an abortion so that she could get radiation and chemotherapy. They said no, deciding that she didn't meet the legal exception for medical emergencies. Gynecological oncologist Dr. Monica Vetter told *Bloomberg News*, "She always told me that she wanted to be alive for the 'kids she already had.' It was heartbreaking."

In Texas, Amanda Zurawski, denied treatment after her water broke too early, nearly died of sepsis. Chelsea Stovall had to travel four hundred miles out of Arkansas to get an abortion for her nonviable pregnancy. She sobbed in an interview with a local television station: "I should be able to say goodbye to her where I want to."

These are just a few examples of what it's like to be a woman in a "pro-life" state. And we haven't even gotten to the girls yet.

After a raped sixth grader in Mississippi was forced to give birth, her mother said she went from shy to nearly mute. Multiple little girls in Florida, victims of incest, were denied abortions. In Ohio, a ten-year-old who was raped and impregnated—forced to leave her home state for care—watched her nightmare story go viral, with Republican leaders calling it a fabrication.

I could go on. The suffering caused by *Roe*'s demise is undeniable and on display every single day. The people being hurt the worst and most often are those who are already vulnerable: young people, poor people, and women of color. Anti-abortion legislators and activists hope that because their laws target those whom this country historically cares about the least, maybe, just maybe, voters won't be as mad.

In spite of the clear and explicit horrors, anti-abortion lawmakers and leaders continue to insist that the abortion bans they've passed are for our own good. They're protecting us, they say. As if they've done us a tremendous favor by stripping us of control of our own bodies, lives, and futures. The truth, of course, is that the anti-abortion movement doesn't care about either women or girls—what happens to pregnant people has never been a concern. Thanks to their bans, we're now living in a country where ob-gyns in anti-choice states advise their patients to buy supplemental life insurance.

I wish they would just come out and say it. Because watching lawmakers pretend as if women's lives being endangered is a mistake—our suffering accidental—is just too damned insulting. None of this is the result of legislative growing pains or of lawmakers having insufficiently "tweaked" their bans.

Anti-abortion lawmakers and activists would have voters believe that they had no idea this is what post-*Dobbs* America would look like. But they had fifty years to plan for the end of legal abortion. They knew this would happen—cancer victims having to beg for radiation, desperate women emptying their savings accounts to flee their states for care. They simply decided women's pain, suffering, and deaths would be an acceptable trade-off for a political win.

Sometimes they say the quiet part out loud and admit it. In 2023 Tennessee state representative Andrew Farmer said on the statehouse floor that "if we can protect the lives of mothers, we're going to do that as much as possible." *If.* This same Republican, in the very same speech, said that babies grow in women's "bellies." That is who is telling our daughters what they can and can't do with their bodies and lives: a guy who talks about pregnancy like a toddler.

Their ignorance is no excuse. After Missouri state representative Brian Seitz proposed a 2022 bill that would make it illegal to end ectopic pregnancies, which are life-threatening, he insisted the legislation was being "misrepresented." And as is the case whenever a male legislator is completely ignorant of the way that pregnancy and bodies work, the ensuing outrage was framed as if women's health were an afterthought. It's not really that these men don't care if women die, you see, it's that they're too stupid to realize it was a possibility.

When will we stop giving them the benefit of the doubt? *Of course* they know that women will die as a result of their laws. They can read statistics. They can see what happened before and what is happening again. For fuck's sake, they've carefully crafted policies that give us fewer rights than a zygote in a country where pregnancy is twenty times more likely to kill you than skydiving. What did they think was going to happen?

Anti-abortion groups and legislators need us to believe that they're not the cruel extremists that their laws show them to be. And they certainly don't want Americans to know that they planned for women's deaths in the same way they scheme over any other "political" issue. I mean this literally: all this pain and suffering was not just "expected"—it was planned for carefully, strategically, and callously.

Over decades, conservatives commissioned polls and prepared talking points. Every raped child forced to give birth, every cancer patient denied care, and every woman arrested after having a miscarriage was accounted for and strategized over. They crafted legislative language, again and again, that would give them exactly what they wanted, even if it meant people would die.

They didn't even bother hiding it very well. Look at any Republican "life of the mother" exception—they all contain a caveat. And that caveat says that women whose lives are at risk can be given abortions, unless the risk is that she's suicidal.

The wording shifts slightly from state to state, but the mandate is the same: pregnant people will be made to stay that way, even if a doctor believes they will kill themselves. Even if they're diagnosed as suicidal.

Let's pause a moment here. Republicans know that forcing people to be pregnant against their will makes them want to kill themselves. And they enshrined, into law, that they don't care.

These caveats have always been one of the most telling bits of policy. What better proof is there that conservative lawmakers know how vital it is to your humanity to have control over your own body? How "reasonable" and "commonsense" can a law be that predicts that women will become suicidal as a result?

We didn't need Republican laws to tell us that women would rather end their lives than be forced into childbirth. Americans remember what happened before *Roe* established the right to abortion, and research makes clear what the mental health consequences of abortion bans are.

A 2022 study from the University of Pennsylvania found that abortion restrictions cause a "significant increase" in the suicide rate among women of reproductive age. This was no causal link. Researchers looked at decades of data and found that the suicide rate among older women didn't increase. Nor did other kinds of deaths, like those by motor vehicle accident. "This association is robust," said one of the study's authors, Ran Barzilay. "It has nothing to do with politics, it's all backed by the data."

This large-scale study was done before we lost *Roe;* imagine what those numbers will look like a year or two from now.

In 2023, the CDC reported that rates of depression and sexual violence among teen girls have skyrocketed over the last decade. Three in five high school girls reported feeling persistently sad and hopeless, up 60 percent since 2011; and more than one in ten report that they've been forced to have sex, a 27 percent increase in just two years. This study, too, was done before the *Dobbs* decision. It's not difficult to predict that those alarming numbers will get even worse now that we've added forced childbirth into the mix.

It's not just teens' mental health that's getting worse. In 2023 the Population Reference Bureau reported that progress in women's health is on a serious backslide: women in their twenties and thirties are more at risk of suicide, dying in childbirth, and being killed than women of previous generations. I'll repeat myself, but it's that important: do we really expect this to get better if women are being forced, against their wills, to carry pregnancies they don't want or that put their health and lives at risk?

A mental health crisis is already unfolding; it began the moment *Roe* was overturned. In 2022, just a few months after the Supreme Court's decision, an Ohio doctor described in an affidavit how a high school senior became so sick during her pregnancy that she couldn't go to school and finish her education. After she was denied an abortion, physicians put her on a suicide watch. In fact, doctors around the country have described women sobbing and threatening to kill themselves after being refused care. This is what happens in the real world to real people when you legally mandate pregnancy.

That's why every Republican passing abortion bans should be asked the same questions: *If you were sitting across the table from a woman who doesn't want to be pregnant, how would you explain to her that she has no choice—and that her lack of choice is* good? *What would you say to her if she started to cry? What if she said she would rather die than remain pregnant?*

If someone believes that women and girls should be forced to carry pregnancies against their wills, surely they should be able to explain why. And I don't just mean repeating a talking point about the "sanctity of life." We need to know what these men would say to someone, specifically, who is forced to remain pregnant.

What would they say to a girl, a child, in the same situation? How would they explain to her what forced pregnancy is?

If they're unprepared to answer these questions, or if they say their answer depends on the situation, then the follow-up question is: *Why, then, do you believe that politicians are the people better suited to make these determinations than doctors, parents, families, and women?*

We cannot let Republicans message their way around the reality of what abortion bans actually do. They need to be asked specific questions about the consequences of their laws.

It's not that I believe they'd answer genuinely, or give some kind of emotional or shamed response. We know they don't care. What I'm interested in is ensuring that voters see what they say—or don't say.

Because even their denials are important and telling. When the University of Pennsylvania study about the link between abortion restrictions and suicide was released, the anti-abortion Charlotte Lozier Institute responded by claiming the research was biased. Why? Because it was published in a journal of the American Medical Association, which has declared that "reproductive health care is essential to women's overall health. Access to abortion is an important component of reproductive health care."

With Americans getting angrier and angrier at what abortion bans are doing to their families and communities, Republicans are desperate to hide the truth from voters. Let's make it harder for them. And we can start by pointing out that their "science" and "expertise" is anything but.

Seeking Fake Science

In a time when miscarrying women and cancer patients are being denied care, the issues like abortion reporting mandates and data often take a political backseat to the urgent suffering on the ground. But the anti-abortion movement's most insidious and dangerous work is often done in the most "boring" ways. It's fake science and studies that anti-abortion groups used to launch a legal attack against abortion medication that made its way to the Supreme Court. And it's state-level reporting requirements like the one in Texas that both scare patients out of getting care and allow Republican leaders to paint abortion as dangerous despite decades of evidence to the contrary.

Anti-abortion groups know they don't have science on their side, so this kind of fabricated evidence has become increasingly important to their work. The Texas abortion "complication" reporting mandate, for example, lists twenty-eight medical issues as abortion complications—conditions that often have nothing to do with abortion. Still, doctors are required to tell the state about any woman who develops one of these issues if she happens to have had an abortion *at any point in her life.*

Doctors who don't make these reports can be fined for each "violation"; after three violations, they could lose their license. It's a policy that forces doctors to lend their name and medical credibility to the collection of false data—"research" that will be used by the state to claim abortion is unsafe.

The list of "complications" are vague and nonsensical. Some, like "adverse reactions to anesthesia," are risks associated with having any medical procedure. Others, like "infection," could develop in a patient for a reason completely unrelated to abortion. The law also lists complications like "pelvic inflammatory disease," which is a type of infection and therefore could be counted twice.

Other "complications" would require reports to the state *years* after a patient had an abortion. I'll use myself as an example: My daughter was born three months early after I developed severe pre-eclampsia. If I delivered her in Texas tomorrow and happened to mention that I ended a pregnancy a few years previous, my doctor would be required to report my daughter's early birth as a "complication" of abortion. Never mind that there's no link between pre-eclampsia and abortion; because "preterm delivery in subsequent pregnancies" is on the law's list of reportable conditions, my physician would have no choice.

The vague criteria for what constitutes a "complication" means that a doctor who is against abortion can use the system to report nonattributable conditions. Because the law encourages citizens to snitch on each other, doctors have to worry that if they don't adhere to this unscientific political mandate, one of their colleagues will turn them in. (I spoke to one medical professional who witnessed a doctor decline to report a "complication," only to have other staff snitch to hospital administrators, who then pressured the doctor to fill out the form.)

This, of course, is deliberate. The fear, confusion, bad science and vague language is meant to drive up the number of reportable "complications." Planned Parenthood put it plainly in their 2018 lawsuit challenging Idaho's near-identical abortion complication reporting mandate: "The Idaho legislature cobbled together the new law to poison the data."

Dr. Ushma Upadhyay, professor and public health scientist at the University of California, San Francisco, says, "That's exactly the point, to create really inflated abortion statistics." Indeed, the "complications" list in the Texas law wasn't created by doctors or experts but by Americans United for Life (AUL), a powerful anti-abortion organization that drafts model legislation for Republican politicians.

Idaho, Indiana, South Carolina, and Mississippi all have laws with identical or similar reporting mandates.

In 2023, North Carolina Republicans proposed a bill that uses the AUL "complications" list, including "psychological complications." That means if you live in North Carolina and go to a doctor for insomnia, and mention you've had an abortion in the past, your sleep problems could be counted as an abortion "complication."

Desperately Seeking Credibility

Unable to use legitimate research to argue for the end of abortion, conservative activists have resorted to creating their own science. They've founded organizations posing as independent research groups, and they've cultivated groups pretending to be researchers to testify in support of anti-abortion legislation, publish bad data, and present themselves as experts despite having questionable qualifications.

For a movement that's seeped in evangelical Christianity, this kind of pretend credibility is important. They don't hide their religious motivations, per se, but they know they can't use them in legal arguments or laws. Instead, lawmakers and lobbyists need to pretend that all of the bans and restrictions they're pushing are scientifically and medically sound.

Still, every time anti-abortion organizations spread a new lie about the dangers of abortion, the scientific community shuts them down. When activists tried to assert a link between abortion and breast cancer, for example, the National Cancer Institute and the American Cancer Society called it bunk. When the movement created a fake mental health condition, "post-abortion syndrome," the American Psychological Association convened a task force to report that no link existed between mental health issues and abortion.

That's the thing: while anti-abortion activists have successfully seeded misinformation in conservative legislation and culture, actual experts have never found their "science" credible. Nor have voters. That's what makes abortion "complication" reports—and similar abortion reporting mandates—so politically valuable. This is data submitted by independent doctors, not anti-abortion groups. That means when Republicans put out a report on how abortion is dangerous, they can claim the reports were objectively collected. They won't mention, of course, that the doctors were pressured to report under threat of losing their jobs.

Killing Real Data

Anti-abortion groups aren't just fabricating their own bad data; they're attacking good, credible studies, and preventing the collection of data they don't like. In Texas, where Republicans have enabled this convoluted way of collecting fake numbers around abortion "complications," the state isn't collecting any information on deaths caused by abortion bans.

This is part of a broad move to hide the real consequences of anti-abortion policies, along with calling maternal mortality data into question to preemptively claim that the rising deaths of pregnant women has nothing to do with abortion bans. We've even seen Republicans in states like Idaho disband their maternal mortality review committees entirely.

Anti-abortion groups are also manipulating the information given to pregnant women. Anti-abortion groups regularly counsel patients who've been given devastating diagnoses, telling them the test could be wrong and that they might abort a healthy fetus. The idea is to either give false hope or to shame—whichever is more effective. But if you're trying to prevent an abortion, the best-case scenario is that the patient never finds out her fetus is endangered at all. And so the anti-abortion movement has launched a disinformation campaign about prenatal testing: claiming that the tests aren't accurate, that the "testing industry" is corrupt, and that women need to be "protected" from genetic tests and ultrasounds.

Some of this isn't new. For years, anti-abortion activists have criticized prenatal testing as part of their efforts to pass legislation prohibiting abortion based on a Down syndrome diagnosis. But since *Roe* was overturned, conservatives have significantly ramped up their efforts to undermine prenatal testing. That's because they know women need prenatal tests more than ever; knowing what's happening with your pregnancy has never been more important, especially if you live in a state with an abortion ban.

In fact, a 2024 report from the Associated Press found that since *Dobbs,* more patients had been asking their doctors for testing—and they're asking for those tests earlier in their pregnancies. Patients' hope, obviously, is to catch any issues as quickly as possible—and to be able to get an abortion under the wire if necessary. In response, the anti-abortion movement has launched an attack on what it calls the "prenatal testing industry," claiming it's hurting women in order to turn a profit.

In 2022 nearly one hundred Republican lawmakers sent a letter to the FDA complaining about labeling requirements and regulatory measures for prenatal tests. They claimed, as the anti-abortion movement does, that the tests were often wrong and were putting healthy pregnancies in danger. Senator Steve Daines (R-MT) said, "It is unacceptable that the FDA is not conducting proper oversight on these inconsistent prenatal tests that often pressure women into making a life-ending decision for their baby."

Legislators also wrote that the companies producing the tests "continue to see their profits grow." This is exactly how Republicans started to target abortion medication—by saying the FDA hadn't properly regulated the drug. The fact that they're using the same strategy to target prenatal tests—which are widely used and accepted—should scare all of us.* How many different ways can conservatives make clear that they don't care about us? They're not just watching women suffer and shrugging—they're working overtime to make it worse.

---

* It's true that some genetic and prenatal testing isn't 100 percent accurate. That's why, when a pregnant person goes to get a particular test, the doctor will explain the different probabilities and percentage rate of accuracies. But the anti-abortion groups' intent on forcing women to carry doomed pregnancies to term greatly exaggerates false positives, making it sound as if the tests can't be trusted at all. They can't remove access to the tests, so instead they try to dissuade women from seeking them out or trusting them.

Chapter 9

They're Not Stopping with Our Bodies

There was a point during their eleven-hour car ride home when Terry's boyfriend debated whether or not to bring her to an emergency room. Terry was pale and lightheaded, and had terrible blueish bags under her eyes. "She was looking really, really bad," Eric, twenty-two, told me. "At a certain point she just faded."

But at three a.m. the couple were only halfway home, and Eric didn't want to stop at a hospital in one of the reddest parts of Texas. Not when they were coming from a New Mexico abortion clinic. "He was worried that they would call somebody and report us," Terry, twenty-one, said. And so they drove on.

Terry and Eric's nightmare had begun a few days earlier when they went for Terry's fifteen-week ultrasound appointment, where they expected to find out the gender sex of their baby. Instead, the Texas couple was delivered unthinkable news: Terry's fetus had not developed at all above the neck—there was no head. The abnormality was one in a million, a specialist told them. Yet while the fetus obviously had no chance of survival, there was still a heartbeat present. In Texas, that was a problem: the state has no exception for fetal abnormalities, not even lethal ones.

Pressuring or forcing women to carry doomed pregnancies

to term is a growing anti-abortion tactic. Even Terry's own ob-gyn advised her to remain pregnant for as long as possible—whether she carried to term or gave premature birth—claiming it would be emotionally better for her to have a moment with her baby.

"As much as I wish I had the chance to hold my baby," Terry said, "I don't think anyone would want to see something that has no head."

So she made multiple calls to out-of-state clinics, finally finding one in New Mexico where the waiting list wasn't too long. The Texas couple, who worked in a coffee shop, emptied out their savings and told their families and friends they were going on a camping trip.

Terry and Eric didn't ask anyone for help with money, and they didn't tell anyone about the pregnancy. They were afraid, they said, that their loved ones would turn them in. After all, the state's so-called bounty hunter law allows private citizens to sue anyone suspected of being involved in an abortion for at least $10,000. That applies to doctors, nurses, and even people who drive someone to an out-of-state clinic, as Eric did. "It felt as if we were robbing a bank," he told me. Terry said the same. "We lied to everyone we knew to get out," she said. "I felt like a criminal."

That fear and isolation, of course, is the point. Conservatives desperately don't want women to leave anti-choice states to obtain care, but abortion bans can't physically prevent a patient from leaving (at least not yet). And so Republicans enact policies that terrorize and terrify: travel bans, curbs on speech, and laws like the one in Texas that allow people to bring civil suits targeting anyone who has anything to do with an abortion.

They were never going to stop at our bodies, and this never was just about abortion. Once you understand that abortion bans are just one tool in a much broader campaign to put women back in their place—and to strengthen white male control over everyone else—all the other, related Republican attacks make much more sense.

Given all the horrors I've written about since *Roe* was overturned, you might be surprised to learn that these laws and ordinances were what put me over the edge. Around the time when the fourth Texas county made it illegal to help someone leave the state for an abortion, I started to truly despair.

In truth, it wasn't the news of the travel ban itself; what did me in was the absolute mundanity with which the press reported that news. It was just another article in just another paper, as if women being prevented from leaving their state is just another story. As if this were a normal occurrence.

The problem, of course, is that it is. What was once unthinkable is now commonplace—the Overton window shattered in thousands of pieces beneath the feet of Republicans and anti-abortion activists. It took them less than two years to sprint from the end of *Roe* to publicly planning to trap women in states where they're not seen as full human beings. Can you imagine the outcry if a law restricted men's ability to leave their state?

What horror, I wonder, will America think is ordinary two years from today?

They're Killing Women

Gerri Santoro was just twenty-eight years old when she died having an illegal abortion. The Connecticut mother of two, who was trying to leave an abusive marriage, died in a motel in 1964. The police photo of her body—slumped over, bloody, and naked—became an iconic pro-choice image. The picture was published in the pages of *Ms.* magazine with the headline "Never Again," and plastered on protest signs when feminists marched for abortion rights before *Roe v. Wade.*

The photo is terrible to look at—Gerri was a human being who was loved—but it's also powerful, putting the consequences of banning abortion on grim display.

What may be most disturbing is the fact that there is a woman out there right now, completely unaware that her image will become a horrific symbol of post-*Roe* America. Maybe she lives in Texas, or Ohio, or Tennessee.

This very second, she could be laughing with a friend or packing her kids' school lunches. Or maybe she's heading off to school herself. Whatever she's doing, she has no idea that her face will one day adorn the posters we march with. Or that images of her broken body will be desperately displayed to politicians in an attempt to get them to care about what their laws do to women.

Maybe her family will pick out the photograph, sharing an image that reminds them of her the most, hoping that a glimmer of who she really was will shine through. Or maybe, like Gerri's, the photo will be the last one ever taken of her—captured in her final and most vulnerable moment.

What photo would you want used if you knew it would be you?

Whoever she is, wherever she lives, chances are that her death won't be caused by an illegal abortion, but a denial of care. The advent of medication abortion has meant that women can self-manage ending their pregnancies without much risk. But that doesn't mean we'll no longer hear the kinds of grisly experiences that were so common before *Roe,* just that there will be fewer of them. I'm grateful for that, at least.

I don't know what's worse: dying in the darkness of a back alley, or in full view under fluorescent lights. They're both tragic, but there's something particularly cruel about the idea of dying while surrounded by those with the ability to save you.

That's what happened in 2012 when Savita Halappanavar died in Ireland. Seventeen weeks into her pregnancy, the thirty-one-year-old Indian dentist was hospitalized after she started miscarrying. At the time, Irish law only allowed abortion when a woman's life was imminently at risk. And even though there was no hope for her fetus, it still had a heartbeat.

If this sounds familiar, it's because it's exactly the excuse we hear in horror story after horror story coming out of states like Texas and Tennessee, where the law mandates women be on death's door before they qualify for care.

Indeed, over the course of three days, Savita begged for help again and again and was refused—even as her health rapidly deteriorated. She died of septic shock, in pain and surrounded by medical professionals who could have saved her life but didn't.

Savita's death sparked renewed outrage in Ireland, fury that led to the repeal of the country's anti-abortion Eighth Amendment a few years later. In the lead-up to that vote, pictures of Savita were everywhere, from protest signs to murals. Her face became the image of Ireland's shame.

I've been thinking about both Savita and Gerri often these days. Their pictures—one smiling, the other a horrific bloody scene—cross my mind anytime I hear about someone who has died—been killed—by an abortion ban.

A teenager with an ectopic pregnancy who died en route to an out-of-state hospital after being denied care in her home state. The young mother of a disabled toddler who slipped into a coma after trying to end her own pregnancy, never waking up. I've heard these stories from abortion fund volunteers, reproductive rights lawyers, hospital workers, and everyday citizens who contact me in my DMs, desperate for help.

I'm not alone: you'd be hard-pressed to find anyone who works in abortion rights who doesn't have at least one story of a death since *Dobbs*.

Women and girls are absolutely dying in America—abortion

bans are killing them. So why aren't we hearing their stories? Where are their pictures?

Preparing for the First Post-*Dobbs* Death

It was clear from the get-go that once *Roe* was overturned, it was only a matter of time before someone died. The avalanche of horrors started immediately after *Roe* was overturned: patients left bleeding for days, raped children forced to travel hundreds of miles for care, people denied vital medications, and women forced to carry dead and dying fetuses. Republicans had spent decades scoffing at feminist warnings, but these very public stories were much harder to ignore.

Faced with the knowledge that women's lives were in imminent and acute danger, did Republicans spring into action to amend their legislation? Did they rush to speak to medical boards, or to meet with hospital legal teams to assure them that providing life-saving care won't get their doctors sent to prison? No. Rather, conservatives launched a preemptive public relations campaign to prepare for the first reported death-by-abortion-ban.

Conservative politicians, activists, and pundits wasted no time floating the idea that abortion bans weren't stopping doctors from providing care. Instead, they said, any harm that came to women was the fault of pro-choicers who frightened medical professionals and their lawyers into misreading the state laws. (In other words, they set the world on fire and wanted to blame the people pointing out that shit is burning.)

In October 2022, the policy director of the conservative group Independent Women's Forum said the cause of all this delayed and denied care wasn't Republican laws but "abortion alarmism." Anti-abortion writer Hadley Heath Manning said the new abortion bans had clear health and life exceptions; it was simply the "baseless fears" of pro-choicers influencing doctors that put women's lives at risk.

After a Louisiana woman whose fetus was missing a part of its head and skull was denied an abortion, State Senator Katrina Jackson, who wrote the state ban, said the hospital had "grossly misinterpreted" the law. When Texas women started to be denied miscarriage treatment, the president of Texas Right to Life claimed the denials were "a failure of our medical associations" and "a breakdown in communication of the law, not the law itself." Conservative columnist Ross Douthat even argued the problem was "hospitals' decision-making" and "activist-journalist misrepresentation."

They wanted Americans to believe that doctors and lawyers—professionals with years of education and experience—either didn't understand abortion laws or were being brow-beaten into fearing them. They hoped voters would ignore the simpler and truer answer: that their laws were written exactly as planned, that the people reading them understood what they meant perfectly, and that women are suffering and dying as a result.

What made this strategy so insidious was that conservatives weren't just shirking blame, they were offloading it onto their biggest threats. The feminists shining a light on the very real human toll of abortion bans and the doctors who were desperate to save their patients' lives made Republicans look extraordinarily bad. And while feminists had been on the receiving end of conservative ire for decades, the targeting of doctors was particularly painful.

After all, healthcare providers are also being victimized by abortion bans. Republicans' deliberately vague "health and life" exceptions have put physicians in the impossible position of deciding—in the already-fraught momenta of medical urgency—just how close to dying someone needs to be before their condition warrants an abortion. And horrifically, forcing them to weigh that possibility against their medical licenses and very freedom.

As callous as it is to blame doctors and hospitals, it isn't thoughtless. The end of *Roe* came at a moment when physicians were being targeted with Covid-era misinformation. The same is true for the way Republicans pointed a finger at the media publishing stories of abortion ban cruelty; "fake news" is a much simpler message than "we're willing to accept women's deaths in order to keep our political win."

This tactic that started just weeks after *Roe*'s demise has only grown stronger since. In 2023, when a Louisiana woman shared her story of being denied miscarriage treatment, a representative from Louisiana Right to Life blamed doctors: "It was just a gross misunderstanding of the law from the practitioners handling the case, unfortunately."

That same week doctors in North Carolina held a press conference begging legislators not to pass any more abortion bans. Dr. Alison Stuebe, a maternal-fetal medicine physician, said, "We're going to see more women die in this state if we can't provide standard of care." Republicans passed a ban a few months later.

When women whose lives were endangered by Texas's ban sued the state, anti-abortion groups didn't come to their aid or express regret for the harm their policy caused. Instead, Susan B. Anthony Pro-Life America released a statement claiming that "every pro-life law in the country allows necessary and timely medical treatment to save the life of a pregnant woman in an emergency" and that "[no] matter how many times we correct the record, pro-abortion activists continue spreading misinformation, confusing physicians and the general public."

Republicans and anti-abortion lobbyists show no sign of slowing this strategy. As I write in the spring of 2024, they continue to claim that Democrats and pro-choice groups are merely fearmongering— and even, most offensively, that doctors are deliberately putting women's lives at risk in order to make a political point. When a group of women sued Tennessee after their health and lives were endangered by the state's abortion ban, the Republican attorney general, Jonathan Skrmetti, hit back by blaming ob-gyns. The state's abortion ban wasn't what had put these women's lives at risk, Skrmetti wrote in a brief; rather it was "other factors like doctors' independent choices not to provide permissible abortions." And in Idaho, attorney general Raul Labrador claimed that doctors were lying about having to airlift patients out of the state to get care elsewhere. He said they were trying to make a "political statement."

Here's the thing. Doctors, as a rule, are not stupid. They understand exactly what the law says. They have hospital lawyers who tell them what the law says and what they are legally allowed to do. Anti-abortion groups and politicians would have us believe that trained doctors, lawyers, and experts are all wrong—or that they're purposely denying women health- and life-saving care because they're pro-choice. It's everyone's fault but their own.

I would almost have more respect for anti-abortion activists and lawmakers if they just said it plainly: they're willing to accept a certain amount of women's suffering and deaths in order to keep abortion illegal.

Where Are Their Stories?

I don't know when the first post-*Roe* death happened, but the first one I learned about occurred just a few short weeks after the Supreme Court decision. I wish I could tell you about it. I want you to know all about this young woman—girl, really—whose death devastated her family and the medical providers who treated her. But as is the case with so many of the deaths caused by abortion bans, her family doesn't want to go public. And I can't blame them.

One of the major reasons abortion deaths aren't being reported is that activists and legal organizations are working hard to protect victims and their families, shielding them from the inevitable backlash should they go public. Pushing them to share their stories would be politically useful: putting faces to the horror and pain caused by bans is the single most compelling way to motivate voters. But activists who care deeply about this issue know that these people aren't just stories or political tools; they're loved ones. They're people whose lives could be forever changed by widely sharing what's happened.

In this way, I'm proud that more stories haven't been reported; it means that the abortion rights movement is being honest with those who come forward, telling them what to expect should they decide to share.

Coming forward about a post-*Roe* death means not only that a loved one's name will be forever attached to this issue, but also—more likely than not—that it will be dragged through the mud. That's especially true for women of color, immigrants, poor people, or members of any other marginalized community. People who are more likely to be killed by a ban to begin with are also more likely to be scapegoated.

Anti-abortion activists and lawmakers are eager to shirk responsibility, and they're not above blaming others for the deaths that they caused.

The other reason we're not hearing these stories is because Republican lawmakers and leaders have made it near-impossible for doctors to go public. For physicians, nurses, and other healthcare workers, coming forward with a patient's story means risking your job and any future employment. Maybe even your freedom.

Look at what happened to Dr. Caitlin Bernard, the Indiana abortion provider who revealed that she treated a ten-year-old rape victim from Ohio. Dr. Bernard didn't disclose any identifying or personal information about the girl—she just told a reporter that such a victim existed. Yet Republican officials targeted her with the full power of the state. Indiana attorney general Todd Rokita launched a year-long harassment campaign against Dr. Bernard, going after her license and attacking her professional reputation. It was punishment for embarrassing GOP leaders and telling the truth about the consequences of abortion bans.

Republicans were sending a very clear message to any medical professional thinking about coming forward: *Do so at your own risk.*

The final reason we're not hearing about post-*Roe* deaths is the most distressing but also the most fixable: mainstream media outlets are too afraid to report plainly on what's happening.

The truth is that we've already read about the first reported post-*Dobbs* death. In January 2024, *The New Yorker* shared the story of Yeniifer Alvarez-Estrada Glick, a twenty-nine-year-old woman who was killed by an abortion ban in Texas. But the publication refused to say that outright—instead, it framed the headline as a question: "Did an Abortion Ban Cost a Young Texas Woman Her Life?" So chances are you've never heard Yeni's name.

The reporter, Stephania Taladrid, did an amazing job of piecing together what happened to Yeni, telling her story with expertise and care. Taladrid's reporting also made very, very clear that Texas's abortion ban killed Yeni. Still, the editors hedged, doing the article a grave injustice in the process. They had the most important story in the country—the first reported post-*Dobbs* death—and they buried it in equivocation.

Anyone who works in journalism can see what likely happened here. At some point in the process of putting this article out into the world—maybe in editing or fact-checking but most likely when the lawyers weighed in—someone made the decision that *The New Yorker* wouldn't conclusively blame Texas's ban for Yeni's death.

So let me say it: Yeni would be alive today if she had been given an abortion. This young woman had diabetes, hypertension, and a history of pulmonary edema. She went to the emergency room with breathing problems just seven weeks into her pregnancy and multiple times thereafter with ever-increasing issues.

Yet even as Yeni got sicker and sicker, at no point did a doctor advise an abortion, not even the affiliated ob-gyn who told Yeni she was at risk of having a heart attack and stroke. When she got so ill that she had to be transferred to a bigger hospital, she was, as records there stated, at "high risk for clinical decompensation/death." But because of the state's ban—and the Catholic hospital's— no one even mentioned the possibility of abortion. As ob-gyn Joanne Stone, former president of the Society for Maternal-Fetal Medicine, told *The New Yorker,* "If she weren't pregnant, she likely wouldn't be dead."

I'm sympathetic to the position that publications are in. Abortion-ban deaths don't happen in a straight or straightforward line, and abortion bans don't exist in a vacuum. They're part of a broader system that fails women in multiple ways. Whether it's healthcare costs, racial and gender bias, maternal health deserts, or the proliferation of religiously affiliated hospitals, there are an infinite number of dangerous combinations that can contribute to deaths like Yeni's.

For mainstream outlets eager for an "objective" unambiguous story, those intersecting factors can be a challenge. And I know how important it is to be precise and careful—especially with a story like this one. But what happened to Yeni isn't debatable, and nuance doesn't erase the obvious truth: abortion bans kill. We have to be willing to say it, and readers have to demand that publications do the same.

I'm sure that by framing its headline as a question, *The New Yorker* leaders believed they were declining to take a particular stand on abortion rights. But by neglecting to say plainly that Texas's ban killed someone, the magazine set a dangerous precedent—one that suggests the media will cover women's deaths only if they're perfect victims.

If American media are waiting for a "perfect" story, they're going to be waiting forever. And it does not bode well for us when *The New Yorker*—a publication with incredible power and credibility, exceptional reporting, and access to legal protection—hedges on saying outright what its reporting proves. What hope can we possibly have for other publications? How many other mainstream outlets have powerful stories waiting in the wings, being picked apart by lawyers or put on hold by scared editors?

Anti-abortion legislators and activists are counting on traditional media outlets being too timid to say exactly what bans are doing to women. And as more of these stories emerge, the anti-abortion movement will pressure outlets to equivocate.

Even with the reticent headline attached to Yeni's story, anti-abortion activists pounced: Dr. Christina Francis, head of the radical American Association of Pro-Life Obstetricians and Gynecologists (AAPLOG), blamed Yeni's local hospital for not having adequate "resources," Yeni herself for being overweight—and even the weather, which prevented a helicopter from transferring her to a bigger hospital. They're desperate to shirk blame, and they'll use the nuances of pregnancy and healthcare to do it. We can't let that happen.

Anatomy of a Post-*Dobbs* Death

Most post-*Dobbs* deaths won't end up in newspapers or magazine spreads; most of the women who die will never have their name known or picture featured on a protest sign. The vast majority of those killed by abortion bans will be nameless statistics in maternal death reports. Because for as many people with stories like Yeni's, or Gerri's, or Savita's, there will be exponentially more deaths that never get connected to abortion bans at all, even when they are directly related.

Suppose a woman in Idaho is twenty-eight weeks pregnant, not due for a few months. She's feeling under the weather, with some swelling and a headache. But it's summer, and she figures it's normal to get a little bloated and uncomfortable in the last trimester. Besides, now that her local medical center has closed their maternity ward, the closest hospital with an ob-gyn is over an hour away.

A few days later this woman starts to feel like she has a terrible flu and starts vomiting. Since her ob-gyn is slammed with other patients, she calls her primary care doctor just to be safe. He tells her it's likely a bug and to rest and take it easy.

But then she starts to feel deep pain radiating to her back, and headache blurs her vision. Only then does she call her husband at work and ask him to drive her to the hospital. She must wait another hour for him to get home, and they have to find someone to borrow a car from. They don't have one right now because money is tight.

By the time she's admitted to the hospital, it's too late: she's suffered a major stroke, her liver is failing, and she dies from HELLP syndrome, a deadly but treatable condition. A death like hers will never be attributed to an abortion ban, but what else do you call something that could have been prevented by adequate access to care?

I tell this story because it's close to my own; when I was twenty-eight weeks pregnant, I felt ill—just a little off, really. I was able to see my ob-gyn immediately, and within minutes of taking my blood pressure, which was sky high, she had me admitted to the hospital across the street. Within three days, my liver was failing. A doctor would later tell me it was as if my health and body "fell off a cliff."

Without the quick care I received, I wouldn't have my daughter and likely wouldn't be here either.

Since *Roe* was overturned, Idaho has lost nearly 25 percent of its ob-gyns, half of its maternal-fetal medicine specialists, and multiple major maternity wards—all because doctors are too afraid to work in a state with a strict abortion ban.

As maternal deserts increase exponentially across the country, a predictable consequence of abortion bans, these are the kinds of deaths we are going to see more and more of. And while they may never get counted as abortion ban deaths, that's what they are.

When Bonner General Health hospital in Idaho shut down its maternity department, the administration couldn't have been clearer about the cause: "Highly respected, talented physicians are leaving. Recruiting replacements will be extraordinarily difficult. In addition, the Idaho Legislature continues to introduce and pass bills that criminalize physicians for medical care nationally recognized as the standard of care. Consequences for Idaho Physicians providing the standard of care may include civil litigation and criminal prosecution, leading to jail time or fines."

The ob-gyns who leave are not being replaced. Medical students and residents don't want to move to states with abortion bans because they know they can't give their patients the standard of care. They also know that if they do treat their patients appropriately, they could be risking their careers and literal prison time.

This exodus isn't limited to Idaho. Every state that has an abortion ban is losing ob-gyns, hospitals are shuttering their maternity wards, and reproductive and maternal health deserts are proliferating.

Doctors and medical students can't get adequate training in anti-choice states. In states with bans, it's illegal to learn how to perform an abortion even though such training is required in order to be an accredited ob-gyn (because abortion is healthcare!).

A 2023 report from ABC News and Boston Children's Hospital found that over 1.7 million American women live in "double deserts"—counties with access neither to abortion nor to maternity care. Another 3.7 million women live in counties without access to abortion and with "no or low" access to maternity care. In other words, millions of American women are being forced into pregnancy in places where they can't even safely give birth.

The connection is no coincidence. Eugene Declercq, a professor at Boston University School of Public Health who studies maternal mortality, said, "The same states that are most likely to be restrictive are also states that have been providing minimal services for a long time to women."

Another 2023 report, this one from the March of Dimes, found that more than 5.6 million women live in counties with limited or no access to maternity care services, and that American hospitals lost three hundred maternity wards in the previous five years.

Other research shows that states with heavily restricted abortion access have maternal death rates that are a whopping 62 percent higher than states where abortion is accessible. Still another study found that women who live in anti-choice states are three times more likely to die during pregnancy and that babies born in those states are 30 percent more likely to die in the first month of life.

Multiple studies, in fact, show that infant mortality is higher in anti-choice states. Research published in the *American Journal of Preventive Medicine* found that states with abortion restrictions had a 16 percent increased infant mortality rate, and after Texas passed its abortion ban, infant mortality shot up by nearly 12 percent.

All this is happening while the maternal mortality rate is rising nationwide. According to the CDC, maternal death rates went up

40 percent in 2021. The highest jump in the death rate was among Black women: non-Hispanic Black women died during and right after pregnancy at a rate 2.6 times that of non-Hispanic white women. These numbers, too, were gathered before the end of *Roe* and the spread of abortion bans. What do we think the 2024 or 2025 numbers will look like?

The truth is, we may not end up knowing: the anti-abortion movement is working to stop the reporting of maternal deaths and to sow distrust in the numbers we do have. They know that women are dying as a result of their policies, and they don't want Americans to know.

In Idaho, Republican leaders disbanded the mortality review committee so that people won't know when the death rate increases. And in Texas, a newly formed maternal mortality committee reported it's being prevented from counting deaths caused by the state's abortion ban. (As I finished editing this book, Ingrid Skop, a well-known anti-abortion activist who doesn't believe abortion bans impact maternal mortality, was appointed to the committee.)

Anti-abortion groups have also been seeding doubt through media quotes and policy papers about the veracity of maternal mortality numbers from the CDC and other sources. They are preemptively claiming that the numbers aren't correct—that you can't trust that data—so that when those new rates come out showing that states with abortion bans have increased maternal deaths, they can say, *We told you not to trust this data.*

Even worse, these groups are betting that when the maternal mortality data does come out, people won't care because the women overwhelmingly impacted—the women who are going to be dying— are disproportionately women of color, Black women especially.

They're hoping that if they can't hide the truth from voters, American racism will win out and people won't care regardless.

In fact, in anticipation of women of color dying at disproportionate rates, anti-abortion groups like the Charlotte Lozier Institute blamed Black women themselves. In a paper calling maternal mortality studies into question more broadly, the organization has suggested that the reason Black women have higher maternal mortality rates is that they're more likely to be obese and unmarried.

Republican politicians have also been spreading misinformation, both to preempt a rise in maternal deaths and to defend their own dangerous bans. When asked about Ohio's abortion ban and the risk it poses to women, for example, Republican state representative Bill Dean told the *Dayton Daily News* in 2022 that "there's no great risk of dying from pregnancy.

"Pregnancy is a natural thing that women are made for," he continued. "That's the way God made them. The myth is that it is dangerous; it's no more dangerous than living every day. I'm not a physician. But I would imagine, a lot of times, it's the lifestyle of the lady that's having the pregnancy. We also have the most obese people in the whole world. It's just individual cases."

The Most Beautiful Story

Edgar Allan Poe once wrote, "The death of a beautiful woman [is] unquestionably the most poetical topic in the world." I think of this quote every time I see a new story from a conservative or anti-abortion outlet about a woman who died while pregnant. No, these stories don't bemoan lives lost thanks to abortion bans or the abysmal American maternal healthcare system—they're celebrating the women who die.

Conservative Christian groups have long glorified women dying during and for their pregnancies, but since *Roe* was overturned, they're pushing out these "feel good" stories at record pace, published in right-wing news outlets, featured on crisis pregnancy center blogs, and highlighted on cable television stations.

We know why: Conservatives are increasingly glorifying dying for pregnancy because they know that post-*Roe* maternal mortality rates are going to skyrocket and they want to make women's deaths as palatable as possible. They hope that if they can make getting sick and dying during pregnancy into something positive, Americans won't react quite so horribly as the maternal death rate shoots up.

Those who put the health of their pregnancy above their own lives are martyred, depicted as the ultimate mothers and perfect women. Just as bad, now it's not only women who die who are being valorized, but women who defied the odds and beat their fatal conditions (for the time being) despite forgoing medically recommended abortions.

In the summer of 2023, *Pregnancy Help News*—an outlet for crisis pregnancy centers and anti-abortion activists—published a piece about a "brave mom who refused abortion after a cancer diagnosis." I'm glad she had a choice to do what she thought best for her and her family. Fox News was even more explicit in one of its stories: "Killing my baby wouldn't 'take my cancer away.'"

Families should choose what medical care is best for them, but consider how dangerous this message is to young women who've been given a serious diagnosis: *If you're a really good mom, a good person, you'll be willing to risk your life.*

In the anti-abortion imagination, the most noble thing a pregnant woman can do is die so that a fetus can live. But it's more than that. To the politicians pushing anti-choice laws, women dying isn't collateral damage—it's just our job.

It's enshrined right there in abortion bans. They believe that if we were real mothers and real women, we'd give up anything for pregnancy: our education, our finances, our safety, our health, and even our lives.

It's a belief so strong they've enshrined it into law. That's why I don't believe in mincing words. Why call abortion rights a difference of opinion or an issue up for debate? This is about a group of people who believe women exist to give birth, and that anything we do that deviates from that expectation makes us unnatural—and ultimately expendable.

So no, it's not an exaggeration to say that the people who create these laws want us dead. They know what their policies have done and will do. And we know what they really think of women. That's why when feminists fight to make sure abortion remains legal and accessible, we're not just fighting for "choice" or for our rights and our bodies—we're fighting for our lives.

I want to live in a country that sees women's lives as valuable beyond their ability to have babies. But right now, it seems like that's too much to ask.

Chapter 10

Conclusion

Abortion Is Everything

Before Dr. George Tiller was murdered in 2009, gunned down in his Kansas church, the abortion provider was known for wearing a button that read, "Trust Women." The slogan relayed perhaps the most important tenet in reproductive healthcare: when it comes to abortion, no one is better suited to make a decision than the person carrying the pregnancy.

I've thought of "Trust Women" often in the years since *Roe* was overturned. I thought of it when Kate Cox was denied an abortion for a doomed and dangerous pregnancy in Texas, especially as lawyers for the state argued that she was no more at risk "than the countless women who give birth every day." I thought of it when I first read about Brittany Watts being prosecuted for miscarrying at home, wondering what "trust" means for Black women who can't get reproductive or maternal healthcare without knowing if they'll die or be arrested in the process.

But when the 2022 story of a ten-year-old girl being raped and impregnated was called a fabrication by Republican politicians and "too good" to be true by journalists, it wasn't "Trust Women" that I thought of. It wasn't even "Trust Girls." I thought, *They will never believe us.*

The girl's abortion provider, Dr. Caitlin Bernard, hadn't shared any meaningful details about her patient, just that the patient existed and that she had been forced to leave her home state of Ohio for care. For abortion rights advocates, the story epitomized what we had spent decades warning about: that the consequences of banning abortion would be swift, widespread, and most harmful to the most marginalized among us.

The response from Republican lawmakers, anti-choice groups, and right-wing media was predictive of how they'd respond to every post-*Roe* horror story: denial and disdain. A host at Fox News suggested the story was a "hoax," while a writer at the *National Review* called it a "a fictive abortion and a fictive rape." Ohio attorney general Dave Yost said the story was likely a "fabrication" and that the newspaper that ran the article should feel "shame." The fact that the doctor who performed the girl's abortion was on the record meant nothing; nor did the idea that an abused minor might have privacy protections in place, or the fact that most rapes go unreported.

Even the mainstream media's reaction told us something. Glenn Kessler, the fact checker at *The Washington Post,* questioned the story because he claimed raped children are "pretty rare," because no rapist had been arrested, and because law enforcement hadn't said anything about it. The only source thus far, he said, was an "activist on one side of the debate." He meant Dr. Bernard, who had treated the young girl.

Why would a police officer's account, or a state official's, be more reliable than one from the doctor who was in the room? Are we really to believe that in a state where abortion is criminalized, law enforcement and government officials are objective? But in a misogynist country, all women are suspect. Even doctors.

It was a glimpse into what was to come: suffering shrugged off as rumor or political fodder, and the picking apart of any experience that makes abortion bans look bad. To too many Americans—men especially—there is no story good enough and no woman or girl credible enough. If the country doesn't believe a ten-year-old rape victim, in what universe would they believe any of us?

Freedom on the Line

I'm writing this almost two years since *Dobbs,* and everything we worried about and warned of has happened. In fact, it's worse than we anticipated. This was never just about abortion, or our bodies, or reproductive health. Abortion is a democracy issue, an economic issue, a workers' rights and racism issue. It's a speech issue and a parents' issue. Reproductive justice groups, particularly those led by Black women, again and again told the country what would happen.

As I write this, we are speeding toward November 2024, when we'll know whether Donald Trump will be elected president again—something that would be a disaster for everyone but especially for women. And even as popular as abortion rights are with voters, political experts and the press are telling us that Americans care about economic, "kitchen table" issues more. There's still not an understanding that abortion *is* an economic issue. (As feminist writer Moira Donegan has said, "Who sets the kitchen table anyway?") In the interest of making plain exactly how far-reaching abortion and the laws that ban it are, let's look at just a few of the ripple effects we've seen since *Roe* was killed.

Despite Republicans' insistence that they would never criminalize women for leaving an anti-abortion state, moves to do just that are underway. In a 2023 court filing defending Alabama's right to prosecute those who help women get out-of-state abortions, Attorney General Steve Marshall argued that while Alabama doesn't yet "forbid" a woman from leaving the state, the state *is* allowed to "restrict" travel when it has "strong, legitimate interests including preserving unborn life." To be clear, this is the Alabama attorney general, writing in a legal brief not only that it's illegal to help someone get an out-of-state abortion, but that it's legal to impose restrictions on individual women's travel as well.

How is that possible? Marshall's argument is that Alabama could restrict travel for pregnant people in the same way it can restrict travel for sex offenders. He says that if the state can track and restrict the whereabouts of predators in order to protect children, they can do the same to pregnant women in order to protect their fetuses.

Marshall's argument isn't an anomaly; he is simply making explicit what anti-abortion legislators and groups have been planning for decades. In 2023 a *Washington Post* reporter asked the anti-abortion activist who was responsible for proposing travel bans in Texas counties why he called them "anti-trafficking" ordinances, given that they would apply to grown women leaving the state of their own free will. His response: "The unborn child is always taken against their will."

And there it is, plain as day. This was never about protecting women or girls. If a fetus is a person, and abortion is murder, of course Republicans are going to outlaw women from "trafficking" their pregnancies out of state to end them. Intentionally or not, they are giving us a heads up about the next attack on our freedom. We would do well to listen.

For Republicans, it's not enough to legislate what women do with our bodies and where we can travel. Their next tactic is to regulate what we can *say* about abortion. After Idaho passed its abortion ban, the University of Idaho sent out an unusual memo to staff, telling them that the school would no longer be offering students birth control. The university's general counsel wrote that "we are advising a conservative approach here." In addition to no longer providing birth control, the memo recommended that the school provide condoms only "for the purpose of helping prevent the spread of STDs . . . [but not] for purposes of birth control." It also dictated that it would be illegal for employees to "promote" abortion or talk about birth control.

You could chalk this up to an overzealous interpretation of the state's law, but the legal team at the university wasn't wrong to be concerned. Idaho's No Public Funds for Abortion Act banned state employees—like those who work at public universities—from "promot[ing] abortion; counsel[ing] in favor of abortion," or referring someone for an abortion. The penalties include a fourteen-year prison sentence, termination of employment, and restitution of public funds.

The backlash to the law was swift. The ACLU sued the state on behalf of a group of public university professors, who noted that the policy left them with "an impossible—and unconstitutional—choice." They could either avoid any speech that someone might interpret as pro-abortion or risk going to prison and losing their livelihoods. An assigned article by a pro-choice writer, a classroom discussion, *anything* could be used to jail a professor.

Idaho is not an anomaly. Since the demise of *Roe,* the attacks on free speech have been everywhere: from bills in South Carolina and Texas that would make pro-choice websites illegal, to moves from the attorneys general of Idaho and Alabama to criminalize simply telling someone how to get an out-of-state abortion. They wanted to make doctors' referrals illegal. Oklahoma librarians were even instructed not to help anyone coming in looking for information on abortion. They were told they couldn't say the word "abortion," either, and if they used the word or helped patrons seeking abortion-related information, they could face possible jail time and a $10,000 fine. In short, banning abortion has set off a domino effect that slams into every other one of our rights.

What to Say to Anti-Abortion Politicians

I could write an entire other book about ripple effects of banning abortion, including the mental health impact on pregnant people, or the way that abortion bans are undermining not only democracy but medical privacy. And at the time of this writing, Republicans like Indiana's attorney general are arguing that abortion reports aren't medical records and should be available to the public in the same way that birth and death certificates are. An anti-abortion group in the state is suing Indiana's health department for the same reason— they say private citizens have the right to scour women's abortion records. These policies strip us of our humanity and have an impact that goes far beyond abortion. That's why the people who enact and defend these laws need to be able to answer for them.

Republicans are desperate to run from questions on abortion rights, distracting from the way that their laws would endanger and criminalize women. That's why the people who would have abortion be illegal need to be put on the spot, whether they're a U.S. senator or a city council member. And they need to answer more than just simple policy questions: they need to be confronted with the real-life impact of abortion bans and to be asked why, on a fundamental human level, they believe it's reasonable to force someone to be pregnant. To sidestep that core issue is to accept the notion that this is all just politics, that the suffering and harm don't matter.

So yes, candidates and representatives should be able to talk about mifepristone, national bans, and federal funding, but they also need to be able to answer questions that get to the heart of what is happening in this country: *What would you say to someone who doesn't want to be pregnant?* Republicans themselves have antici-pated that women will become suicidal as a result of their laws; and doctors, in affidavits, have described women crying and threatening to kill themselves upon finding out they would be denied abortions.

This is what happens in the real world to real people when you legally mandate pregnancy.

Republicans need to be asked specific questions about the consequences of their laws: Under what circumstances should a woman be allowed an abortion if her fetus has an abnormality? What kind of abnormalities should be included in an abortion ban exception? What would you say to women who have been forced to carry doomed pregnancies to term, only to watch their babies suffer and die right after birth?

What about the women who have ended up in the ICU with sepsis after being denied an abortion?

How sick must a person be in order to legally qualify for an abortion?

How much damage to their body is considered acceptable before they'll be allowed to end their pregnancy?

If these politicians believe that they know better than women and doctors, they should be able to answer without hesitation. If they want to dictate a person's most personal health decisions, they have to be prepared to answer difficult, detailed questions.

One broader question I haven't seen anyone answer is this: *How do you defend banning abortion against the wishes of voters?* Over 80 percent of Americans believe abortion should be a decision between a woman and her doctor; they don't want pregnancy regulated at all. Support for abortion rights is broadly increasing across the country, even in red states. How do these numbers square with their belief in democracy?

If politicians believe they're best suited to make these decisions, there is no reason they shouldn't be able to clearly articulate their vision for a post-*Roe* world: If you believe there should be exceptions to abortion bans, what do you think about the fact that these so-called exceptions aren't actually usable? How would you change that?

Do you believe that emergency contraception and hormonal birth control are abortifacients?

How do you respond to the country's biggest anti-abortion groups who believe hormonal birth control should be illegal?

Why do you think a woman might seek out an abortion later in pregnancy?

Do you know how many clinics in the country perform abortions in the third trimester?

Can you tell us how much money an abortion costs?

A pregnant woman in Alabama, accused of using marijuana, was jailed in order to "protect" her fetus. An Indiana woman was charged with murder after she attempted suicide and her pregnancy ended. What do you think about these cases?

There are an infinite number of questions, circumstances, and nuances that come along with banning abortion. Are Republicans prepared to answer all of them? If not, why not? Could it be because pregnancy is too complicated to legislate?

What to Say to Anti-Abortion Women

When the *Dobbs* decision was announced, it broke my heart to see women—some of them so very young—celebrating outside of the Supreme Court, jubilant that the right to abortion was no longer protected. I was incredulous that they could betray other women with actual smiles on their faces. Was the patriarchal pat on the head really worth it? How could they possibly live with themselves? Most of all, did they really not understand that their own bodies were on the line, too?

Somehow these women have convinced themselves that their collaboration with the men who made this happen—and their submission to the misogyny that fuels anti-abortion beliefs—will keep them safe. But their complicity won't protect them. The women who fought to overturn *Roe* are beholden to the same laws that ban all of us from getting essential care. And while they may not realize right now how their lives will be impacted, they're sure to find out how wrong they are.

Fighting alongside anti-choice lawmakers—most of whom have little understanding about the bodies they are legislating—won't save a conservative woman if she has an ectopic pregnancy and lives in a state that bans abortion. Her collusion won't allow doctors to move faster as they assess whether they'll lose their medical license or be jailed if they offer her help. Protesting outside of an abortion clinic won't stop a woman from being denied cancer treatment if she gets sick while pregnant and lives in a state that says an embryo is more important than her health and life.

A "pro-life" woman who is miscarrying will still have to risk infection, sepsis, and death if her doomed fetus has a lingering heartbeat. If a woman has a pregnancy that is incompatible with life, she will have to carry a suffering, dying baby no matter what her politics are.

And like the many, many, conservative women who have quietly gotten abortions despite their public beliefs, it is very likely that one of those women celebrating outside the Supreme Court will get pregnant and simply not want to be. Like the rest of us, she will have no choice.

It's true that privilege can protect you to a certain extent. If you are white, have money, and have the ability to travel to a state where abortion is legal—you will have a much easier time than those from marginalized communities. But there is nothing that will make anyone immune. We are all in danger, even the women who got us here.

Even if anti-abortion women are lucky enough to never need abortion care, the same lawmakers who fought to make abortion illegal are also coming for birth control—something that 99 percent of American women will use in their lifetimes. These are the legislators who vote against paid maternity leave, pay equity, and funding for domestic violence shelters. The women who align themselves with them are supporting an ideology that would also happily ban them from voting, having credit, or the freedom to divorce.

When you codify the lie that our bodies are not our own, everything is on the table. And when you collaborate with men who believe you are fundamentally less than, and you throw other women under the bus, you can't be surprised or hurt when your body gets run over along with the rest of us.

We Need to Save Ourselves

As I wrote this book, the Supreme Court was considering a case that will determine whether conservative states can refuse to give women life-saving abortions in hospital emergency rooms. I wish that was hyperbole, but it's not: Idaho and Texas have sued over the Emergency Medical Treatment and Labor Act (EMTALA), a federal law that says emergency departments have to give patients life-saving and stabilizing treatment—even if that means giving someone an abortion.*

It's surreal and yet somehow completely predictable. If feminists would have warned that less than two years after *Roe*'s demise we'd be fighting for our right to life-saving care, no one would have ever believed us. And yet, here we are: listening to the nation's highest court debate just how many organs a woman can lose before a state

---

* In January 2024, the Fifth Circuit ruled in favor of Texas, stating that EMTALA "does not provide an unqualified right for the pregnant mother to abort her child." An unqualified right. In other words, *How dare we expect to live!*

should be legally required to give her care. That's why we can't count on being believed. We can't depend on the men in charge seeing our humanity. We need to save ourselves.

The organization Shout Your Abortion got it right after the *Dobbs* decision was leaked. They said, "Fuck SCOTUS, we're doing it anyway." We can try to get politicians and media to believe us, but we can't depend on it. We can and will fight to change the laws, but that may not work. In the end, we need to take care of ourselves and each other.

That's part of the reason I started *Abortion, Every Day;* I didn't trust that traditional journalism would catch on to the nuances of the attacks on our bodies. I wanted to do my part to take care of us. It's the same reason that while incredible activist organizations are working within the system to change policies and fight injustices, others are working outside of it—ensuring that people get the abortions they need no matter what.

And it doesn't matter if you're a seasoned activist or new to the issue, it doesn't matter if you do this full time or if reading this book is the most you've ever been involved. We all have the ability and the responsibility to do something: to remind people that we are not overreacting, we are not exaggerating and that what is happening right now is that bad and that it can absolutely get worse; to make sure people know the truth about abortion misinformation; to help people get care when they need it; to tell the truth about how pro-choice America really is; to hold our local media and politicians accountable. My hope is that everything you've read so far will help you at least take a step forward. Most of all, we can make sure that this post-*Roe* nightmare is never normalized. The danger of the ordinary is what keeps me up nights.

There's No Such Thing as Abortion "Compromise"

What's happening with abortion has nothing to do with the middle. There's nothing moderate about women in the ICU with sepsis, there's no compromise to be made with those who would force raped ten-year-olds to give birth. The "center" on abortion disappeared the first time a woman underwent a hysterectomy because it was the only legal way for doctors to end her life-threatening pregnancy.

That's why the mainstream pro-choice movement needs to get out of their defensive crouch. The consequences of widespread abortion bans are no longer theoretical. We don't have to ask voters to imagine how bad it would be if abortion was restricted, we can simply point to what is already in progress: cancer patients denied care, mothers forced to carry dead and dying fetuses, states losing half of their ob-gyns. That sort of horror is immune to talking points.

That said, in a moment when we're hearing so many extreme stories, it can be difficult to bring the issue back to this foundational truth: Every abortion denied is a tragedy. That's why it's vital to highlight all the harm caused by bans—not just the most tragic. Too often, pro-choice politicians will focus almost exclusively on the extreme stories they believe will be most sympathetic: sexual violence victims and women with wanted pregnancies denied abortions despite the risk to their lives. Those stories matter, that's why we tell them. But concentrating on the few experiences that we believe are most palatable at the expense of the majority of cases is a grave moral and strategic error.

It's vital that we remember and remind others that to force someone to be pregnant against their will, for any reason, at any point, causes profound existential harm. Abortion is healthcare, but it is also freedom. That's why we can't get caught in the trap of supporting restrictions. I understand the fear some pro-choicers have. They believe pushing for abortion rights without restrictions will give conservatives ammunition to call us extremists who want abortion "up until birth." But here's the thing: they're going to say that anyway.

When Ohio abortion rights activists drafted Issue 1, they did so with a "viability" limitation. They didn't want conservatives to attack them for supporting abortion "up until birth." But anti-abortion activists and groups opposing the campaign said it anyway; the president of Susan B. Anthony Pro-Life America even wrote in *Newsweek* that the amendment proposal would allow for abortion "right up until birth."

Conservatives' "abortion up until birth" attack may be graphic, but it's not based in reality. It assumes women are cruelly and deliberately waiting around for the opportunity to end a pregnancy as late as is legally possible. We need to ask Republicans, *Does that sound like any of the women you know? Is this what you think women are like?* Let them say it out loud.

So when conservatives say our objective is "no limits abortion," we have to counter with the truth: The goal is a culture that supports people throughout their pregnancies, no matter how long they last or how they end. Sometimes that means helping someone become a parent, ensuring they have access to safe and unbiased prenatal care. Sometimes it means taking a friend to get an abortion a few weeks after a missed period or securing compassionate care for a raped and impregnated child.

We want to live in a country where a devastated woman who has received tragic news about her pregnancy doesn't have to put her grief on hold for a week so she can find a doctor. A country where a teenager doesn't have to convince a judge that she's responsible enough not to have a baby. And yes, a country where someone who needs an abortion later in their pregnancy—for whatever reason—is able to get one.

Because we trust women. And we know that what happens during pregnancy is complicated, personal, and impossible to dictate by law. Increasingly, Americans understand that. They don't want the government involved in their decisions about pregnancy at any point. Not at six weeks, not at twenty-six weeks. Not in New York, and not in Alabama.[*]

This is no time for equivocating. We need to work for full access to abortion. So, if there was ever a time to fight for what we want, and for the world that women and girls deserve, this is it. There's no middle ground on our freedom, and we can't leave anyone behind.

---

[*] A few weeks before I wrote this, a Democrat flipped an Alabama House seat—campaigning not just on abortion but *her* abortion. She shared her abortion story and won by 25 points. In Alabama.

Resources

Countering the Propaganda

We've seen the way anti-abortion fake science has made its way into the cultural lexicon—from "partial-birth abortion" to "chemical abortion," neither of which is a real medical term.* The longer these lies are repeated unchecked, the more easily they become part of American life.

Nowhere is this more evident than in what Americans believe about pregnancy itself.

All of us—even those of us who support abortion rights—have been influenced by anti-abortion propaganda. If you've ever been pregnant and signed up for one of those apps that sends you weekly updates of what kind of fruit your baby is the size of, you've likely seen it. If you've googled pregnancy or fetus images and seen diagrams that look like little babies, you've seen it too. The truth is that Americans largely don't know what pregnancy and abortion really look like.

---

* "Chemical abortion" is a political phrase that's been deliberately crafted by conservative groups seeking to make abortion medication seem dangerous or poisonous.

In 2022 the abortion providers at the MYA Network published photos of early pregnancy tissue taken from the abortions they performed. (With patient permission, of course.) The broad response to these images was incredulity.

When I posted the images on TikTok, people flooded my comments to accuse me of digitally altering them. They said I photoshopped the fetus out or was lying about what the images actually were. Even pro-choice people couldn't believe it.

5 weeks

7 weeks

9 weeks

Americans have been so fully misinformed about abortion that they couldn't fathom that this—these small white blobs with no visible embryo—was what everyone was making all this fuss over. Even after a Stanford University pathologist weighed in to say, yes, the images were real, many people refused to believe it.

Even Alliance Defending Freedom—the extremist organization responsible for the end of *Roe*—published an article attacking the images and the clinicians who released them. They claimed that the doctors at the MYA Network "deliberately removed or strategically covered up" the embryo in their pictures of early pregnancy.

For others, the images of early abortion put the issue in perspective. Some women contacted me to express relief; they said the images made them feel better about their miscarriages or abortions. The shame they felt didn't feel quite so heavy.

To this day, whenever I repost these images, I'm attacked with hate. The last time I published them to Twitter, the website put a content warning on them suggesting that they were fake. Imagine how powerful these images must be if people are so desperate to suppress them.

The anti-abortion movement knows that if Americans see the truth—that they're stripping women's rights in favor of a quarter inch piece of tissue—they might rethink their stance or get even angrier and more pro-choice. They're right to be afraid: studies show that the more educated someone is about pregnancy, the more likely they are to support abortion rights. To me, that means science, facts, and information are more important than ever.

Here is a list of resources—facts, organizations, explanations of anti-abortion terms, and books for further reading—that I hope will serve you moving forward.

Facts About Abortion

Abortion is a medical intervention to end a pregnancy—for whatever reason.

- One in four American women[*] will have an abortion in her lifetime.
- Most abortion patients are parents. Six in ten women who get abortions already have children.
- Ninety-nine percent of women who have had abortions don't regret it, and the most common emotion that women have after an abortion is relief.
- Decades of research have shown that both procedural and medication abortions are safe.
- In 2023 abortion medication accounted for 63 percent of abortions, up from 53 percent in 2020.
- An analysis of more than one hundred studies on abortion medication found that "more than 99 percent of patients who took the pills had no serious complications."
- Abortion medication via telehealth is safe. A study that looked at more than sixty thousand medication abortions across twenty states found that 98 percent of the abortions were effective, and that 99.8 percent were free from serious adverse events.

Voters have overwhelmingly supported abortion rights for decades, and their support has only grown since *Dobbs*. Abortion rights are now more popular than they've ever been in American

---

[*] We don't yet have statistics that include trans men, nonbinary people, and others with the ability to get pregnant.

history. Americans increasingly understand that pregnancy is too complicated to legislate at any point.

- Eighty-one percent of Americans don't want abortion regulated by the government at all, but believe it should be a decision between a patient and their doctor.
- Eighty-five percent of voters say abortion should be legal in some or all circumstances.
- Fifty-five percent of voters, including one-third of Republicans, want abortion legal "for any reason."
- More than 70 percent of voters want abortion medication to be legal.
- Support for abortion throughout pregnancy is the highest it's ever been and has risen by nearly 10 percentage points in the last five years.
- Seventy-four percent of adults under thirty believe abortion should be legal in most or all circumstances, and nearly 40 percent believe it should be legal in all circumstances.
- Adults under thirty are twice as likely to describe themselves as "pro-choice" than "pro-life."
- Despite Republican insistence to the contrary, fifteen-week abortion bans are just as unpopular as six-week bans.
- Americans reject the notion that fifteen-week bans are "reasonable compromises" by a more than two-to-one margin.
- Even Republicans support abortion access. In 2023, 65 percent of Republicans in Tennessee wanted their state ban to be loosened, and nearly one in four white evangelicals in Ohio voted in support of enshrining abortion rights in the state constitution.

The consequences of banning abortion are dire: skyrocketing maternal and infant mortality, increased poverty, maternal health deserts, and brain drain. The most serious of those consequences impact the most marginalized communities.

- States with abortion restrictions have maternal death rates that are 62 percent higher than states with abortion access.
- Women who live in anti-choice states are three times more likely to die during pregnancy.
- The maternal mortality rate is increasing twice as fast in states with abortion restrictions.
- Restricting abortion is linked to an increased suicide risk among women of reproductive age.
- Bans on abortion will lead to a 21 percent increase in pregnancy-related deaths overall, with a 33 percent increase among Black women.
- Anti-abortion groups are trying to sow distrust in maternal mortality data because they know the numbers are going up post-*Dobbs*.
- Being forced to carry a pregnancy to term quadruples the odds that a patient's family will live below the poverty line and triples the chance the pregnant person will end up unemployed.
- The states most likely to have abortion bans and restrictions are also providing minimal services for women and mothers.
- States that restrict abortion have a 16 percent greater infant mortality rate.

Every state with an abortion ban is losing ob-gyns, with the result that hospitals are shuttering their maternity wards, and reproductive and maternal health deserts are spreading.

- As of 2024, 25 million women live in a state with an abortion ban.

- Some 3.7 million women live in a county without access to abortion and with "no or low" access to maternity care.
- More than 5.6 million women live in counties with limited or no access to maternity care services.
- Over 1.7 million American women live in "double deserts"—counties that lack both abortion care and maternal healthcare.
- American hospitals lost three hundred maternity wards in the last five years.
- Anti-abortion crisis pregnancy centers outnumber real health clinics by a factor of three to one—and the number is still growing.
- In the two years since Idaho passed its abortion ban in 2022, the state has lost nearly 25 percent of its ob-gyns. Idaho has also lost half its maternal-fetal medicine specialists and multiple major maternity wards.
- Hospitals and health centers in states with abortion bans are unable to recruit new ob-gyns and maternal-fetal medicine specialists.
- Medical students and residents don't want to move to states with abortion bans because they know they can't give their patients the standard of care.

Anti-abortion groups and lawmakers are targeting birth control—not in the future but right now.

- Conservatives are trying to redefine IUDs and emergency contraception (morning-after pills) as "abortifacients," when in fact these forms of contraception don't end a pregnancy but prevent one.
- They are using confusion over birth control to push the lie (which 73 percent of Americans believe) that emergency contraception can end a pregnancy. It can't.

- Republicans are chipping away at birth control access by attacking insurance coverage and protection for younger people, and by overfunding crisis pregnancy centers that steer patients away from contraception.
- Anti-abortion groups have launched a cultural campaign to sow distrust in hormonal contraception in order to convince young women that birth control is "unnatural" or bad for them.
- Birth control is extremely popular. A 2024 survey reported that 80 percent of voters say protecting access to contraception is "deeply important" to them—and that even 72 percent of Republicans support birth control.

Abortion ban "exceptions" are largely not real. While some people may be able to access them—and all should try!—these policies are written deliberately to be unusable.

- Despite anti-abortion claims that pregnancy from rape is rare, a 2024 study estimated that since *Roe* was overturned, there were 65,000 rape-related pregnancies in anti-choice states.
- The shame, fear of victim-blaming, and trepidation over the criminal justice system keeps more than two-thirds of rape victims from going to police. Yet most rape "exceptions" require victims to have filed a police report or to bring some other kind of documentation "proving" their attack.
- Mississippi's abortion ban has an "exception" for rape, but not one doctor in the entire state is willing to give a rape victim an abortion because of the severity of the law.
- As of 2024, most abortion bans don't have an "exception" for fatal fetal abnormalities.
- About 120,000 pregnancies are diagnosed with fetal abnormalities every year, and congenital malformations are responsible for thousands of infant deaths every year.

Republicans claim that they don't want to arrest women, but women were criminalized even while *Roe* was in effect. Legislators are increasingly introducing bills that would make having an abortion publishable as a homicide.

- The people most likely to be targeted in pregnancy criminalization cases are from marginalized communities: women of color (Black women especially), poor women, those who are unhoused, and those with substance abuse issues.
- Criminalization relies on communities turning on each other and "snitch culture." A 2023 report found that when people were turned in for self-managing their abortions, 45 percent of the time it was a healthcare provider who reported them. The next most likely group to report was acquaintances, at 26 percent.
- Prosecutors who want to charge women will get around prohibitions on arresting abortion patients by bringing seemingly unrelated charges like "abuse of a corpse" or "chemical endangerment."

Anti-Abortion Language

Standard, consensus: These terms mean abortion ban. Republicans don't want to use *ban* because they know bans are incredibly unpopular. If you hear a politician say they support a "national minimum standard," that means they're for a federal abortion ban. Other terms you might hear that mean *ban* are "reasonable restrictions" and "commonsense restrictions."

Previable: This term refers to a fatal fetal abnormality, a nonviable pregnancy. Anti-abortion groups want to trick women

into carrying doomed pregnancies to term, so they're changing *nonviable* to "previable" to give women false hope and
confuse them.

Maternal-fetal separation: Anti-abortion activists don't want
to admit that abortions are sometimes necessary to save a
patient's health or life. So instead of calling pregnancy termination in those cases abortion, they call it "maternal-fetal
separation." It is not a medical term, yet it has made its way
into multiple pieces of legislation. Most dangerously, under
"separation," Republicans legislated life-threatening pregnancies are to be ended with either a C-section or an induce-
ment of vaginal labor. They are thus forcing doctors to give
women major surgery instead of a ten-minute, safer, less-
traumatic abortion.

Perinatal hospice care, prenatal counseling: Anti-abortion
groups have co-opted counseling services in an effort to
force women to carry doomed pregnancies to term. In Republican legislation, these terms refer to crisis pregnancy
centers. These centers force women who've been diagnosed
with a fatal fetal abnormality to speak to anti-abortion
"counselors"—who most often have no license or training in
mental health. The "counselors" try to convince patients that
carrying a doomed pregnancy to term is better for them.
They lie about the danger of abortion and try to shame patients who want to end their pregnancies.

Maternal health centers, maternal wellness centers: These
are newer terms for anti-abortion crisis pregnancy centers.
Because Americans are increasingly aware of these centers

and their anti-abortion agenda, Republicans are trying to cloak the organizations under new terminology.

Late abortion: Anti-abortion groups and lawmakers are trying to define "late abortion" as any abortion that occurs after twelve weeks. It is not a medical or scientific term.

Viability: This too is not a medical term. The ability of a fetus to survive outside a person's body is not a set standard but varies from pregnancy to pregnancy.

Anti-trafficking, abortion trafficking: These terms refer to travel bans—laws that prevent people in anti-abortion states from helping others go to another state for abortion care. Republicans hope that by hiding travel bans in language that sounds protective of women and girls, voters won't notice.

Organizations

If you need help finding a trusted and verified abortion provider, head to Abortion Finder, I Need An A, Abortion Care Network, or Planned Parenthood.

If you need abortion medication now, or want to have pills on hand for the future, contact Aid Access, Plan C Pills, Abortion Finder, I Need An A.

The organization that you order your medication from will have resources on how to take it, but you can also find information at Hey Jane (heyjane.com) or We Testify (abortion.shop).

If you're self-managing an abortion and need medical advice, contact the Miscarriage and Abortion Hotline: (833) 246-2632.

To protect your digital privacy when planning your abortion, look at the resources and guides from the Electronic Frontier Foundation and the Digital Defense Fund.

If you need help affording abortion care, contact an abortion fund or practical support fund near you. (For those who want to offer help, donating to your local fund is also a great idea!)

If you need to know the abortion law in your state, an abortion fund can help, or you can check out the Center for Reproductive Rights.

For free legal help as a patient or health practitioner, call If/When/How's Repro Legal Helpline: (844) 868-2812.

If you want to dive deeper into abortion research, look to Advancing New Standards in Reproductive Health (ANSIRH, home of the Turnaway Study), Ibis Reproductive Health, the Guttmacher Institute, and the National Institute of Reproductive Health.

For important abortion rights activism, check out Pregnancy Justice, Sister Song, WE TESTIFY, and WhoNotWhen.

If you need help right now, call or text 988 for the National Suicide Prevention Lifeline. The National Domestic Violence Hotline is (800) 799-7233. And you can reach the National Sexual Assault Hotline at (800) 656-4673.

For Further Reading

Foster, Diana Greene. *The Turnaway Study: Ten Years, a Thousand Women, and the Consequences of Having—or Being Denied—an Abortion*. New York: Scribner, 2021.

Littlejohn, Krystale E., and Rickie Solinger. *Fighting Mad: Resisting the End of Roe v. Wade*. Berkeley: University of California Press, 2024.

Marty, Robin. *New Handbook for a Post-Roe America: The Complete Guide to Abortion Legality, Access, and Practical Support.* New York: Seven Stories Press, 2021.

Roberts, Dorothy. *Killing the Black Body: Race, Reproduction and the Meaning of Liberty.* New York: Pantheon, 1997.

Ross, Loretta, and Rickie Solinger. *Reproductive Justice: An Introduction.* Berkeley: University of California Press, 2017.

Shah, Meera. *You're the Only One I've Told: The Stories Behind Abortion.* Chicago: Chicago Review Press, 2020.

Sherman, Renee Bracey, and Regina Mahone. *Liberating Abortion: Claiming Our History, Sharing Our Stories, and Building the Reproductive Future We Deserve.* New York: HarperCollins, 2024.

Ziegler, Mary. *Roe: The History of a National Obsession.* New Haven, CT: Yale University Press, 2023.

Acknowledgments

This book would not exist in any way, shape, or form without my first editor, best supporter, and incredible husband, Andrew Golis. My daughter, Layla, has lent out her mom to this work for the better part of two years and cheered me on the whole way. She's the reason I do this work.

There are three women who deserve thanks until the end of time. My editor, Libby Burton, knows exactly what needs to get done and how to do it. I'm so grateful for her wisdom, patience, and vision. Everyone should have an agent as good as Laurie Liss, who will hear out any gripe and go to war if you ask her to. Grace Haley has worked tirelessly on *Abortion*'s endnotes, ensuring that every one of my arguments was supported, and every word backed up. She's been an incredible support this past year.

Thanks also go to my assistant, Cassidy Howard, for keeping my life in order, and the team at Crown for their amazing work. The readers and community at *Abortion, Every Day* have been a constant source of inspiration. I'm so thankful that in this terrible moment in time, I have a community like the one at *AED* to rely on and commiserate with.

Finally, thank you to the people who shared their stories with me for *Abortion* and *Abortion, Every Day*. Your trust in me means everything.

Notes

Introduction

ix   ***Dobbs* decision was leaked** Josh Gerstein and Alexander Ward, "Supreme Court Has Voted to Overturn Abortion Rights, Draft Opinion Shows," *Politico,* May 2, 2022.

ix   **the Supreme Court made it official** *Dobbs v. Jackson Women's Health Organization,* 597 U.S. (2022).

x   **white supremacist patriarchy** bell hooks, Ain't I a Woman? Black Women and Feminism (Boston, MA: South End Press, 1981).

x   **a law adopted in 1864** Katherine Davis-Young, "The Arizona Supreme Court Allows a Near-Total Abortion Ban to Take Effect Soon," NPR, April 9, 2024.

xi   **led by a man who liked to marry twelve- and fourteen-year-old girls** Monica Hesse, "Meet the 'Pursuer of Nubile Young Females' Who Helped Pass Arizona's 1864 Abortion Law," *Washington Post,* April 10, 2024.

xi   **eroding birth control access, running ob-gyns out of town** Jessica Valenti, "The Anti-Abortion Blueprint," *Abortion, Every Day,* February 19, 2024.

xi   **a network of religious "maternity homes"** Charles A. Donovan, "Expanding State and Federal Support for Decisions for Life," Charlotte Lozier Institute, May 31, 2023.

xi   **secret campaign to force women to carry** Rep. Chip Roy et al. to Acting Commissioner Janet Woodcock, "FDA Approval of Prenatal Testing," January 21, 2022.

xi   **charge women with murder** See, for example, the Alabama bill introduced by lawmakers the year after *Roe* was overturned: Alabama House of Representatives, H.B. 454, Equal Protection Act (2023).

xi   **defending women of color being arrested** "Confronting Pregnancy Criminalization: A Practical Guide for Healthcare Providers, Lawyers, Medical Examiners, Child Welfare Workers, and Policymakers," Pregnancy Justice, July 2022.

Chapter 1: Abortion Is Good, Actually

1   **forcing children to give birth** For an example of an abortion ban enforcing restrictions on minors, see the North Carolina one, in which state legislators defined woman as "A female human, whether or not she is an adult." North Carolina General Assembly, S.B. 20, Care for Women, Children, and Families Act (2023).

1   **devastated women carry dead and dying fetuses** Nadine El-Bawab et al., "In Post-Roe America, Women Detail Agony of Being Forced to Carry Nonviable Pregnancies to Term," ABC News, December 14, 2023.

1   **mandating that rape victims sign affidavits** West Virginia's abortion ban contains a rape exception with strict conditions, including law enforcement requirements and an eight-week gestational limit. Prohibition to Perform an Abortion, W. Va. Code §16-2R-3 (2022).

1–2 **Over 80 percent of Americans don't want the government** "Abortion," Historical Trends, Gallup, n.d.

2   **they said abortion should be "safe, legal and rare"** Anna North, "How the Abortion Debate Moved Away from 'Safe, Legal, and Rare,'" *Vox,* October 18, 2019.

3   **the ability to choose if and when** Adam Sonfield et al., "Social and Economic Benefits of Women's Ability to Determine Whether and When to Have Children," Guttmacher Institute, March 2013.

3   **those who are denied abortions** Sarah C. M. Roberts et al., "Risk of Violence from the Man Involved in the Pregnancy After

Receiving or Being Denied an Abortion," *BMC Medicine* 12, no. 144 (September 2014).

3   **abortion is safe (much safer than pregnancy)** Elizabeth G. Raymond and David A. Grimes, "The Comparative Safety of Legal Induced Abortion and Childbirth in the United States," *Obstetrics and Gynecology* 119, no. 2 (February 2012): 215–19.

3–4   **one in four American women** Rachel K. Jones and Jenna Jerman, "Population Group Abortion Rates and Lifetime Incidence of Abortion: United States, 2008–2014," *American Journal of Public Health,* no. 12 (December 2017): 1904–9.

5   **Most often, though, we're both** Katherine Kortsmit et al., "Abortion Surveillance—United States, 2021," *Morbidity and Mortality Weekly Report,* Centers for Disease Control and Prevention, November 22, 2023.

6   **Abortion is a medical intervention** "ACOG Guide to Language and Abortion," American College of Obstetricians and Gynecologists, September 2023.

7   **Most people in the United States who end their pregnancies** Rachel K. Jones and Amy Friedrich-Karnik, "Medication Abortion Accounted for 63% of All US Abortions in 2023—An Increase from 53% in 2020," Guttmacher Institute, March 19, 2024.

7   **25 million women live in a state with an abortion ban** Geoff Mulvihill, Kimberlee Kruesi and Claire Savage, "A Year After Fall of Roe, 25 Million Women Live in States with Abortion Bans or Tighter Restrictions," Associated Press, June 22, 2023.

7   **also called a manual uterine aspiration (MUA) abortion** "What is Manual Uterine Aspiration (MUA)?," MYAbortion Network, December 2023.

7   **This kind of abortion has a history** For more, see Hannah Dudley-Shotwell, *Revolutionizing Women's Healthcare: The Feminist Self-Help Movement in America* (New Brunswick, NJ: Rutgers University Press, 2020).

8   **Those in the second trimester and beyond** "Abortion in the Second Trimester," Abortion Care FAQs, American College of Obstetricians and Gynecologists, August 2022.

8   **Most abortions happen in the first trimester** Kortsmit et al., "Abortion Surveillance—United States, 2021."

9   **Research shows that some patients don't learn** Ivette Gomez, Alina Salganicoff and Laurie Sobel, "Abortions Later in Pregnancy in a Post-Dobbs Era," *KFF Health News,* February 21, 2024.

9   **If Republicans weren't enacting restrictions** Ushma D. Upadhyay, "Barriers Push People into Seeking Abortion Care Later in Pregnancy," *American Journal of Public Health* 112, no. 9 (September 1, 2022): 1280–81.

9   **there would be fewer abortions after** Ibid.

9   **Children and teens are more likely** "Statistics In-Depth," National Intimate Partner and Sexual Violence Survey, National Sexual Violence Resource Center.

9   **more likely to be victims of incest** Howard N. Snyder, "Sexual Assault of Young Children as Reported to Law Enforcement: Victim, Incident, and Offender Characteristics," Bureau of Justice Statistics, U.S. Department of Justice, July 2000.

9   **less likely to have the resources and support** Quoctrung Bui and Claire Cain Miller, "The Age That Women Have Babies: How a Gap Divides America," *The New York Times,* August 4, 2018.

9   **They have to overcome additional financial** Ibid.

9   **You're more likely to have a complication** Ushma D. Upadhyay et al., "Incidence of Emergency Department Visits and Complications After Abortion," *Obstetrics and Gynecology* 125, no. 1 (January 2015): 175–83.

9   **99 percent of them won't regret it** Corinne H. Rocca et al., "Decision Rightness and Emotional Responses to Abortion in the United States: A Longitudinal Study," *PLoS One* 10, no. 7 (July 8, 2015).

9   **because they live in a community** M. Antonia Biggs, Katherine Brown, and Diana Greene Foster, "Perceived Abortion Stigma and Psychological Well-Being over Five Years After Receiving or Being Denied an Abortion," *PLoS One* 15, no. 1 (January 29, 2020).

10   **Decades of research have shown** National Academies of Sciences, Engineering, and Medicine, *The Safety and Quality of Abortion Care in the United States* (Washington, DC: The National Academies Press: 2018).

10   **safer than Tylenol or Viagra** Ibid.

10   *The New York Times* **examined more than one hundred studies**

Amy Schoenfeld Walker et al., "Are Abortion Pills Safe? Here's the Evidence.," *The New York Times,* March 25, 2024.

10   **restrict access to mifepristone** David S. Cohen, Greer Donley and Rachel Rebouché, "Abortion Pills," *Stanford Law Review* 76 (February 2024): 317.

10   **retracted by their publishers** Brendan Pierson, "U.S. Publisher Retracts Studies Cited by Texas Judge in Suspending Abortion Pill's Approval," Reuters, February 6, 2024.

10   **women who take abortion medication** Jeanne Mancini, "Declaring a Publish Health Emergency Over Abortion Would be Reckless," *Newsweek,* March 7, 2023.

10   **among women of reproductive age, only 0.01 percent** Ushma D. Upadhyay et al., "Abortion-Related Emergency Department Visits in the United States: An Analysis of a National Emergency Department Sample," *BMC Medicine* 16, no. 88 (June 24, 2018).

10   **another showed that less than 1 percent** Ushma D. Upadhyay et al., "Incidence of Emergency Department Visits and Complications After Abortion," *Obstetrics and Gynecology* 125, no. 1 (January 2015): 175–183.

11   **simply sent home** Lisa Rapaport, "Few U.S. Women Have Serious Complications After Abortions," Reuters, July 11, 2018.

12   **"These telemedicine providers are entirely virtual"** Carrie N. Baker quoted in Dahlia Lithwick, "The Anti-Abortion Movement's Biggest Fear," *Slate,* March 25, 2024.

13   **A 2024 study from** Ushma D. Upadhyay et al., "Effectiveness and Safety of Telehealth Medication Abortion in the USA," *Nature Medicine* 30, (February 15, 2024): 1191-1198.

13   **A 2023 study from** Fekede Asefa Kumsa et al., "Medication Abortion Via Digital Health in the United States: A Systematic Scoping Review," *npj Digital Medicine* 6, no. 128 (2023).

13   **the most comprehensive research on the impact** Diana Greene Foster *The Turnaway Study: Ten Years, a Thousand Women, and the Consequences of Having—or Being Denied—an Abortion* (New York: Scribner, 2021).

14   **forcing a woman into pregnancy quadruples the odds** Diana Greene Foster et al., "Socioeconomic Outcomes of Women Who Receive and Women Who Are Denied Wanted Abortions in the United States," *American Journal of Public Health* 112, no. 9 (September 1, 2022): 1290–96.

14   **"The things they worry about coming"** Diana Greene Foster
     quoted in Ronnie Cohen, "Denial of Abortion Leads to
     Economic Hardship for Low-Income Women," Reuters,
     January 18, 2018.

15   **"We have the data to show"** Diana Greene Foster quoted in
     Annalisa Merelli, "Measuring the Long-Term Cost of Restricting
     Abortion Access," *STAT,* October 17, 2023.

15   **bans on abortion in the United States will lead** Amanda Jean
     Stevenson, "The Pregnancy-Related Mortality Impact of a Total
     Abortion Ban in the United States: A Research Note on Increased
     Deaths Due to Remaining Pregnant," *Demography* 58, no. 6
     (December 1, 2021): 2019–28.

15   **abortion restrictions have maternal death rates** Eugene
     Declercq et al., "The U.S. Maternal Health Divide: The Limited
     Maternal Health Services and Worse Outcomes of States
     Proposing New Abortion Restrictions," Commonwealth Fund,
     December 14, 2022.

15   **abortion restrictions cause a "significant increase"** Jonathan
     Zandberg et al., "Association Between State-Level Access to
     Reproductive Care and Suicide Rates Among Women of
     Reproductive Age in the United States," *JAMA Psychiatry* 80, no.
     2 (December 28, 2022): 127–34. The researchers—who came
     from the University of Pennsylvania's department of psychology,
     the Perelman School of Medicine, and the Wharton School—
     looked at data between 1974 and 2016. They found a "significant
     increase" in the suicide rate among women of reproductive age
     after abortion restrictions were enacted.

Chapter 2: America Supports Abortion

16   **voters have overwhelmingly supported** "Abortion," Historical
     Trends, Gallup, n.d.

16   **Abortion rights are more popular** Lydia Saad, "Broader Support
     for Abortion Rights Continues Post-Dobbs," Gallup, June 14,
     2023.

16   **Eighty-five percent of voters say abortion** "Abortion," Historical
     Trends, Gallup, n.d.

17   **more than 70 percent want abortion medication** "Abortion,"
       Historical Trends, Gallup, n.d.

17   **over 80 percent believe abortion** Mallory Newall,
       Charlie Rollason, and Bernard Mendez, "Most Americans
       Support Access to Medication Abortion," Ipsos, March 29,
       2024.

17   **55 percent of voters, including one-third of Republicans, want
       abortion legal "for any reason"** Julie Wernau, "Support for
       Abortion Access Is Near Record, WSJ-NORC Poll Finds," *Wall
       Street Journal,* November 20, 2023.

17   **A 2023 poll out of Tennessee** Donald Levy, "Tennesseans
       Strongly Support Red Flag Law and Safe Storage, Call for Less
       Restrictive Abortion Law," Siena College Research Institute,
       December 17, 2023.

17   **In Florida, most Republican voters** "FL Fall Statewide Omnibus
       Survey, Nov 2023," Public Opinion Research Lab, University of
       Florida, November 30, 2023.

17   **when voters passed Ohio's abortion rights amendment** "Ohio
       Exit Polls," *2023 Exit Polls,* CNN, November 7, 2023.

17   **they claim that voters want some kind of restriction** Susan B.
       Anthony Pro-Life America, an influential organization, has
       pushed this narrative in the first place. For how it incorporate
       polling into its activism, see "Where Do Americans Stand on
       Abortion?," Susan B. Anthony Pro-Life America, April 9, 2024.

18   **As of the spring of 2024** Protecting Pain-Capable Unborn
       Children from Late-Term Abortions Act, S. 4840, 117th Cong.
       (2022).

18   **support for the right to abortion throughout pregnancy** Amelia
       Thomson-DeVeaux, "Dobbs Turned Abortion into a Huge
       Liability for Republicans," *FiveThirtyEight,* June 22, 2023.

18   **abortion up until "viability"** The "viability" standard was created
       by a Supreme Court clerk during Roe, which has been used
       throughout the legislative process for many states after the Dobbs
       decision. For more on this history, see Alyssa Edes, "Part 1: The
       Viability Line," More Perfect (podcast), June 8, 2023.

18   **respondents were 15 percentage points** "Exploring the Impact of
       a Viability Limit on Support for Ballot Measures," PerryUndem,
       July 12, 2023.

18   **"people are saying, 'I don't want the government involved'"**
     Tresa Undem quoted in Amelia Thomson-DeVeaux, "A Growing
     Share of Americans Think States Shouldn't Be Able to Put Any
     Limits on Abortion," *FiveThirtyEight,* July 25, 2023.

19   **about women who get a devastating diagnosis** Another public
     example is the Center for Reproductive Rights lawsuit
     representing women who had been denied abortions in
     Tennessee despite threats to their life, health, and future fertility.
     Among them, K Monica Kelly was denied care after her fetus was
     diagnosed with trisomy 13. Carter Sherman, "'I Wasn't Allowed
     to Get the Healthcare I Needed': The Women Suing Tennessee for
     Being Denied Abortions," *Guardian,* February 1, 2024.

19   **they were refused treatment** Christina Zielke is one of
     many women who nearly died after being refused care for a
     miscarriage. She was discharged from the hospital and denied
     treatment while passing blood clots "the size of golf balls." Kylie
     Cheung, "Woman Denied Emergency Abortion in Ohio Filled
     Diapers with Blood, Almost Died," *Jezebel,* November 16, 2022.

19   **74 percent of adults under thirty** "Nearly a Year After Roe's
     Demise, Americans' Views of Abortion Access Increasingly Vary
     by Where They Live," Pew Research Center, April 26, 2023.

19   **nearly 80 percent responded that abortion** Gary Langer, "More
     Say Politics, Not the Law, Drive Supreme Court Decisions: Poll,"
     ABC News, May 9, 2023.

19   **81 percent of Americans agreed** Newall, Rollason, and Mendez,
     "Most Americans Support Access."

20   **Abortion was on the ballot in five different states** Elizabeth
     Nash and Isabel Guarnieri, "In the US Midterm Elections,
     Resounding Victories for Abortion on State Ballot Measures,"
     Guttmacher Institute, November 9, 2022.

20   **Exit polls showed** Janice Kai Chen, Chris Alcantara, and Emily
     Guskin, "How Different Groups Voted According to Exit Polls
     and AP VoteCast," *Washington Post,* November 10, 2022.

20   **who supported Democrats by over 70 percent** "The Youth Vote
     in 2022," Center for Information and Research on Civic Learning
     and Engagement, Tufts University, April 2023.

20   **abortion was a top issue for voters** Aditi Sangal et al., "2022
     Midterm Election Results," CNN, November 9, 2022.

20   **27 percent of respondents** "Exit Polls 2022," NBC News, November 8, 2022.

21   **focused on the anti-abortion extremism** Sylvia Goodman, "Beshear Attacks Cameron over Abortion Restrictions in Kentucky's Race for Governor," WKMS, September 7, 2023.

21   **"because of her courage, this commonwealth"** Andy Beshear, Victory Speech, November 7, 2023.

21   **Lands didn't campaign just on abortion** Colby Itkowitz, "Democrat Who Ran Heavily on Abortion Rights, IVF Wins Alabama Special Election," *Washington Post,* March 26, 2024.

21   **pro-choice ad featuring** Grace Panetta, "Two Abortion Stories, Two Decades Apart, Fuel a Special Election in Alabama," *19th,* March 21, 2024.

22   **anti-abortion organizations and conservative activists** "Abortion Policy/Anti-Abortion Summary," OpenSecrets, March 6, 2024.

23   **before Roe was overturned, a study found** "The Supreme Court's *Dobbs* Decision on Public Opinion," PerryUndem, June 14, 2023.

23   **Studies show that for years** "Accurate and Unbiased," NARAL Pro-Choice America, June 11, 2020.

24   **only 9 percent of articles about abortion** Ibid.

24   **"For some, the changes are joyful"** Julie Vitkovskaya and Susan Svrluga, "Terrified, Elated, Anxious," *Washington Post,* November 23, 2022.

24   **Three-quarters of eighteen-to-thirty-year-olds** "The Youth Vote in 2022," Center for Information and Research on Civic Learning and Engagement, Tufts University, April 2023.

24   **adults under thirty are twice as likely** "Harvard Youth Poll," Institute of Politics, Harvard Kennedy School, December 5, 2023.

24   **cardiac activity isn't possible** Jennifer Gunter, "Dear Press, Stop Calling Them 'Heartbeat' Bills and Call Them 'Fetal Pole Cardiac Activity' Bills," *HuffPost,* December 12, 2016.

25   **language "personifying the fetus"** Katie Woodruff, "Coverage of Abortion in Select U.S. Newspapers," *Women's Health Issues* 29, no. 1 (January 2019): 80–86.

25   **half the news articles** Laura Nixon et al., "Shaping Stigma: An Analysis of Mainstream Print and Online News Coverage of

Abortion, 2014–2015," *Berkeley Media Studies Group,* no. 23 (January 2017).

26   **Half the states also allow** Ryan Byrne, "What States Allow Citizens to Initiate Ballot Measures?," *Ballotpedia,* February 5, 2024.

27   **Mississippi Republicans decided to restore** Michael Goldberg, "Mississippi Could Renew Initiatives but Ban Them on Abortion," Associated Press, February 28, 2023.

27   **voters had overwhelmingly rejected** Frank James, "Mississippi Voters Reject Personhood Amendment by Wide Margin," NPR, November 8, 2011.

27   **Republicans there passed a six-week abortion ban** Laura A. Bischoff, "Ohio Bans Abortions After Six Weeks. Here's What You Need to Know," *Columbus Dispatch,* June 27, 2022.

27   **pro-choice groups started collecting** Anna Staver and Jessie Balmert, "Abortion in Ohio: What Does Proposed Constitutional Amendment Say?," *Cincinnati Enquirer,* February 23, 2023.

27   **tried to raise the standard for ballot measures** Julie Carr Smyth and Samantha Hendrickson, "Ohio Constitution Question Aimed at Thwarting Abortion Rights Push Heads to August Ballot," Associated Press, May 10, 2023.

28   **Republicans were so intent** Karen Kasler, "Total Tab for Ohio's August Special Election to Decide 60% Voter Approval Amendment Goes Up," Statehouse News Bureau, October 31, 2023.

28   **drafted an incendiary and false summary** Marilou Johanek, "LaRose Pushes Unfair, Inaccurate Language for Voters on November Ohio Reproductive Rights Amendment," Ohio Capital Journal, August 29, 2023.

28   **LaRose later admitted** Andrew J. Tobias, "Secretary of State Frank LaRose Says Abortion Opponents Helped Craft Ballot Language to Aid Defeat of Issue 1," Cleveland.com, November 29, 2023.

29   **abortion "up until birth"** This is a common phrase used by the anti-abortion movement to inaccurately characterize pro-abortion policies. Julie Rovner, "Abortion 'Until the Day of Birth' Is Almost Never a Thing," *KFF Health News,* November 15, 2023.

30   **Attorney General Ashley Moody petitioned** CBS Miami Team,

"Florida Attorney General Ashley Moody to Fight Abortion Amendment," CBS News, October 9, 2023.

30   **the majority of Republicans oppose** Matt Dixon, "Florida's Legislature Passes a 6-Week Abortion Ban," NBC News, April 13, 2023.

30   **In Missouri, Republicans tried to stop** Aaron Blake, "With Abortion Rights Looming, Missouri GOP Advances Slanted Ballot Rules," *Washington Post,* February 24, 2024.

30   **Bailey claimed that restoring** Jason Hancock, "Ashcroft Says Initiatives Seek to 'Nullify Missouri Laws Protecting the Right to Life,'" *Missouri Independent,* October 20, 2023.

31   **Bailey had to be forced by the state supreme court** Kaycen Bayless, "Missouri Supreme Court Rules Against Bailey in Abortion Petition Case," *Kansas City Star,* July 20, 2023.

31   **the state would need to hire** Hancock, "Ashcroft Says Initiatives."

31   **"how it's possible that you can have a state"** Alexis McGill Johnson on *The ReidOut,* MSNBC, August 23, 2022.

32   **readers had been contacting her** Stephanie Grace, "In Some States, People Get to Vote on Things Like Abortion Rights. Not in Louisiana," *New Orleans Advocate,* September 2, 2023.

32   **Louisiana voters were so interested** Brooke Thorington, "Candidates for Governor Weigh In on Abortion and If Voters Should Have Final Say on the Issue," Louisiana Radio Network, September 10, 2023.

32   **"stripped away our ballot initiative process"** Emily Wagster Pettus, "Mississippi Should Revive Process to Put Issues on Ballot, Secretary of State Watson Says," Associated Press, September 13, 2023.

32   **Watson changed his ballot measure stance** Emily Wagster Pettus, "Mississippi Should Revive Process to Put Issues on Ballot, Secretary of State Watson Says," Associated Press, September 13, 2023.

32   **readers were increasingly questioning** Laura Belin, "Why Iowans Can't Force a Statewide Vote on Abortion Rights," *Bleeding Heartland,* November 11, 2023.

32   **"Come on, North Carolina Republicans"** Editorial Board, "NC Republicans Won't Let Us Vote on Abortion. They Know They'd Lose," *Charlotte Observer,* November 12, 2023.

33   **"Thank goodness that most of the states"** Rick Santorum quoted in "OH Passes Measure to Legalize Marijuana," Newsmax, November 7, 2023.

Chapter 3: "Pro-Life" Language Is a Sham

34   **Senator Mitch McConnell (R-KY)** et al., "Republicans are Trying to Find a New Term for 'Pro-Life' to Stave off More Electoral Losses," NBC News, September 7, 2023.

34   **"being against all abortions"** Kevin Cramer quoted ibid.

35   **watching cancer patients** Shefali Luthra, "State Abortion Bans are Preventing Cancer Patients from Getting Chemotherapy," *19th,* October 7, 2022.

35   *abortion* **refers only to** For an example of this language in legislation, see Oklahoma House of Representatives, H.B. 3216, Life is a Human Right Act (2024).

36   **"I believe it would probably impact her life"** Catherine Glenn Foster quoted in Jennifer Bendery, "An Abortion Is Not an Abortion if a 10-Year-Old Gets One, Says Anti-Abortion Leader," *HuffPost,* July 14, 2022.

36   **"If a ten-year-old became pregnant"** Ibid.

36   **"That's not an abortion"** Erin Hawley quoted in U.S. House Oversight and Reform Committee, *Abortion Access and the Law: Hearing on Abortion Rights and Access,* 118th Cong., July 13, 2022.

36   **"Abortion is an elective choice"** Beth Whitehead, "10 Ways the Pro-Abortion Left Proves It Isn't Pro-Choice or Pro-Women," *Federalist,* July 19, 2022.

36   **"difference between necessary women's health care"** "Important to note: Abortion supporters are the ones conflating abortion with miscarriage care and care for ectopic pregnancy. Pro-lifers know the difference between necessary women's health care and intentionally killing a baby. It's abortion supporters who won't distinguish." Alexandra DeSanctis Marr (@xan_desanctis), X post, July 16, 2022.

37   **denied miscarriage care or being left** Amanda Seitz, "Emergency Rooms Refused to Treat Pregnant Women, Leaving One to Miscarry in a Lobby Restroom," Associated Press, April 19, 2024.

37   **Lawmakers in states like South Dakota and Idaho said they were going to "clarify"** Kimberlee Kruesi, "Asked to Clear Up Abortion Bans, GOP Leaders Blame Doctors and Misinformation for the Confusion," Associated Press, March 11, 2024; and Kelcie Moseley-Morris, "Idaho Legislators Pass Contentious Bill That Adds Clarification Language to Abortion Ban," *Idaho Capital Sun,* March 29, 2023.

38   **"trying to make it look like something happened"** Ibid.

38   **"medically indicated separation procedure"** Iowa General Assembly, H.F. 510, Human Life Protection Act (2023).

38   **"When you're looking at a case"** Kristan Hawkins quoted in Carter Sherman, " 'They Hate God': US Anti-Abortion Activists Aim to Fight Back on 51st Roe Anniversary," *Guardian,* January 22, 2024.

39   **abortion is never necessary to save** Every few years this post from the anti-abortion group Live Action goes viral: Lila Rose, "Abortion Is NEVER Medically Necessary," Facebook, August 16, 2019.

39   **induction of vaginal birth and C-sections** Planned Parenthood v. State of Idaho, No. 49615, 49817, 49899, 2023 Idaho 92 (Idaho Sup. Ct. 2023).

40   **"be done by labor induction or c-section"** Mary E. Harned and Ingrid Skop, "Pro-Life Laws Protect Mom and Baby: Pregnant Women's Lives Are Protected in All States," Charlotte Lozier Institute, September 11, 2023.

40   **they call "medically standard"** Ingrid Skop, "Response to Media Allegations that Abortion Restrictions Cause Maternal Mortality and Female Suicides," Charlotte Lozier Institute, March 21, 2023.

40   **"a more appropriate method of separation"** "Abortion Policy Allows Physicians to Intervene to Protect a Mother's Life," Charlotte Lozier Institute, May 16, 2023.

40   **Louisiana woman's water broke** Emily Woodruff, " 'It's a Minefield': Louisiana's Abortion Laws Leave Doctors Fearful of Violations," *New Orleans Advocate,* July 22, 2022.

40   **"was screaming—not from pain"** Ibid.

40   **doctors were increasingly giving patients** "Criminalized Care: How Louisiana's Abortion Bans Endanger Patients and Clinicians," Lift Louisiana, Physicians for Human Rights, Reproductive Health Impact, Center for Reproductive Rights, March 23–24, 2024.

40   **"Our attorney general, Jeff Landry, sent us all a letter"** Ibid.

41   **Doctors who perform abortions can face** Ibid.

41   **"preserve the appearance of not doing an abortion"** Ibid.

41   **"This person has had a c-section"** Ibid.

41   **what happened with "partial-birth abortion"** "State Bans on So-called 'Partial Birth' Abortion," State Health Facts, *KFF Health News,* May 1, 2022.

41   **Anti-abortion groups coined** Julie Rovner, " 'Partial-Birth Abortion': Separating Fact from Spin," NPR, February 23, 2006.

42   **"dangerous and extreme late-term abortions"** Jeanne Mancini, "Three More States Move to Put Reasonable Limits on Abortion," *Hill,* May 31, 2023.

42   **a paper in support** Ingrid Skop, "Why We Need Federal Limits on Late Abortion to Protect Both Mother and Child," Charlotte Lozier Institute, October 2, 2023.

43   **"no standard medical definition" for "late abortion"** Ibid.

44   *Nonviable* **has become** For a list of terms anti-abortion groups are bringing to medical professionals and legislators, see "Glossary of Medical Terms for Life-Affirming Medical Professionals," American Association of Pro-Life Obstetricians and Gynecologists, June 2023.

44   **Conservatives have even started** Michael New, Mary Szoch, and Jennifer Bauwens, "Biden's Tragic Misjudgment: Disabled Lives Matter," *Hill,* March 12, 2024.

44   **"prenatal counseling" and "perinatal hospice"** Jessica Valenti, "The GOP's Next Target? Prenatal Tests," *Abortion, Every Day,* February 13, 2024.

44   **"The only way we're going to do it** Nikki Haley quoted in Christian Hall, "Nikki Haley Sees Possibility of a Federal Ban on Late-Term Abortions," *Bloomberg,* January 8, 2024.

46   **"We will oppose any presidential candidate"** Marjorie Dannenfelser quoted in Michael C. Bender, "Anti-Abortion Group Urges Trump to Endorse a National Ban," *The New York Times,* April 20, 2023.

46   **"When Ambassador Haley talks about national consensus"** Marjorie Dannenfelser quoted in "SBA Response to Nikki Haley Interview," Susan B. Anthony Pro-Life America, May 14, 2023.

46   **"introduce legislation soon"** Lindsey Graham quoted in Live 5

Web Staff, "Sen. Graham Discusses Abortion, Hunter Biden During Stop in Lowcountry," WCSC-TV, June 23, 2023.

46   **"building consensus" on abortion** Elise Stefanik quoted in Gabrielle M. Etzel, "House GOP Conference Chairwoman Calls for 15-Week Federal Abortion Ban Post-Dobbs," *Washington Examiner,* June 20, 2023.

47   **"I want to see that consensus"** Eric Bradner and Gregory Krieg, "Takeaways from CNN's Town Hall with Chris Christie," CNN, June 13, 2023.

47   **a message of "consensus" and "reasonable limitations"** Ronna McDaniel on *Meet the Press,* NBC News, November 12, 2023.

47   **a fifteen-week ban that he called** Gary Grumbach, "Virginia Gov. Youngkin Eyes a 15-Week Abortion Ban as a 'Consensus' Voters Would Back," NBC News, August 27, 2023.

47   **"*Banning* is not the word"** Marjorie Dannenfelser quoted in "The New Terms of Abortion Politics," *The New York Times,* June 1, 2023.

47   **"the dictionary definition of 'ban'"** Marjorie Dannenfelser, "How the Media Mislead About Americans' Consensus on Abortion," *Hill,* July 11, 2023.

47   **"To be clear, you're using that word, I'm not"** Bernie Moreno quoted in "Ohio U.S. Senate Republican Primary Candidates Debate Abortion," WJW, January 22, 2024.

47   **"I don't use the word *ban*"** Frank LaRose quoted ibid.

48   **"This is a pro-life plan, not an abortion ban"** Joyce Krawiec quoted in Ashley Anderson, Joseph Holloway, Michael Hyland, Joe Jurney, and Lillian Donahue, "NC Senate Approves Bill That Bans Abortions After 12 Weeks," WNCN, May 5, 2023.

48   **"We think the use of the word"** Andy Harris quoted in "NEW: At Friday's March for Life breakfast, @RepAndyHarrisMD told my colleague 'Rose' how Republicans could pass a federal abortion ban if they win majorities in Congress this year. One key: Don't ever say the word 'ban,'" Lauren Windsor (@lawindsor), X post, January 21, 2024.

48   **"the big ban word"** James Bopp quoted in Amy Littlefield, "The Anti-Abortion Movement Gets a Dose of Post-Roe Reality," *Nation,* June 28, 2023.

48   **"We want to talk about 'protections'"** Karen Cross quoted ibid.

49 **"I wouldn't use the word *ban*"** E.V. Osment quoted in Caroline Vakil and Julia Manchester, "GOP Candidates Navigate Abortion Minefield," *Hill,* June 23, 2023.

49 **"restrictions on the procedure at 15 weeks"** Ibid.

49 **covered a proposed fifteen-week ban** Gregory S. Schneider and Michael Scherer, "Youngkin Bets 15-Week Abortion Limit Is Winner in Virginia and Beyond," *Washington Post,* October 25, 2023.

49 **proposal for a national ban** Tal Axelrod, "'This Is the Beginning, Not the End': Republicans Brace for Continued Abortion Rights Fallout," ABC News, March 28, 2024.

49 **"encouraging Republicans to clearly state"** Michael Scherer, "Divisions over Abortion Roil 2024 GOP Presidential Field," *Washington Post,* October 8, 2023; and "How Kari Lake's Tactical Retreat on Abortion Could Point the Way for the G.O.P.," *The New York Times,* October 14, 2023.

Chapter 4: They're Banning Birth Control

53 **Ninety-nine percent of American women** "Contraceptive Use in the United States by Demographics," Guttmacher Institute, May 2021.

53 **"transforms the endometrium"** Brian Clowes and Marisa Cantu, "Birth Control: Is the Pill an Abortifacient?," Human Life International, October 24, 2023.

53 **the Centers for Disease Control and Prevention** January W. Payne, "Forever Pregnant," *Washington Post,* May 15, 2006.

54 **laws that allow insurers to deny coverage** Mabel Felix, Laurie Sobel, and Alina Salganicoff, "The Right to Contraception: State and Federal Actions, Misinformation, and the Courts," *KFF Health News,* October 26, 2023.

54 **claiming that the IUDs, the morning-after pill, and sometimes even the Pill** In a prominent example, Samuel Alito, in a speech to the Federalist Society, conflated contraception and abortion. Justice Samuel Alito, Keynote Address to the 2020 National Lawyer Convention, November 12, 2020.

55 **"She can't cite a piece of legislation"** Marty Schladen, "LaRose Says 'No Reasonable Person' Is Talking About Banning

Contraceptives. But His Allies Are," *Ohio Capital Journal,*
August 7, 2023.

55   **If your pharmacist has the right** Arizona, Arkansas, Georgia,
Idaho, Mississippi, and South Dakota allow pharmacists to refuse
to fill prescriptions for contraceptives, including emergency
contraception, and at least twenty-six states have reported
instances of pharmacy refusals. "Refusals to Provide Health Care
Threaten the Health and Lives of Patients Nationwide," National
Women's Law Center, December 2020.

55   **live in an area with just one or two pharmacies** Millions of
patients across the country live in pharmacy deserts without
access to the medications they need. A 2015 study found that one
in three U.S. city neighborhoods were pharmacy deserts, and
Black and Latino residents were disproportionately impacted by
them. Jenny S. Guadamuz et al., "Fewer Pharmacies in Black and
Hispanic/Latino Neighborhoods Compared with White or
Diverse Neighborhoods, 2007–15," *Health Affairs* 40, no. 2
(May 2021).

56   **ob-gyns have been fleeing** Maryn McKenna, "States with
Abortion Bans Are Losing a Generation of Ob-Gyns," *WIRED,*
June 20, 2023.

56   **state support for crisis pregnancy centers** Anna Claire Vollers,
"Abortion-Ban States Pour Millions into Pregnancy Centers with
Little Medical Care," *19th,* August 24, 2023.

56   **Florida raised it** Laura C. Morel and Clara-Sophia Daly, "Florida
Legislators Want to Vastly Expand State Funds for Anti-Abortion
Pregnancy Centers," *Reveal,* March 22, 2023.

56   **Texas went from giving the groups** Cynthia McFadden, Maite
Amorebieta, and Didi Martinez, "In Texas, State-Funded Crisis
Pregnancy Centers Gave Medical Misinformation to NBC News
Producers Seeking Counseling," NBC News, June 29, 2022.

56   **"supporting healthy families"** Kim Reynolds quoted in Caleb
McCullough, "Abortion Rights Activists Oppose Republican
Proposal to Fund Crisis Pregnancy Centers," *Gazette,*
February 15, 2023.

56   **"everything in its power"** Shelby Wilcher quoted in Anne
Flaherty and Katie Kindelan, "One Year Post-Roe, Crisis
Pregnancy Centers Expand Footprint in Mississippi," ABC News,
June 23, 2023.

56   **"eligible maternal wellness centers"** Louisiana State Legislature, S.B. 41, Establishes a Tax Credit for Certain Maternal Wellness Centers (2023).

56   **must be affiliated** Julie O'Donoghue, "Tax Credit Approved for Donors to Louisiana Anti-Abortion Centers," *Louisiana Illuminator,* July 2, 2023.

57   **The law in Texas is similar** Ed Pilkington, "'Death Star Law' to Abortion: The New Rightwing Laws Taking Effect in Texas," *Guardian,* September 1, 2023.

57   **crisis pregnancy centers spread misinformation** "Crisis Pregnancy Centers Lie: The Insidious Threat to Reproductive Freedom," NARAL Pro-Choice America, January 2015.

57   **A 2023 report on centers in Ohio** "Ohio Crisis Pregnancy Centers Revealed," Pro-Choice Ohio, August 2023.

57   **"next to aborting your baby"** "Crisis Pregnancy Centers Lie: The Insidious Threat to Reproductive Freedom," NARAL Pro-Choice America, January 2015.

57   **"young, unmarried female client"** Kiera Butler, "The Anti-Abortion Movement's Next Target: Birth Control," *Mother Jones,* May 5, 2022.

57   **"about the side effects and risks of hormonal birth control"** Ibid.

57   **they already outnumber real health clinics** Jack Dobkin, "In the Grand Scheme: Six Sinister Tactics Employed by Anti-Abortion Centers," *Equity Forward,* April 19, 2022.

58   **your local Planned Parenthood clinic shuttered** Iowa's clinic closures are one instance of many. See Katarina Sostaric, "Planned Parenthood Closing Three Iowa Clinics, Expanding Abortion Services at Others," Iowa Public Radio, June 23, 2023. Researchers found that in the first one hundred days after *Dobbs,* sixty-six clinics in fifteen states stopped providing abortion care. Marielle Kirstein et al., "100 Days Post-Roe: At Least 66 Clinics Across 15 US States Have Stopped Offering Abortion Care," Guttmacher Institute, October 6, 2022.

58   **discontinue its participation** William Petroski, "Iowa Legislature Gives Final OK to Bill Defunding Planned Parenthood; Heads to Branstad," *Des Moines Register,* April 20, 2017.

58   **a nearly 83 percent drop in Iowans** Michaela Ramm, "Few Are Using Iowa's Family Planning Program Started to Thwart Planned Parenthood," *Des Moines Register,* October 12, 2023.

59   **conservative organizations, activists, and lawmakers** For an
example of the use of anti-abortion rhetoric to push false
narratives about oral contraceptives, see Brian Clowes, "The
Birth Control Pill: Unintended Consequences," Human Life
International, May 11, 2017.

59   **disrupt the implantation of a fertilized egg** Alexandra
McPhee, "A Synopsis: Contraception v. Abortion," Concerned
Women for America Legislative Action Committee, June 14,
2023.

59   **"that leads to pregnancy"** "How Your Fetus Grows During
Pregnancy," American College of Obstetricians and
Gynecologists, January 2024.

59   **the retail chain Hobby Lobby argued** Hobby Lobby v. Burwell,
573 U.S. 682 (2014).

59   **lawsuits seeking to protect pharmacy workers** Ian Lopez,
"Reproductive Rights Clash with Religious Ones in Abortion
Wars," *Bloomberg Law,* January 30, 2023.

59–60   **Oregon Right to Life sued the state** Julia Shumway, "Oregon
Right to Life Sues State Over Birth Control, Abortion Insurance
Mandate," *Oregon Capital Chronicle,* September 6, 2023.

60   **In Colorado they tried** Megan Verlee, "Colorado Debates
Whether IUDs Are Contraception or Abortion," NPR, March 5,
2015.

60   **in Missouri they fought** Michael Ollove, "Some States Already
Are Targeting Birth Control," *Stateline,* May 19, 2022.

60   **opposed the effort** Ashton Pittman, "Fact Check: Senator Falsely
Claims Protecting Birth Control Allows 'Morning-After
Abortions,'" *Mississippi Free Press,* October 19, 2023.

60   **all language referring to IUDs** Indiana General Assembly, H.B.
1426, An Act to Amend the Indiana Code Concerning Human
Services (2024).

60–61   **"we are a strong pro-life state"** Cindy Ledbetter quoted in Mary
Claire Molloy, "What You Need to Know About Indiana's
Controversial Birth Control Bill," *Mirror Indy,* March 7, 2024.

61   **"pay for abortion-inducing drugs"** U.S. Senate Judiciary
Committee, *Confirmation Hearing on the Nomination of Hon.
Amy Coney Barrett to be an Associate Justice of the Supreme Court
of the United States,* 116th Cong. (2020) (statement of Senator
Ted Cruz).

61   **"The morning-after pill, as we know"** Mike Johnson quoted in
      Tessa Stuart, "House Speaker Mike Johnson's Long Crusade
      Against Birth Control," *Rolling Stone,* October 30, 2023.

61   **Every major anti-abortion group and activist** Joerg Dreweke,
      "Contraception Is Not Abortion: The Strategic Campaign of
      Antiabortion Groups to Persuade the Public Otherwise,"
      Guttmacher Policy Review 17, no. 4 (Fall 2014): 16.

61   **Some groups, like Students for Life** "Contraception," Students
      for Life of America, April 7, 2024.

63   **73 percent of Americans** Grace Sparks et al., "KFF Health
      Tracking Poll: Early 2023 Update on Public Awareness on
      Abortion and Emergency Contraception," *KFF Health News,*
      February 1, 2023.

63   **colleges both in pro- and anti-choice states** Itzel Luna, "As
      Abortion Bans Grow, Colleges Find Answer to Easy
      Contraceptive Access: Vending Machines," *USA Today,* July 22,
      2023.

63   **"providing dangerous abortion pills"** Breccan F. Thies, "Plan B
      Vending Machines Installed on Colleges Campuses Across the
      Country," *Washington Examiner,* June 6, 2023.

63   **"Abortion-by-Vending-Machine"** Kristan Hawkins, "Abortion-
      by-Vending-Machine Is Much Worse Than it Sounds," Fox News,
      July 12, 2023.

64   **The birth control pill is the most popular** "Contraceptive Use in
      the United States," Guttmacher Institute, May 2021.

64   **urged not to use hormonal birth control** Madeline Peltz and
      Jacina Hollins-Borges, "Career Women in Right-Wing Media Tell
      Young Girls to Give Up Their Dreams at Young Women's
      Leadership Summit," *Media Matters,* June 11, 2023.

65   **"outside of their natural roles"** Alex Clark quoted in ibid.

65   **"majorly impacting relationships"** Mikhaila Peterson quoted in
      Agustin Hays " 'Toxic Masculinity' Fear, Media Portrayal as
      'Fools' Contributing to Men Leaving Workforce," Fox News,
      February 5, 2023.

65   **the rise of "tradwives"** For more on "tradwife" history, see Moira
      Donegan, "Wife Sentences," *Bookforum,* April 16, 2024.

66   **influencers are also talking about the dangers** Sarah Sloat,
      "Birth Control TikTok is a Symptom of Medicine's Bigger
      Problem," *WIRED,* August 15, 2022.

66 **researchers at the University of Delaware** Emily J. Pfender and
M. Marie Devlin, "What Do Social Media Influencers Say About
Birth Control? A Content Analysis of YouTube Vlogs About Birth
Control," *Health Communication* 30, no. 14 (January 15, 2023):
3336-3345.

67 **most viral "tradwife" videos of 2022** "We lowkey got scammed"
Brittany Martinez (@BritMartinez), X post, September 1, 2022.

67 **launched a billionaire-backed wellness company** Emily
Shugerman, "Peter Thiel, Right-Wing Billionaire, Sinks More
Cash Into Women's Health," *Daily Beast,* June 16, 2023.

67 **dates of their menstrual cycles** Anna Merlan, "Peter Thiel's
Investment Firm is Backing a Menstrual Cycle-Focused 'Femtech'
Company," *Vice,* September 6, 2022.

67 **"similar to PTSD"** Sabrina Kosmas, "The Pill Gives Women a
Cortisol Response Similar to PTSD—What Other Negative Side
Effects Aren't We Being Told About?," *Evie,* April 11, 2023.

67 **other kinds of birth control use were decreasing** Jamie Smyth and
Oliver Roeder, "Demand for Morning-After Pill Rises in US as
Abortion Restrictions Spread," *Financial Times,* February 16, 2023.

67 **a third of women who weren't on birth control** "Why So Many
Women are Getting Off Birth Control," *The Skimm,* October 11,
2023.

67 **"There is a lot of distrust"** Smyth and Roeder, "Demand for
Morning-After Pill Rises."

68 **80 percent of voters say protecting access** Annie Karni,
"Republican Opposition to Birth Control Bill Could Alienate
Voters, Poll Finds," *The New York Times,* February 26, 2024.

68 **64 percent of voters** Ibid.

68 **"Don't shy away from talking"** Ibid.

68 **glossy profile on Students for Life president** Elaine Godfrey,
"The New Pro-life Movement Has a Plan to End Abortion,"
Atlantic, April 19, 2023.

Chapter 5: "Exceptions" Don't Exist

70 **Mississippi has an abortion ban exception** The exception
language in Mississippi's ban reads: "For the purposes of this
section, rape shall be an exception to the prohibition for an

abortion only if a formal charge of rape has been filed with an appropriate law enforcement official." Abortion Prohibited; Exceptions, Miss. Code R. § 41-41-45 (2015).

70   **But in 2022, when investigative reporters** Isabelle Taft, "Can Rape Victims Access Abortion in Mississippi? Doctors, Advocates Say No," *Mississippi Today,* September 15, 2022.

70   **a woman was denied an abortion** Ashley White, "Her Unborn Baby Was Developing Without a Skull. She Had to Leave Louisiana to Get an Abortion.," *Acadiana Advocate,* June 13, 2023.

70   **Amanda Zurawski wasn't given an abortion** "Zurawski v. State of Texas," Texas Abortion Ban Emergency Exceptions Case, Center for Reproductive Rights, November 28, 2023.

70   **told by doctors she'd need to have a stroke** Courtney Carpenter, "League City Family in 'Nightmare' Situation Under Texas Abortion Law," KTRK-TV, September 22, 2022.

71   **"Exceptions function mainly as PR tools"** Elizabeth Nash, "Focusing on Exceptions Misses the True Harm of Abortion Bans," *Ms.,* December 12, 2022.

71   **keep more than two out of three victims** "The Criminal Justice System: Statistics," Rape, Abuse and Incest National Network, 2019.

71   **They include a requirement** See, for example, the language in Wyoming's ban: "Prior to the performance of any abortion under this paragraph the woman, or the woman's parent or guardian if the woman is a minor or subject to a guardianship, shall report the act of incest or sexual assault to a law enforcement agency and a copy of the report shall be provided to the physician." Wyoming House of Representatives, H.B. 0152, Life is a Human Right Act (2023).

71   **it often takes rape and incest victims** Denise-Marie Ordway, "Why Many Sexual Assault Survivors May Not Come Forward for Years," *Journalist Resource,* October 5, 2018.

71   **add in a time limitation** Indiana General Assembly, S.E.A. 1, An Act to Amend the Indiana Code Concerning Health (2022).

72   **they have to inform the patient** South Carolina General Assembly, S.B. 240, Human Life Protection Act (2023).

72   **any woman who the state** Tennessee Legislature, S.B. 857, An Act to Amend Tennessee Code (2023).

72   **Women have been accused** Rachel de Leon, "'If the Police Don't Believe You, They Might Prosecute You': How Officers Turn Victims of Sexual Assault into Suspects," *Reveal,* September 25, 2023.

73   **Iowa's state medical board guidelines** Iowa Board of Medicine, 653-13.17, Proposed Notice of Intended Action to H.F. 732 (2024).

73   **Tennessee Republicans voted to force children** Chris Salvemini, "Bill That Would Have Allowed Children Under 13 Years Old to Get Abortion Care in TN Fails in House Subcommittee," WBIR, February 20, 2024.

73   **"sexual assault actually helps prevent"** Kristan Hawkins quoted in Jessica Valenti and Grace Haley, "Students for Life President Kristan Hawkins: 'Rape Prevents Pregnancy,'" *Abortion, Every Day,* June 19, 2023.

73   **65,000 rape-related pregnancies** "Rape-Related Pregnancies in the 14 States with Total Abortion Bans," *Jama Internal Medicine* 184, no. 3 (January 24, 2024): 330–332.

74   **"Sexual assault is incredibly common"** Samuel Dickman quoted in Selena Simmons-Duffin, "Raped, Pregnant and in an Abortion Ban State? Researchers Gauge How Often it Happens," NPR, January 24, 2024.

74   **One of the more brutal Republican policies** Some states write a list of fatal fetal conditions into their restrictions, see Louisiana State Legislature, S.B. 342, An Act to Enact R.S. 1:15.1, Relative to Abortion (2022). Other bans write in generalized fatal fetal exceptions if they are "universally lethal," see Utah State Legislature, S.B. 174, Abortion Prohibition Amendments (2020).

74   **stories like Kate Cox's** Eleanor Klibanoff, "Texas Woman Asks Judge to Let Her Terminate Pregnancy After Lethal Fetal Diagnosis," *Texas Tribune,* December 5, 2023.

74   **With the help of the Center for Reproductive Rights** "Texas Emergency Abortion Case: *Cox v. Texas,*" Center for Reproductive Rights, December 13, 2023.

74   **"countless women . . . give birth every day"** Ken Paxton quoted in Ryan Autullo "Texas Woman Granted Emergency Abortion Over State's Wishes," *Bloomberg Law,* December 7, 2023.

75   **"genuine miscarriage of justice"** Maya Guerra Gamble quoted
      in Susan Rinkunas, "Texas Judge Rules Woman with Non-Viable
      Pregnancy Can Have an Abortion," *Guardian,* December 7, 2023.

75   **threatening them with criminal charges** "Attorney General Ken
      Paxton Responds to Travis County TRO," Press Release,
      December 7, 2023.

75   **the senator took off in a sprint** Ellie Quinlan Houghtaling, "Ted
      Cruz Really, Really Does Not Want to Talk About That Texas
      Abortion Case," *The New Republic,* December 14, 2023.

75   **Nikki Haley said she believed the Texas law** Amy B Wang, "GOP
      Candidates Sidestep Questions about Texas Abortion Case,"
      Washington Post, December 13, 2023.

76   **fetal abnormalities to be "uniformly diagnosable"** The full text
      of the exception states that, "The diagnosis by a qualified
      physician of a physical or genetic condition that (i) is defined as a
      life-limiting disorder by current medical evidence and (ii) is
      uniformly diagnosable." North Carolina General Assembly, S.B.
      20, Care for Women, Children, and Families Act (2023).

76   **define a nonviable pregnancy** See Indiana General Assembly,
      S.E.A. 1, Senate Enrolled Act 1 (2022).

76   **states that deliberately include no language** Alabama State
      Legislature, H.B. 314, Human Life Protection Act (2022).

77   **Every year about 120,000 pregnancies** "Data & Statistics on
      Birth Defects," Centers for Disease Control and Prevention,
      June 28, 2023.

77   **not to be treated as "walking coffins"** Marlena Stell, a Texas
      woman forced to carry her dead fetus for weeks after being
      denied an abortion, said, "I felt like a walking coffin. You're just
      walking around knowing that you have something that you
      hoped was going to be a baby for you, and it's gone. And you're
      just walking around carrying it," quoted in Timothy Bella,
      "Woman Says She Carried Dead Fetus for 2 Weeks After Texas
      Abortion Ban," *Washington Post,* July 20, 2022.

77   **Take Indiana's abortion ban** Indiana General Assembly, S.E.A. 1,
      An Act to Amend the Indiana Code Concerning Health (2022).

77   **"If an abortion is performed"** "Perinatal Hospice," Indiana State
      Department of Health Perinatal Hospice and Palliative Care
      Information Center, Indiana State Department of Health,
      October 2022.

78   **"There is no footprint too small"** Ibid.

78   **If you had any remaining doubts** Katie Yoder, "Perinatal Hospice and Palliative Care Offers Alternative to Abortion, Experts Say," *Catholic Spirit,* January 2, 2024.

78   **"I love reminding them"** Ibid.

78   **"training and increasing the number"** Ibid.

79   **ban contains no exception** Protecting Pain-Capable Unborn Children from Late-Term Abortions Act, S. 4840, 117th Cong. (2022).

80   **the state's infant mortality rate** Isabelle Chapman, "Nearly Two Years After Texas' Six-Week Abortion Ban, More Infants are Dying," CNN, July 20, 2023.

80   **"preventing unborn children"** Michael J. New, "CNN Misleads on Texas's Infant-Mortality Rate," *National Review,* July 20, 2023.

81   **Tennessee woman with an ectopic pregnancy** Steve Cavendish, "Sarah Needed an Abortion. Her Doctors Needed Lawyers.," *Nashville Scene,* December 20, 2022.

81   **"It's a felony, what they did"** Ibid.

81   **accused Republicans of trying** Will Brewer quoted in Stephanie Kirchaessner, "How Close to Death Must a Woman be to Get an Abortion in Tennessee," *Guardian,* March 20, 2023.

82   **"objective" medical standard** Will Brewer quoted in Kavitha Surana, "Tennessee Lobbyists Oppose New Lifesaving Exceptions in Abortion Ban," *ProPublica,* February 24, 2023.

82   **"intended to be ambiguous and confusing"** Sarah Osmundson, "All-of-Nothing Abortion Politics Will Leave Women with Nothing," *The New York Times,* March 16, 2023.

82   **"We have denied abortion care"** Ibid.

82–83   **committee members send each other** Kavitha Surana, "Maternal Deaths Are Expected to Rise Under Abortion Bans, but the Increase May Be Hard to Measure," *ProPublica,* July 27, 2023.

83   **Republicans wrote language to "clarify"** Kelcie Moseley-Morris, "Idaho Legislators Pass Contentious Bill that Adds Clarification Language to Abortion Ban," *Idaho Capital Sun,* March 29, 2023.

83   **"The list was endless"** Julianne Young quoted in Ryan Suppe, "As Doctors Flee State, Idaho Bill Expands Exceptions for Abortion. Health Isn't One," *Idaho Statesman,* March 30, 2023.

84   **The polling is astronomical** Nearly 80 percent of Americans support rape and incest exceptions, even in conservative areas. "Abortion," Historical Trends, Gallup, n.d.

Chapter 6: The Punishment Is the Point

86   **Brittany Watts cried** Jericka Duncan et al., "Brittany Watts, Ohio Woman Charged with Felony After Miscarriage at Home, Describes Shock of Her Arrest," CBS News, January 26, 2024.

86   **claimed that they have no interest** When reporters do ask anti-abortion groups about abortion criminalization, they typically reply as this spokesperson for Susan B. Anthony Pro-Life America did, when questioned about post-*Roe* arrests: "Pro-life leaders across the country unequivocally reject any efforts to subject women to criminal punishment following an abortion." Quoted in Cary Aspinwall, "What the End of Roe Looks Like in Real Time," *Marshall Project,* December 9, 2023.

87   **Purvi Patel was sentenced to twenty years** Jessica Valenti, "It Isn't Justice for Purvi Patel to Serve 20 Years in Prison for an Abortion," *Guardian,* April 2, 2015.

87   **Melissa Ann Rowland was arrested** Alexandria Sage, "Mom Arrested After Utah Stillbirth," CBS News, March 12, 2004.

87   **Rennie Gibbs was just sixteen years old** Nina Martin, "A Stillborn Child, a Charge of Murder and the Disputed Case Law on 'Fetal Harm,' " *ProPublica,* March 18, 2014.

87   **A Louisiana woman was charged** Lynn M. Paltrow and Jeanne Flavin, "Pregnant, and No Civil Rights," *New York Times,* November 7, 2014.

87   **Christine Taylor was charged** Christophe Haubursin, "An Indiana Woman is Facing 20 Years in Prison for 'Feticide,' " *Vox,* April 3, 2015.

87   **Bei Bei Shuai lost her pregnancy** Julie Rovner, "Woman Who Tried to Commit Suicide While Pregnant Gets Bail," NPR, May 18, 2012.

87   **Alabama charged Marshae Jones** Sarah Mervosh, "Alabama Woman Who Was Shot While Pregnant Is Charged in Fetus's Death," *The New York Times,* June 27, 2019.

88   **abortion patients could be given** South Carolina General Assembly, H.B. 3549, A Bill to Amend the South Carolina Code of Laws by Enacting the South Carolina Prenatal Equal Protection Act of 2023 (2023).

88   **"no one that I know wants"** Amanda Shaw, "Abortion Death Penalty Bill is 'Lunacy,' SC Governor Says," WHNS, March 23, 2023.

88   **woman in his state had been arrested** Lyn Riddle and Joseph Bustos, "SC Woman Charged After Allegedly Consuming Abortion Pills to End Pregnancy," *State,* March 2, 2023.

88   **The bill in Alabama** Alabama House of Representatives, H.B. 454, Equal Protection Act (2023).

88   **the bill also deliberately defined personhood** Alabama's abortion ban reads: "This bill would expand the definition of person for the purposes of the criminal code to include an unborn child from the moment of fertilization." Alabama House of Representatives, H.B. 454, Equal Protection Act (2023).

88   **"the actor intentionally or recklessly"** Ibid.

89   **"we do not support any measure"** Carol Tobias to State Lawmakers, "An Open Letter to State Lawmakers from America's Leading Pro-Life Organizations," May 12, 2022.

89   **"equal protection" movement has rapidly gained traction** Lila Rose et al., "The Pro-Life Movement Should Follow Its North Star: Equal Protection," *National Review,* June 15, 2023.

90   **"significant risk"** Jericka Duncan et al., "Brittany Watts, Ohio Woman Charged with Felony After Miscarriage at Home, Describes Shock of Her Arrest," CBS News, January 26, 2024.

91   **"My recommendation instead of waiting"** An anonymous doctor quoted in Maham Javaid and Kim Bellware, "She Miscarried in Her Bathroom. Now She's Charged with Abuse of a Corpse," *Washington Post,* December 15, 2023.

91   **"out of respect for patient privacy"** Ibid.

92   **45 percent of the time** Laura Huss and Goleen Samari, "Self-Care Criminalized, The Criminalization of Self-Managed Abortion from 2000 to 2020," If/When/How: Lawyering for Reproductive Justice, 2023.

92   **Black women in particular** "Black Mamas Matter: Advancing the Human Right to Safe and Respectful Maternal Health Care," Black Mamas Matter Alliance, Center for Reproductive Rights, 2018.

92   **people of color are more likely** "Inmate Race," Federal Bureau of Prisons, April 13, 2024.

92   **"left in that toilet"** Lewis Guarnieri quoted in Maria Sole Campinoti, Holly Yan and Zenebou Sylla, "A Woman Who Had a Miscarriage Is Now Charged with Abusing a Corpse as Stricter Abortion Laws Play Out Nationwide," CNN, December 19, 2023.

93   **"subjective personal factors"** Huss and Samari, "Self-Care Criminalized."

93   **"found a baby stuck in a toilet"** Kim Lampkins, "Rally Planned in Support of Brittany Watts, Woman Charged After Miscarriage," WKBN, January 9, 2024.

93   **reported that police were called** Chris McBride, "Woman's Abuse of Corpse Case Heads to Grand Jury," *Tribune Chronicle*, November 4, 2023.

93   **"I just want to know what"** Grace Howard quoted in Julie Carr Smyth, "A Black Woman Was Criminally Charged After a Miscarriage. It Shows the Perils of Pregnancy Post-Roe," Associated Press, December 16, 2023.

94   **they pursued charges** Purvaja S. Kavattur et al., "The Rise of Pregnancy Criminalization: A Pregnancy Justice Report," Pregnancy Justice, September 2023.

94   **"This is a very disturbing case"** Huss and Samari, "Self-Care Criminalized."

95   **"concealing or abandoning a dead body"** Margery A. Beck, "Nebraska Mother Sentenced to 2 Years in Prison for Giving Abortion Pills to Pregnant Daughter," Associated Press, September 22, 2023.

95   **"this bill would provide"** Alabama State Legislature, H.B. 314, Human Life Protection Act (2022).

95   **"is not a criminal offense"** Steve Marshall quoted in "Alabama Attorney General Explains Alabama's Abortion Law," WAKA Action 8 News, July 1, 2022.

95   **Alabama attorney general's office told him** Craig Monger, " 'Self-Managed' Abortions Could Still Bring Criminal Prosecution Under Child Chemical Endangerment Laws," *1819 News*, January 7, 2023.

95   **"does not provide an across-the-board exemption"** A spokesperson for Steve Marshall quoted ibid.

95   **"an environment in which"** Chemical Endangerment of
Exposing a Child to an Environment in Which Controlled
Substances Are Produced or Distributed, Ala. Code § 26-15-3.2
(2024).

96   **Ashley Banks, who slept on a jail floor** Amy Yurkanin,
"Pregnant Women Held for Months in One Alabama Jail to
Protect Fetuses from Drugs," AL.com, September 7, 2022.

96   **Another woman, Stacey Freeman** Amy Yurkanin,
"Alabama Woman Jailed for Using Drugs During Pregnancy
Wasn't Pregnant, Lawsuit Says," AL.com, November 20,
2022.

97   **Abortion funds raising money** Andrea González-Ramírez,
"Abortion Funds Confront Post-Roe Chaos," *The Cut,* July 8,
2022.

97   **doctors taking legal risks** Abigail Brooks and Dasha Burns,
"How a Network of Abortion Pill Providers Works Together in
the Wake of New Threats," NBC News, April 7, 2024.

97   **volunteer pilots flying women** Kim Brooks, "The Pilots
Flying Abortion Patients Across State Lines: Elevated Access Is
Circumventing Restrictive Legislation and All-Out Bans from
High in the Air," *The Cut,* November 10, 2022.

97   **like proposing legislation** For an example of "drug-trafficking"
attacks against abortion medication, see Oklahoma State
Legislature, H.B. 3013, An Act Relating to Abortion-Inducing
Drugs (2023).

98   **The first so-called abortion trafficking law** Idaho Legislature,
H.B. 242, An Act Relating to Abortion (2023).

98   **make it a felony** Tennessee Legislature, H.B. 1895, An Act to
Amend Tennessee Code Relative to Abortion (2023).

98   **"recruits, harbors, or transports"** Idaho Legislature, H.B. 242,
An Act Relating to Abortion (2023).

98   **the Idaho law was blocked** Rebecca Boone, "Federal Judge Puts
Idaho's 'Abortion Trafficking' Law on Hold During Lawsuit,"
Associated Press, November 9, 2023.

98   **"A teenage girl in Moscow, Idaho"** Amicus Brief of the State of
Washington et al. in Support of the Plaintiff's Motion for a
Temporary Restraining Order Or, in The Alternative, a
Preliminary Injunction, Matsumoto v. Labrador (2023) (No.
23-cv-00323-DKG).

99　**"If they did it knowingly"** Nathan Dahm quoted in Mckenzie Richmond, "'You're an Accessory in the Violation of a Crime'; Dahm Defends Controversial Abortion Bill," KTUL, February 5, 2024.

99　**Multiple Texas counties have passed** Caroline Kitchener, "Texas Highways Are The Next Anti-Abortion Target. One Town Is Resisting," *Washington Post,* September 1, 2023.

99　**"One cannot seriously doubt that"** Steve Marshall quoted in Alander Rocha, "Alabama Attorney General Doubles Down on Threats to Prosecute Out-of-State Abortion Care," *Alabama Reflector,* August 31, 2023.

100　**legislation to make pro-choice** Texas Legislature, H.B. 2690, An Act Relating to Abortion, Including Civil Liability for Distribution of Abortion-Inducing Drugs and Duties of Internet Service Providers (2023).

100　**allow them to remove** For an example of legislation that makes it easier for states to remove district attorneys who refuse to prosecute abortion-related cases, see Texas Legislature, S.B. 20, Relating to the Enforcement of Criminal Offenses by District Attorneys, Criminal District Attorneys, and County Attorneys (2023).

100　**Governor Ron DeSantis suspended** Jose Pagliary, "Gov. Ron DeSantis' Controversial Power Grab Gets Its Day in Court," *Daily Beast,* December 1, 2022.

100　**fifteen Republican state attorneys general** Brief of Amici Curiae States of Ohio et al. Supporting Appellee, Warren v. DeSantis (2023) (No. 23-10459).

101　**"bounty hunter" laws** Texas Legislature, S.B. 8, The Texas Heartbeat Act (2021). Texas's abortion ban allows private citizens to sue anyone they suspect of being involved in an abortion (doctors, nurses, even people who drove to the out-of-state clinic) for at least $10,000. The architect of the state's "bounty hunter" mandate, Jonathan Mitchell, has helped develop similar statutes across the country and is one of the chief lawyers behind the anti-abortion movement.

103　**about how "she can't wait"** Gloria Oladipo, "Nebraska Teen and Her Mother Charged for Aborting and Burying Fetus," *The Guardian,* August 9, 2022.

103   **that lie was repeated again and again** "Nebraska Mom Pleads Guilty to Giving Daughter Pills for an Abortion and Helping Bury the Fetus," Associated Press, July 7, 2023.

Chapter 7: Teens Are the Canaries in the Coal Mine

105   **voted to force child rape victims** Chris Salvemini, "Bill That Would Have Allowed Children Under 13 Years Old to Get Abortion Care in TN Fails in House Subcommittee," WBIR, February 20, 2024.

105   **"Please think of the children"** Gloria Johnson quoted in "WATCH: 'We should not be forcing children to carry a pregnancy,' Tennessee Holler @TheTNHoller," X post, February 20, 2024.

105   **the so-called anti-trafficking law** Idaho Legislature, H.B. 242, An Act Relating to Abortion (2023).

105   **Tennessee's version of this law** Tennessee General Assembly, H.B. 1895, An Act to Amend Tennessee Code Relative to Abortion (2024).

106   **Bailey brought a lawsuit** Matt Griffith, "Missouri AG Lawsuit Accuses Planned Parenthood of Child Trafficking," KMZU, February 29, 2024.

106   **"Starting with a law"** Mary Ziegler, "Abortion Restrictions Targeted at Minors Never End There," *Atlantic,* April 28, 2023. For more on this concept, see Mary Ziegler, *Roe: The History of a National Obsession* (New Haven, CT: Yale University Press, 2023).

107   **"We are running an important"** "The Governor of CA continues to deceive and gaslight. Tennessee is standing on strong conservative principles. We are running an important parental rights bill. The bill prohibits an adult who is not the parent/guardian of a minor from facilitating an abortion for that minor without the parent's consent. The bill doesn't prohibit providing healthcare to any pregnant woman, period. There are zero criminal penalties against any pregnant minor young lady/woman." Jason Zachary quoted in Tori Gessner, "Ad Targeting TN 'Abortion Trafficking' Bill Depicts Inaccuracies, Sponsor Says," WKRN, February 26, 2024.

108   **Republicans were stoking** Kate Sosin, "'Don't Say Gay' Bills Aren't New. They've Just Been Revived," *19th,* April 20, 2022.

108   **three separate anti-abortion groups** Susan Tebben, "Strategies Emerge as Abortion Rights Fight Ramps Up," *Ohio Capital Journal,* March 6, 2023.

108   **calling the measure a "Trojan horse"** Sarah Parshall Perry and Thomas Jipping, "Ohio Ballot Initiative Is a Trojan Horse—and a 'Right' to Abortion Is Just the Beginning," Heritage Foundation, August 28, 2023.

108   **"non-marital teen birth rate"** Robert Rector, "Marriage, Abortion, and Welfare," Heritage Foundation, May 22, 2023.

109   **Republicans' refusal to vote** Nikki McCann Ramirez, "West Virginia Republicans Block Child Marriage Ban," *Rolling Stone,* March 9, 2023.

109   **"assault on parental rights"** Theresa Gavarone quoted in Susan Tebben, "Abortion Rights Groups Ask Ohio Supreme Court to Order Full Amendment Text for November Ballots," *Ohio Capital Journal,* September 7, 2023.

109   **"Until recently, one thing"** Frank LaRose, "Frank LaRose: Protect Parents by Voting No on Issue 1," *Richland Source,* October 18, 2023.

109   **Democrats "compromised" on minors' reproductive rights** Andrew Selsky, "Oregon Senate Republicans End 6-Week Walkout That Blocked Bills on Abortion, Gun Bills," Associated Press, June 15, 2023. See Oregon Legislative Assembly, H.B. 2002, An Act Relating to Health (2023).

110   **"There's a morning-after pill"** Paul Blest, "Child Rape Victims Have 'Options' and Other Wild Things the GOP Says About Abortion," *Vice News,* September 7, 2022.

110   **judicial bypasses allow teens** For what this can look like, see Lizzie Presser, "She Wanted an Abortion. A Judge Said She Wasn't Mature Enough to Decide," *ProPublica,* November 29, 2022.

110   **judges were approving fewer abortions** Caroline Catherman, "Florida Judges Arbitrarily Denied Minors' Requests for Abortions Last Year, Report Finds," *Orlando Sentinel,* February 9, 2023.

111   **the Fifth Circuit Court of Appeals upheld** Chris Geidner, "Religious Supremacy, Not Supremacy Clause, Is Key to Fifth Circuit Contraception Ruling," *Law Dork,* March 14, 2024.

111   **"If she did receive contraceptives"** Kyle Duncan quoted in
Shefali Luthra, "For Teens in Texas, Getting Birth Control
Without Parental Consent Just Got Even Tougher," *19th,*
March 12, 2024.

112   **ban gender-affirming care for minors** Lindsey Dawson and
Jennifer Kates, "Policy Tracker: Youth Access to Gender
Affirming Care and State Policy Restrictions," *KFF Health News,*
April 17, 2024.

112   *the same law* **as the state's abortion ban** Nebraska State
Legislature, L.B. 574, An Act Relating to Public Health and
Welfare (2023).

113   **accused groups like Planned Parenthood** For an example
of a "grooming" accusation against Planned Parenthood,
see Michael J. New, "Planned Parenthood Is Grooming
Our Kids to Be Sexually Active," *Christian Post,* October 6,
2018.

113   **"faulty science standards"** Brooke W. Stanton, "Abortion's
Winning Streak Fueled by Faulty Science Standards," *Newsweek,*
August 24, 2023.

114   **"widespread scientific ignorance"** Ibid.

114   **74 percent of adults under thirty** "Nearly a Year After Roe's
Demise, Americans' Views of Abortion Access Increasingly
Vary by Where They Live," Pew Research Center, April 26,
2023.

114   **found that adults under thirty** "Harvard Youth Poll," Institute of
Politics, Harvard Kennedy School, December 5, 2023.

115   **a video produced by Live Action** "Meet Baby Olivia," Live
Action, April 6, 2024. For more on the Live Action video and the
anti-abortion education plan, see Jessica Valenti, "Anti-Abortion
Propaganda in Schools," *Abortion, Every Day,* January 26,
2024.

115   **multimillion-dollar judgment levied against him** Sabrina
Tavernise, "Planned Parenthood Awarded $2 Million in Lawsuit
over Secret Videos," *New York Times,* November 15, 2019.

115   **designated as a hate group** "American College of Pediatricians,"
Southern Poverty Law Center, n.d.

116   **bring civil action against any public school district** Kentucky
General Assembly, H.B. 346, An Act Relating to Human Growth
and Development Instruction (2024).

116   **the more someone knows about pregnancy** Steven Greene et al., "Public Opinion on Abortion in Post-Roe America" Conference, Southern Political Science Association, January 2024.

116   **"reach[ing] young people during"** "Students for Life reaches young people during crucial developmental years, inviting them to belong to a growing movement that respects the value of human life and stands up for the voiceless. Students for Life gives them a movement to belong to." "2019-2020 Annual Report," Students for Life of America, 2021.

116   **"have lost their value"** "Protecting Value: Middle School Curriculum," Students for Life of America, 2020.

116   **"one million children"** Ibid.

116   **"If you are against abortion"** Ibid.

117   **offer free sports physicals** Nedra Rhone, "Beware of Crisis Pregnancy Centers In Post-Roe Era," *Atlanta Journal-Constitution,* January 13, 2023.

Chapter 8: They Don't Care About Women

118   **Jaci Statton was told to wait** Selena Simmons-Duffin, "In Oklahoma, a Woman Was Told to Wait Until She's 'Crashing' for Abortion Care," NPR, April 25, 2023.

118   **couldn't come back for an abortion** Courtney Carpenter, "League City Family in 'Nightmare' Situation Under Texas Abortion Law," ABC13 Eye Witness News, September 29, 2022.

118   **"I felt like a walking coffin"** Bella, "Woman Says She Carried Dead Fetus for 2 Weeks."

118   **even though her fetus had anencephaly** Chris Rosato, "Mother Claims She Was Denied an Abortion Despite Baby's Condition," WAFB, August 15, 2022.

118   **The same thing happened to Heather Mayberry** Mary Kekatos, "Woman Says She Was Forced to Travel for an Abortion Despite Her Fetus's Fatal Condition," ABC News, June 15, 2023.

118   **had to carry a dying baby to term** Aria Bendix, "Woman Suing Texas Over Abortion Ban Vomits on the Stand in Emotional Reaction During Dramatic Hearing," NBC News, July 19, 2023.

118   **denied treatment for an ectopic pregnancy** Caroline Kitchener, "An Ectopic Pregnancy Put Her Life at Risk. A Texas Hospital Refused to Treat Her," *Washington Post,* February 23, 2024.

119   **"in extreme danger of losing her life"** Ibid.

119   **emergency hysterectomy** Kavitha Surana, "Doctors Warned Her Pregnancy Could Kill Her. Then Tennessee Outlawed Abortion," *ProPublica,* March 14, 2023.

119   **Ashley Caswell was forced to sleep** Sam Levin, "An Alabama Woman Was Imprisoned for 'Endangering' Her Fetus. She Gave Birth in a Jail Shower," *Guardian,* October 13, 2023.

119   **a mother of five with cervical cancer** Jeannie Baumann, "Abortion Restrictions Weakening Cancer Care, Other Treatments," *Bloomberg Law,* August 14, 2023.

119   **"She always told me"** Ibid.

119   **In Texas, Amanda Zurawski** "The Plaintiffs and Their Stories: Zurawski v. State of Texas," Center for Reproductive Rights, November 14, 2023.

119   **Chelsea Stovall had to travel** Nadine El-Bawab et al., "Meet 18 Women Who Shared Heartbreaking Pregnancy Journeys in Post-Roe World," ABC News, December 16, 2023.

119   **"I should be able to say goodbye"** Chelsea Stovall quoted in "The Unseen Impact of Arkansas's Abortion Ban," THV11, September 21, 2022.

119   **sixth grader in Mississippi forced to give birth** Charlotte Alter, "She Wasn't Able to Get an Abortion. Now She's a Mom. Soon She'll Start 7th Grade," *Time,* August 14, 2023.

119   **Multiple little girls, impregnated** Anna Betts, "A Young Victim of Incest Was Denied an Abortion in Florida and Forced to Travel for Care, Planned Parenthood Said," *Buzzfeed News,* October 13, 2022.

119   **ten-year-old who was raped and impregnated** Shari Rudavsky and Rachel Fradette, "Patients Head to Indiana for Abortion Services as Other States Restrict Care," *Indianapolis Star,* July 1, 2022.

120   **advise their patients to buy** Nicole Karlis, "'It Doesn't Make Sense': What Happens When Life-Saving Abortion Isn't Protected, Despite Federal Law," *Salon,* January 10, 2024.

120   **desperate women emptying** Kimya Forouzan, Amy Friedrich-Karnik and Isaac Maddow-Zimet, "The High Toll of US Abortion Bans: Nearly One in Five Patients Now Traveling Out of State for Abortion Care," Guttmacher Institute, December 7, 2023.

120   **"if we can protect the lives of mothers"** Andrew Farmer quoted in Sam Stockard, "House Passes Abortion Decriminalization Bill Despite Complaints It Will Hurt Women," *Tennessee Lookout,* March 21, 2023.

121   **bill that would make it illegal** Editorial Board, "Missouri Bill to Outlaw Abortion in Ectopic Pregnancies is Effectively a Death Sentence," *St. Louis Post-Dispatch,* March 12, 2022.

121   **the legislation was being "misrepresented"** Melinda Henneberger, "No, Missouri Ban on Ending Dangerous Ectopic Pregnancies Was Not 'Misrepresented,'" *Kansas City Star,* March 16, 2022.

121   **fewer rights than a zygote** "What We See in the Shameful Trends on U.S. Maternal Health," *New York Times,* November 17, 2021.

121   **more likely to kill you than skydiving** Caroline Criado Perez, "Pregnancy Is Riskier Than Skydiving—Birth Control Should Be Harder to Market," CNN, September 20, 2018.

121   **Over decades, conservatives commissioned polls** Mary Ziegler, *Roe: The History of a National Obsession* (New Haven, CT: Yale University Press, 2023).

121   **Look at any Republican** The national abortion ban proposed by Senator Lindsey Graham contains the standard "life of the mother" exception language that excludes suicidal conditions: "In reasonable medical judgment, the abortion is necessary to save the life of a pregnant woman whose life is endangered by a physical disorder, physical illness, or physical injury, including a life-endangering physical condition caused by or arising from the pregnancy itself, but not including psychological or emotional conditions." Protecting Pain-Capable Unborn Children from Late-Term Abortions Act, S. 4840, 117th Cong. (2022).

122   **"significant increase" in the suicide rate** Jonathan Zandberg et al., "Association Between State-Level Access to Reproductive Care and Suicide Rates Among Women of Reproductive Age in the United States," *JAMA Psychiatry* 80, no. 2 (December 2022): 127–34.

122   **"This association is robust"** "Restricted Abortion Access Linked to Increased Suicide Risk in Young Women" (news release), University of Pennsylvania, December 28, 2022.

123   **rates of depression and sexual violence** "U.S. Teen Girls Experiencing Increased Sadness and Violence," Centers for Disease Control and Prevention, February 13, 2023.

123   **progress in women's health** Sara Srygley, "Losing More Ground: Revisiting Young Women's Well-Being Across Generations," *Population Bulletin* 77, no. 1 (2023).

123   **how a high school senior** Affidavit of Dr. Sharon Liner in Support of Plaintiff's Motion for Temporary Restraining Order Followed by Preliminary Injunction, Preterm-Cleveland v. Yost (2022) (No. A2203203).

123   **women sobbing and threatening** Marty Schladen, "Affidavits: More Pregnant Minors Who Were Raped Denied Ohio Abortions," *Ohio Capital Journal,* September 22, 2022.

124   **responded by claiming that the research** Ingrid Skop, "Response to Media Allegations that Abortion Restrictions Cause Maternal Mortality and Female Suicides," Charlotte Lozier Institute, March 21, 2023.

124   **"reproductive health care is essential"** Brief of Amici Curiae American College of Obstetricians and Gynecologists et al. in Support of Respondents, *Dobbs v. Jackson Women's Health Organization* (2022) (No. 19–1392).

125   **launch a legal attack** *Alliance for Hippocratic Medicine v. FDA,* No. 23-10362 (5th Cir. 2023).

125   **lists twenty-eight medical issues** Woman's Right to Know Act, Tex. Code §171.006 (2021).

126   **"The Idaho legislature cobbled together"** Planned Parenthood of the *Great Northwest v. Wasden,* No. 18-35926 (D. Idaho 2015).

126   **"That's exactly the point"** Ushma Upadhyay quoted in Jessica Valenti, "Texas Is Fabricating Abortion Data," *Abortion, Every Day,* May 4, 2023.

127   **North Carolina Republicans proposed a bill** North Carolina General Assembly, S.B. Care for Women, Children, and Families Act (2023).

127   **cultivated groups pretending** Karissa Haugeberg, *Women Against Abortion: Inside the Largest Moral Reform Movement of the Twentieth Century* (Urbana: University of Illinois Press, 2017).

127   **abortion and breast cancer** "Reproductive History and Cancer Risk," National Cancer Institute, November 9, 2016.

127   **"post-abortion syndrome"** The Turnaway Study documents the false narrative of abortion regret and the lack of evidence for "post-abortion trauma syndrome." See Corinne H. Rocca et al.,

"Decision Rightness and Emotional Responses to Abortion in the United States: A Longitudinal Study," *PLoS One* 10, no. 7 (July 8, 2015).

128 **along with calling maternal mortality data** The attacks on maternal mortality research often use statements from the American Association of Pro-Life Obstetricians and Gynecologists. See "AAPLOG Policy Statement: The Women's Health Protection Act of 2021," American Association of Pro-Life Obstetricians and Gynecologists, June 2021.

128 **disband the state's maternal mortality review committees** Rachel Cohen, "Idaho Dissolves Maternal Mortality Review Committee, as Deaths Remain High," Boise Public Radio, July 7, 2023.

128 **the state isn't collecting any information** Maggie Q. Thompson, "Texas Maternal Mortality Task Force Hasn't Counted Abortion Death Cases for 10 Years," *Austin Chronicle,* March 22, 2024.

128 **Anti-abortion groups are also manipulating** For more on anti-abortion attacks on access to accurate information about pregnancy, see Jessica Valenti, "Calculated Cruelty," *Abortion, Every Day,* October 19, 2023; and Jessica Valenti, "Calculated Cruelty (Part II)," *Abortion, Every Day,* January 5, 2024.

129 **disinformation campaign about** The anti-abortion movement has a history of attacking prenatal testing. See, for example, Nora Sullivan, "Non-invasive Prenatal Screening Expands Disability Discrimination Abortion," Charlotte Lozier Institute, December 18, 2024.

129 **more patients had been asking** Laura Ungar et al, "Post–Roe v. Wade, More Patients Rely on Early Prenatal Testing as States Toughen Abortion Laws," Associated Press, February 12, 2024.

129 **a letter to the FDA** Chip Roy et al. to Janet Woodcock, "FDA Labeling Requirements and Regulatory Measures for Prenatal Tests," January 21, 2022.

129 **"It is unacceptable that the FDA"** Steve Daines quoted in Representative Michelle Fischbach, "97 Republican Legislators Demand Answers from FDA on Inaccurate Noninvasive Prenatal Genetic Testing," January 22, 2022.

129 **"continue to see their profits grow"** Roy et al. to Woodcock, "FDA Labeling Requirements."

Chapter 9: They're Not Stopping with Our Bodies

132   **the state's so-called bounty hunter law** Texas Legislature, S.B. 8, The Texas Heartbeat Act (2021).

132   **abortion bans can't physically prevent** Naomi Cahn, June Carbone, and Nancy Levit, "Is It Legal to Travel for Abortion After Dobbs?," *Bloomberg Law,* July 11, 2022.

133   **Texas county made it illegal** J. David Goodman, "In Texas, Local Laws to Prevent Travel for Abortions Gain Momentum," *The New York Times,* October 24, 2023.

133   **Gerri Santoro was just twenty-eight years old** Amanda Arnold, "How a Harrowing Photo of One Woman's Death Became an Iconic Pro-Choice Symbol," *Vice,* October 26, 2016.

134   **women can self-manage ending their pregnancies** American College of Obstetricians and Gynecologists' Committee on Practice Bulletins—Gynecology, Society of Family Planning, "Medication Abortion Up to 70 Days of Gestation: ACOG Practice Bulletin, Number 225," *Obstetrics and Gynecology* 136, no. 4 (October 2020): e31–e47.

134   **Savita Halappanavar died in Ireland** Ben Quinn, "Scandal in Ireland as woman dies in Galway 'after being denied abortion,'" *Guardian,* November 13, 2012.

135   **repeal of the country's anti-abortion** "Eighth Amendment Repealed as Irish President Signs Bill into Law," BBC, September 18, 2018.

136   **wasn't Republican laws but "abortion alarmism"** Hadley Heath Manning, "Abortion Alarmism—Not Dobbs—Is Going to Hurt Women," *Real Clear Health,* October 6, 2022.

137   **"grossly misinterpreted" the law** Katrina Jackson quoted in Emily Woodruff, "Louisiana Lawmakers Say Hospital 'Grossly Misinterpreted' Law That Allows Exceptions to Abortion Ban," *New Orleans Advocate,* August 24, 2022.

137   **"a failure of our medical associations"** "I have seen reports of doctors being confused, but that is a failure of our medical associations." John Seago quoted in Pam Belluck, "They Had Miscarriages, and New Abortion Laws Obstructed Treatment," *The New York Times,* July 17, 2022.

137   **the problem was "hospitals' decision-making"** "There seems to

be both a real problem in some hospitals' decision-making here and a problem of activist-journalist misrepresentation as well." Ross Douthat (@DouthatNYT), X post, August 1, 2022.

137 **doctors who were desperate** Erika L. Sabbath, Samantha M. McKetchnie, and Kavita S. Arora, "US Obstetrician-Gynecologists' Perceived Impacts of Post–Dobbs v Jackson State Abortion Bans," *JAMA Network Open* 7, no. 1 (January 2024).

138 **a Louisiana woman shared her story** Rosemary Westwood, "Bleeding and in Pain, She Couldn't Get 2 Louisiana ERs to Answer: Is It a Miscarriage?," NPR, December 29, 2022.

138 **"It was just a gross misunderstanding"** Poet Wolfe, "Louisiana Anti-Abortion Group Calls on Doctors to Stop Denying Care Exempted by Ban," *Guardian,* February 26, 2023.

138 **doctors in North Carolina** Hana Stepnick, "Doctors Urge Lawmakers Not to Limit Abortion Further," *9th Street Journal,* February 26, 2023.

138 **"We're going to see more women die"** Alison Stuebe quoted in Hana Stepnick, "Doctors Urge Lawmakers Not to Limit Abortion Further," *9th Street Journal,* February 26, 2023.

138 **When women whose lives were endangered** "Zurawski v. State of Texas," Texas Abortion Ban Emergency Exceptions Case, Center for Reproductive Rights, November 28, 2023.

138 **"every pro-life law in the country allows"** "Texas Abortion Lawsuit: Leading Nat'l Pro-Life Group Responds," Susan B. Anthony Pro-Life America, March 9, 2023.

138 **a group of women sued Tennessee** "Blackmon v. State of Tennessee," Medical Emergency Exceptions to State Abortion Bans, Center for Reproductive Rights, April 4, 2024.

139 **"other factors like doctors' independent choices"** Jonathan Skrmetti quoted ibid.

139 **"political statement"** Raul Labrador quoted by Nicole Blanchard, "Idaho Attorney General Labrador Questions Doctors' Accounts of Abortion Emergencies," *Idaho Statesman,* April 24, 2024.

140 **People who are more likely to be killed** Liza Fuentes, "Inequity in US Abortion Rights and Access: The End of Roe Is Deepening Existing Divides," Guttmacher Institute, January 2023.

140 **Dr. Caitlin Bernard, the Indiana abortion provider** Sheryl Gay Stolberg, "An Indiana Doctor Speaks Out on Abortion, and Pays a Price," *The New York Times,* July 28, 2022.

140   **Republican officials targeted her** Moira Donegan, "She
       Performed an Abortion on a 10-Year-Old Rape Victim. The Right
       Vilified Her," *Guardian,* July 10, 2023.

140   **Rokita launched a year-long harassment campaign** Peter Slevin,
       "One of the Last Abortion Doctors in Indiana," *The New Yorker,*
       February 25, 2024.

141   **Yeniifer Alvarez-Estrada Glick** Stephania Taladrid, "Did an
       Abortion Ban Cost a Young Texas Woman Her Life?," *The New
       Yorker,* January 8, 2024.

142   **"If she weren't pregnant"** Joanne Stone quoted ibid.

143   **anti-abortion activists pounced** Samantha Kamman, "Activists
       Blame Abortion Restriction for Pregnant Mother's Death; Pro-
       Lifer responds," *Christian Post Reporter,* January 15, 2024.

145   **Idaho has lost nearly 25 percent** Idaho Physician Well-Being
       Action Collaborative, "A Post Roe Idaho," Idaho Coalition for
       Safe Healthcare, February 2024.

145   **maternal deserts increase exponentially** "Nowhere to Go:
       Maternity Care Deserts Across the U.S.," Maternity Care Deserts
       Report, March of Dimes, October 12, 2022.

145   **When Bonner General Health hospital** Caroline Lobsinger,
       "BGH Shutters Labor, Delivery Services," *Bonner County Daily
       Bee,* March 18, 2023

145   **"Highly respected, talented physicians are leaving"** Erin Binnall
       quoted in Bonner General Health, Press Release, March 17,
       2023.

145   **Medical students and residents** Kendal Orgera, Hasan
       Mahmood and Atul Grover, "Training Location Preferences of
       U.S. Medical School Graduates Post Dobbs v. Jackson Women's
       Health," Research and Action Institute, Association of American
       Medical Colleges, April 13, 2023.

145   **Every state that has an abortion ban** Sheryl Gay Stolberg, "As
       Abortion Laws Drive Obstetricians from Red States, Maternity
       Care Suffers," *The New York Times,* September 7, 2023.

145   **it's illegal to learn** Sara Hutchinson, "Abortion Bans Complicate
       Medical Training, Risk Worsening OB/GYN Shortages,"
       Washington Post, October 13, 2023.

146   **1.7 million American women** Nicole Wetsman, John Brownstein
       and Benjamin Rader, "Maternal Care Deserts Overlap with Lack
       of Abortion Access, Analysis Shows," ABC News, August 1, 2023.

146   **"The same states that are most likely"** Eugene Declercq quoted in ibid.

146   **more than 5.6 million women** "Where You Live Matters: Maternity Care Deserts and the Crisis of Access and Equity," March of Dimes, 2022.

146   **62 percent higher than states** Eugene Declercq et al., "The U.S. Maternal Health Divide: The Limited Maternal Health Services and Worse Outcomes of States Proposing New Abortion Restrictions," Commonwealth Fund, December 14, 2022.

146   **three times more likely to die** "The State of Reproductive Health in the United States: The End of Roe and the Perilous Road Ahead for Women in the Dobbs Era," Gender Equity Policy Institute, January 19, 2023.

146   **a 16 percent increased infant mortality rate** Roman Pabayo et al., "Laws Restricting Access to Abortion Services and Infant Mortality Risk in the United States," *International Journal of Environmental Research and Public Health* 17, no. 11 (2020).

146   **infant mortality shot up** Isabelle Chapman, "Nearly Two Years After Texas' Six-Week Abortion Ban, More Infants are Dying," CNN, July 20, 2023.

146   **maternal death rates went up** Nada Hassanein, "The Rate of Women Dying in Childbirth Surged by 40%. These Deaths Are Preventable," *USA Today,* March 16, 2023.

147   **Republican leaders disbanded** Rachel Cohen, "Idaho Dissolves Maternal Mortality Review Committee, as Deaths Remain High," Boise Public Radio, July 7, 2023.

147   **it's being prevented from counting deaths** Maggie Q. Thompson, "Texas Maternal Mortality Task Force Hasn't Counted Abortion Death Cases for 10 Years," *Austin Chronicle,* March 22, 2024.

147   **disproportionately women of color** "Inequity in US Abortion Rights and Access: The End of Roe Is Deepening Existing Divides," Guttmacher Institute, January 2023.

148   **Charlotte Lozier Institute blamed** Ingrid Skop, "Response to Media Allegations That Abortion Restrictions Cause Maternal Mortality and Female Suicides," Charlotte Lozier Institute, March 21, 2023.

148   **"there's no great risk"** Bill Dean quoted in London Bishop, "Dean Takes Hard-Line Stances on Abortion, Welfare in Statehouse Race vs. Duffee" *Dayton Daily News,* October 19, 2022.

149   **pushing out these "feel good" stories** For a recent example, see Francesca Pollio Fenton, "Jessica Hanna, Catholic Mother Who Chose Life Amid Cancer Battle, Dies," Catholic News Agency, April 8, 2024.

149   **"brave mom who refused abortion"** "'I'm Not Giving Up'— The True Story of a Brave Mom Who Refused Abortion After a Cancer Diagnosis," *Pregnancy Help News,* July 13, 2023.

149   **"Killing my baby"** "Mom Who Refused Abortion to Receive Chemotherapy," Fox News, September 13, 2023.

Chapter 10: Abortion Is Everything

151   **Dr. George Tiller** Joe Stumpe and Monica Davey, "Abortion Doctor Shot to Death in Kansas Church," *The New York Times,* May 31, 2009.

151   **"than the countless women"** Defendant's Plea to the Jurisdiction and Response to Plaintiff's Application for Temporary Restraining Order, Kate Cox v. Texas (2023) (No. D-1-GN-23-008611).

151   **a ten-year-old girl being raped** Shari Rudavsky and Rachel Fradette, "Patients Head to Indiana for Abortion Services as Other States Restrict Care," *Indianapolis Star,* July 1, 2022.

151   **"too good" to be true** Editorial Board, "An Abortion Story Too Good to Confirm," *Wall Street Journal,* July 13, 2022.

152   **suggested the story was a "hoax"** "Jesse Watters: Authorities in Ohio Haven't Even Begun a Criminal Investigation into This Rape," Fox News, July 11, 2022.

152   **"a fictive abortion and a fictive rape"** "Or was making up a fictive abortion and a fictive rape a way of drawing attention to the way abortion has been used to cover up statutory rape for all these years?" Michael Brendan Dougherty (@michaelbd), X post, July 8, 2022.

152   **likely a "fabrication"** Dave Yost quoted in Bethany Bruner, Monroe Trombly and Tony Cook, "Arrest Made in Rape of Ohio Girl That Led to Indiana Abortion Drawing International Attention," *Columbus Dispatch,* January 24, 2023.

152   **raped children are "pretty rare"** Glenn Kessler, "A One-Source Story About a 10-Year-Old and an Abortion Goes Viral," *Washington Post,* July 13, 2022.

153 **"strong, legitimate interests"** Motion to Dismiss, Yellowhammer Fund v. Steve Marshall (2023) (No. 2:23-cv-00450-MHT-KFP).

154 **"The unborn child is always taken"** Kitchener, "Highways Are the Next Antiabortion Target."

154 **"we are advising a conservative approach"** Marina Pitofsky, "Idaho College Says Staff Could Face Felony for 'Promoting' Abortion, Providing Birth Control," *USA Today,* September 27, 2022; Caroline Kitchener and Susan Svrluga, "U. of Idaho May Stop Providing Birth Control Under New Abortion Law," *Washington Post,* September 26, 2022.

155 **"for the purpose of helping prevent"** Ibid.

155 **"promot[ing] abortion; counsel[ing] in favor"** Idaho Legislature, H.B. 17, The No Funds for Abortion Act (2021).

155 **"an impossible—and unconstitutional—choice"** Kelcie Moseley-Morris, "Idaho Educators File Federal Lawsuit Over 'No Public Funds For Abortion' Law," *Idaho Capital Sun,* August 8, 2023.

155 **would make pro-choice websites illegal** South Carolina General Assembly, S. 1373, Equal Protection at Conception—No Exceptions—Act (2021); and Texas Legislature, H.B. 2690, The Women and Child Safety Act (2023).

155 **criminalize simply telling someone** Raúl R. Labrador to Brent Cane, "Letter in Response to Recent Inquiries Regarding Idaho's Criminal Prohibitions on Abortion," March 27, 2023; and "Alabama Attorney General Doubles Down on Threats to Prosecute Out-of-State Abortion Care," *Alabama Reflector,* August 31, 2023.

155 **Oklahoma librarians were even instructed** Claire Woodcock, "Oklahoma Threatens Librarians: 'Don't Use the Word Abortion,'" *Vice,* July 21, 2022.

156 **abortion reports aren't medical records** Abigail Ruhman, "Indiana Attorney General Pushes to Disclose Terminated Pregnancy Reports," Indiana Public Broadcasting, April 12, 2024.

157 **Over 80 percent of Americans believe abortion** "Abortion," Historical Trends, Gallup, n.d.

157 **Support for abortion rights is broadly increasing** "Support for Abortion Access Is Near Record, WSJ-NORC Poll Finds," *Wall Street Journal,* November 20, 2023.

160   **99 percent of American women** "Contraceptive Use in the
       United States by Demographics," Guttmacher Institute,
       May 2021.

160   **legislators who vote against** Jonathan Weisman, "Why Paid
       Family Leave's Demise This Time Could Fuel It Later," *The New
       York Times,* October 31, 2021; Eleanor Mueller "Senate
       Republicans Block Bill Targeting Gender Pay Gap," *Politico,*
       June 8, 2021; and James Walker, "Full List of 172 Republicans
       Who Opposed the Violence Against Women Act," *Newsweek,*
       March 18, 2021.

160   **or the freedom to divorce** Kimberly Wehle, "The Coming Attack
       on No Fault Divorce Laws," *Atlantic,* September 26, 2023.

160   **a case that will determine** Nina Totenberg, "Supreme Court to
       Examine a Federal-State Conflict Over Emergency Abortions,"
       NPR, April 24, 2024.

161   **"Fuck SCOTUS, we're doing it anyway"** Rewire News Group
       Staff, "'It's Time to Raise Hell': Activists Today Are Shouting
       About Abortion Pills," Rewire News Group, December 1, 2021.

Index

Mayberry, Heather, 118
media, false balance in, 23–25
Medicaid, 9, 58, 60
medical sexism, 67
medications. *See* birth control;
    emergency contraception
mental health, 67, 122–24, 127–28,
    156–57
Mercy Health-St. Joseph's
    Hospital, 91
messaging. *See* "pro-life" language
Michigan Proposal 3, 108
Miller, Lauren, 38
minors. *See* teenagers and children
Miscarriage and Abortion Hotline,
    175
miscarriages, 19, 35, 125, 138
    Brittany Watts's case, 86, 90–94,
      102–3, 151
    Halappanavar's case, 134–35
misinformation, 3, 9–10, 12, 29,
    63, 64, 66, 79, 102–3, 116–17,
    138
misogyny, 65, 84, 94, 101, 104, 106,
    152, 158–59
misoprostol, 7
Mississippi
    ballot measures, 27, 32
    birth control bans, 56, 60
    "exceptions," 70, 172
    punishment, 87
Mississippi Today, 70
Missouri, 30–31, 106, 121
Mister Rogers' Neighborhood (TV
    show), 97
Moody, Ashley, 30
Moreno, Bernie, 47
morning after pills. *See* emergency
    contraception

mortality rate. *See* infant mortality
    rate; maternal mortality rate
MYA Network, 166, 167

NARAL Pro-Choice America, 24
Nash, Elizabeth, 71
National Cancer Institute, 127
National Republican Senatorial
    Committee, 49
National Review, 36, 89, 152
National Right to Life
    Committee, 48
"national standard," 46, 50
"natural" family planning, 66–67
Nebraska, 95, 103, 112
New, Michael, 80
New Mexico, 131–32
Newsom, Gavin, 107
Newsweek, 113
New Yorker, 141–43
New York Times, xi, 10, 46,
    49–50, 82
no-fault divorce, 66
nonviable pregnancies, xi, 118, 119
    "exceptions" for, 74–80, 81
    Kate Cox's story, 74–76, 79–80
    use of terms, 44, 76, 173–74
North Carolina, 32–33, 48, 76, 127,
    138
North Dakota, 115

ob-gyns, fleeing anti-choice states,
    56, 120, 145–47, 170–71
objectivity, faux notions of, 24
Ohio
    Bernard's story, 140–41, 151–52
    birth control bans, 54–55, 57
    Brittany Watts's case, 86, 90–94,
      102–3, 151

About the Author

Jessica Valenti is the author of seven books about feminism, politics, and culture. She has had two abortions. She ended her first pregnancy three months before meeting her husband, Andrew. Two years later, they had their daughter, Layla. Even though she desperately wanted another child, Jessica had a second abortion three years later to protect her health and life—and to ensure her daughter grew up with a mother.

Jessica is a terrible sport, a terrific cook, and a mom who spoils her now-thirteen-year-old daughter. She is not a murderer or a criminal, though her country would allow certain states to treat her as such. She is a human being with the unalienable right to decide what happens to her own body, and a mother who has a responsibility to protect her daughter from those who see her as an incubator rather than a person.

Jessica publishes a newsletter called *Abortion, Every Day*, has contributed to publications like *The New York Times*, *The Washington Post*, and *The Guardian*. She speaks about feminism at colleges and organizations across the country and abroad.

Jessica lives in Brooklyn with Andrew, Layla, and their dog, Bruno—enjoying a full life that would not be possible without abortion.